EAST ASIA-ARCTIC RELATIONS

EAST ASIA-ARCTIC RELATIONS: BOUNDARY, SECURITY AND INTERNATIONAL POLITICS

Edited by Kimie Hara and Ken Coates

ISBN 978-1-928096-02-3 (paper)
ISBN 978-1-928096-03-0 (ebook)

Published by the Centre for International Governance Innovation.

Printed and bound in Canada.

Cover and page design by Steve Cross.

The Centre for International Governance Innovation
67 Erb Street West
Waterloo, ON Canada N2L 6C2

www.cigionline.org

Contents

Acronyms

AERC	Arctic Environment Research Center
AMAP	Arctic Monitoring and Assessment Programme
ANWTF	Alaska Northern Waters Task Force
ASEAN	Association of Southeast Asian Nations
BC	British Columbia
CAO	Central Arctic Ocean
CBMs	confidence-building measures
CHARS	Canadian High Arctic Research Station
DFAIT	Department of Foreign Affairs and International Trade (Canada)
EEZ	exclusive economic zone
G2	Group of Two
IASC	International Arctic Science Committee
IMO	International Maritime Organization
INSROP	International Northern Sea Route Programme
IPY	International Polar Year
ITK	Inuit Tapiriit Kanatami
JAMSTEC	Japan Agency for Marine-Earth Science and Technology
JIIA	Japan Institute of International Affairs
JOGMEC	Japan Oil, Gas and Metals National Corporation
KANUMAS	Kalaallit Nunaat Marine Seismic
KIOST	Korea Institute of Ocean Science and Technology
KMI	Korea Maritime Institute
KOGAS	Korea Gas Corporation
KOPRI	Korea Polar Research Institute
KORDI	Korea Ocean Research and Development Institute
LNG	liquefied natural gas
MCO	Mumbai Cooperation Organization
MEXT	Ministry of Education, Culture, Sports, Science and Technology (Japan)
MLIT	Ministry of Land, Infrastructure and Tourism (Japan)
MOF	Ministry of Oceans and Fisheries (Korea)

MoFA	Ministry of Foreign Affairs (Japan)
MOU	memorandum of understanding
NATO	North Atlantic Treaty Organization
NGO	non-governmental organization
NIDS	National Institute for Defense Studies (Japan)
NIPR	National Institute of Polar Research (Japan)
NOC	national oil company
NPOPSS	National Planning Office of Philosophy and Social Science (China)
NSR	Northern Sea Route
NTI	Nunavut Tunngavik Incorporated
NWP	Northwest Passage
NWT	Northwest Territories
OCS	Outer Continental Shelf (Alaska)
OPRF	Ocean Policy Research Foundation
PPs	permanent participants (Arctic Council)
PRC	People's Republic of China
PRIC	Polar Research Institute of China
SAO	Senior Arctic Officials (Arctic Council)
SCAFP	*Statement on Canada's Arctic Foreign Policy*
SCO	Shanghai Cooperation Organization
TEU	twenty-foot equivalent unit
UNCLCS	UN Commission on the Limits of the Continental Shelf
UNCLOS	United Nations Convention on the Law of the Sea
UNDP	United Nations Development Programme
USGS	US Geological Survey
USSR	Union of Soviet Socialist Republics

Acknowledgments

///

This volume emerged from an extensive international collaboration and came to fruition thanks to the generous support of several organizations and many individuals.

Two workshops were held, in Whitehorse, Yukon and Waterloo, Ontario, in March 2013. The events were made possible with the generous funding of the Centre for International Governance Innovation (CIGI) and the Japan Foundation, as well as the kind support of Yukon College, the Balsillie School of International Affairs, the Japan Futures Initiative, St. Jerome's University, the Keiko and Charles Belair Centre for East Asian Studies of Renison University College at the University of Waterloo and the Johnson-Shoyama Graduate School at the University of Saskatchewan.

The editors would like to thank all of the project collaborators. Special thanks are due to the authors of the volume for their contributions. Carin Holroyd also made excellent logistical arrangements for the engaging and effective meeting in Whitehorse. In addition to the authors, the workshop participants provided superb commentary and valuable insights. Many thanks to all of them: Eva Busza, Douglas Goold, Scott Harrison, Elizabeth Hanson, Piers McDonald, Charles Aruliah, Jim Balsillie, Ryan Dean, Jordan Dupuis, Kris Kinsinger, Alistair McIntyre, Ted McDorman, John Higginbotham, Li Fang, Jianfeng Mu, Song Oh and Tetsuya Yoshimoto. The CIGI publications team, especially Sonya Zikic and Jennifer Goyder, showed great patience and provided excellent editorial support.

Introduction

//

Kimie Hara and Ken Coates

Global climate change is reshaping the Arctic region, both physically and in terms of international politics. The dramatic reduction in sea ice cover has provoked images of vast, increasingly viable transpolar shipping and accessible resources, generating significant commentary within and between the circumpolar states (Canada, the United States, Greenland, Iceland, Russia, Finland, Sweden and Norway). As a rising chorus of international voices remind us, changes to the region concern more than the circumpolar states. Three East Asian countries — Japan, South Korea and China — are more attentive to, and interested in, Arctic developments than ever before.

East Asian nations depend on global resources, fund scientific research and move their goods through sea lanes around the world. Accordingly, Asian commentators have expressed concern about Arctic states blocking them from participating in discussions about the future of the circumpolar world. East Asian nations are highly motivated to engage in Arctic affairs because of recent developments such as the great earthquake and nuclear disaster in Japan in 2011, oil price volatility and supply issues from the Arab Spring in the Middle East and North Africa. This led to extensive investigations of alternative energy sources, supply routes and security. These processes reminded East Asian governments about the value of safe and secure shipping routes, access to natural resources, and environmental and scientific knowledge to inform decision making.

Canada, Russia and the United States have extensive commitments to the Far North and long histories of Arctic engagement. As the major polar nations with the gateways to the Asia-Pacific, they have lengthy experience with East Asia. Their northern responsibilities, geography and trans-Pacific engagement, combined with East Asia's growing interest in the Far North, make the nations of both regions key stakeholders in deliberations on the future of Arctic governance. Furthermore, the evolving situation in the Arctic could influence relations among East Asian nations, providing new opportunities for cooperation or additional sources of conflict.

East Asia-Arctic Relations:
Boundary, Security and International Politics

◇◇◇

This volume is an outcome of an international collaborative project, which aimed to launch a focused and detailed conversation about the historical, contemporary and future dimensions of East Asian countries' relationships and interests in the Arctic. The project started from a brainstorming discussion between the editors during the Japanese Studies Association of Canada conference held in Halifax, Nova Scotia in August 2011. Bringing together leading experts from Japan, China, South Korea, Russia, the United States and Canada, the project draws scholarly and policy-making attention to East Asia's growing interests in the Far North and identifies political, economic, legal and security connections between East Asia and the Arctic.

As major phases of the project, two workshops were held in 2013: the first in Whitehorse, Yukon on March 2-3, 2013, and the second in Waterloo, Ontario on March 5, 2013. The Whitehorse workshop provided an opportunity for 16 scholars to reflect on the issues at hand. Intensive discussions took place over two days on 13 papers, which were submitted and circulated prior to the workshop. Those papers examined the roles and impacts of East Asian interests on Arctic politics and diplomacy and those of the contemporary Arctic on East Asian affairs. There were also exchanges of views with local politicians in the Yukon. The second, policy-focused workshop in Waterloo built on the work concluded in Whitehorse. The participants in this workshop included nine scholars who attended the Whitehorse workshop, and an additional 12 individuals who are Arctic experts, foreign affairs specialists or government representatives. The workshop consisted of a series of facilitated discussions in greater detail on Arctic policy alternatives available to Canada, the Arctic Council and East Asian nations. The focus was to identify potential points of conflict and cooperation.

At both workshops, there were lively exchanges among the participants, who gathered from Japan, China, South Korea, Russia, the United States, Norway and across Canada. The workshops also generated significant personal and collective discoveries and inspired participants to consider anew the fundamental political and economic relationships in the Arctic, as well as several research outputs.[1]

This volume consists of the revised Whitehorse conference papers. The two-day Whitehorse conference began with introductory addresses and a paper examining historical influences and forces for change in the Arctic. This was followed by the sessions considering the interests of East Asian powers (in particular, Japan, China

---

[1]   In addition to this volume, outputs of this project include workshop reports and an online paper series. See the CIGI project page for details: www.cigionline.org/series/east-asia-arctic-relations-boundary-security-and-international-politics.

Introduction

and South Korea) in the Arctic; concerns of Arctic powers with gateways to the Pacific (specifically the United States, Canada and Russia) on East Asia-Arctic relations; the changing Arctic and its implications for East Asia, in terms of security, economics and border regions; and East Asia-Arctic affairs from indigenous, global and circumpolar perspectives.

The composition of this volume is similar to that of the Whitehorse conference as a whole. The authors were asked to write papers on their respective areas of expertise. They do not necessarily share the same view on each area. This was reflected in the well-balanced discussions of both the Whitehorse and Waterloo workshops, where participants actively exchanged views and opinions, which are reflected in several parts of the contributed papers. A brief summary of each chapter follows.

In chapter 1, Ken Coates steps back from the current political, economic and diplomatic debates about the Far North to consider the broader patterns in the history and geopolitics of the region. Coates, who was raised in the Yukon, is something of a northern development skeptic, not convinced that the ambitious plans for regional economic development, the opening of the Arctic passageways to commercial shipping and other grand strategies for the region will come to fruition. The North, Coates argues, has disappointed its promoters and advocates in the past and will do so again in the future. At the same time, he points out, the Far North has produced some of the world's most innovative approaches to indigenous empowerment, environmental management and intraregional planning, including the creation of the Arctic Council. It is these institutional reforms and institutions that will likely be the most prominent legacy of the contemporary debates about the Arctic.

In chapter 2, Fujio Ohnishi argues that Japan's Arctic policy is in the process of developing toward more active engagement in the region. Three milestones of Japan's past involvement in the Arctic are discussed, and the current processes formulating Japan's Arctic interests are summarized. The chapter then considers opportunities and challenges for Japan in the Arctic, in areas such as Arctic shipping, oil and gas exploitation, and fisheries. It concludes with a discussion of three strategic considerations that influence Japan's Arctic policy: the need to combine scientific findings with economic interests; possible diplomatic linkages between Arctic and East Asian states; and making diplomatic efforts toward subnational actors, such as indigenous groups in the region.

In chapter 3, China's interests and participation in the Arctic are discussed. As China's presence in the Arctic grows, international attention also increases. Kai Sun clarifies China's interests in the Arctic and touches on future trends in this regard. Beginning with a discussion of China's recent Arctic capacity building and diplomacy, this paper suggests that China looks north for basically four reasons: it is influenced by environmental changes in the Arctic; it is drawn by the business opportunities arising from the opening of the Arctic passages and better access to Arctic resources; and it is also committed to maintaining good governance in the Arctic — which is also in its best interests. At present, China's participation in Arctic affairs is limited, but it is preparing to make greater contributions to good governance in the Arctic.

In chapter 4, Young Kil Park examines South Korea's interest and involvement in the Arctic and analyzes its challenges, summarizing the Arctic-related activities the country has pursued so far; examining specific interests in the fields of science, sea routes and hydrocarbon resources, fishing and governance; and, finally, evaluates the challenges ahead. South Korea has made significant progress in entering the Arctic Ocean, but many challenges must be addressed before the Arctic can become a source of economic prosperity.

Chapter 5, by Jerry McBeath, concerns the US view of East Asian nations' involvement in the Arctic, emphasizing the perspective of Alaska, the only US Arctic state. It treats six different areas of US/Alaska policy: US national strategy for the Arctic; oil and gas exploration and development; marine transportation; fisheries; investment in infrastructure; and governance. McBeath's study finds few differences between the positions of Alaska and the United States, notwithstanding often-hostile rhetoric from leaders in the United States' farthest north frontier.

In chapter 6, P. Whitney Lackenbauer and James Manicom examine Canadian perceptions of East Asia's Arctic interests. Whereas some commentaries conceptualize Asian states, particularly China, as potential threats to Canada's interests in the Arctic, the authors argue that the basis for this alarmist rhetoric (apart from more generalized discourses associated with the "rise of Asia") is speculative and imprecise. Using Canada's Northern Strategy and the Statement on Canada's Arctic Foreign Policy as filters, this chapter suggests where Asia's Arctic interests may converge or diverge with those of Canada. It also recommends various messages that Canada may wish to emphasize in its interactions with Asian states to safeguard its national interests, promote sustainable development for the benefit of Northerners, and enhance cooperation and constructive dialogue in the circumpolar world.

In chapter 7, Tamara Troyakova interprets the Arctic as a key economic resource as the main driver of Russia's activity in the region. Siberia and the Russian Far East, she argues, could be integrated into the conventional Northeast Asian region in economic, social and cultural arenas. Rather than simply exploiting natural resources, she suggests that we should be able to predict where Siberia and the Russian Far East will go, together with the rest of Northeast Asia. Cooperation among Northeast Asian countries would be useful for Russia's plan to transform the Arctic into a "strategic resource base."

In chapter 8, Kimie Hara argues that the evolving situation in the Arctic region could have significant impact on the political relations and the regional security architecture in East Asia, providing new opportunities for cooperation and additional sources of conflict. The chapter considers security implications of the Arctic thaw to East Asia, where the structure of the regional Cold War confrontation remains to this day. It first highlights the post-World War II developments of the regional political and security environment in East Asia, with particular attention to the regional conflicts, considers possible impacts of the emerging Arctic thaw to the status quo, and concludes with some recommendations to prepare for possible climate change in the security environment in East Asia and the Arctic.

In chapter 9, Carin Holroyd looks at East Asia's economic interests in the Arctic. East Asia has discovered the Arctic, both because of a growing global interest in the effects of climate change on the fragile circumpolar ecosystem, and because of the economic potential of resource development in the region. Japan, South Korea and China are determined to be part of Arctic political processes, including the Arctic Council, Holroyd argues, so that they can influence decisions over oil, gas and mineral development. East Asian companies have become increasingly active in the region, developing Arctic-ready commercial ships, supporting Arctic research and exploring opportunities for resource development in the Far North. This chapter reviews current economic activity in the region, identifying areas of East Asian interest and examining the long-term strategies for Japan, South Korea and China in the area.

The Arctic Sea is touted as a new available space as the ice-melting process has accelerated in recent years. Debates over the Arctic are featured in aspects such as military competition, resource hunting and transportation rivalry. Active newcomers such as China, South Korea and Japan (all recently admitted observers to the Arctic Council) are developing, and their southern rivalries over maritime areas now extend to the north. The dual process between conflict and cooperation around the Arctic will feature in relations with those sea border dynamics. Chapter 10, by Akihiro Iwashita, explores the seas around the continent as the "Sea of Eurasia," positing the Arctic as an eastern component of this proposed body of water. After reviewing trends in continental cooperation over border issues, lessons applicable toward maritime affairs are drawn.

In chapter 11, David A. Welch suggests that, contrary to popular belief — and contrary to the views of many politicians and scholars — the Arctic is completely uninteresting geopolitically from a traditional national security perspective. It is somewhat more interesting geopolitically from various non-traditional security perspectives (for example, human security, cultural security, energy security, economic security and environmental security); but it is truly important only in the one respect that attracts the least attention and action from policy makers: namely, ecospheric security.

In chapter 12, James Manicom and P. Whitney Lackenbauer write a second contribution to the volume, focusing, this time, on the applications of East Asian nations for observer status at the Arctic Council. It begins with a general reflection on East Asian nations' interests in the Arctic, followed by a brief background on the Arctic Council and observer status (including the criteria laid out in the 2011 Nuuk Declaration) and the formal applications of China, Japan and South Korea. While East Asian states have offered little explicit rationale for observer status, academic and media commentators in Asian nations have offered reasons why the council should extend it. The authors critically analyze commentators' viewpoints in light of the Nuuk criteria, as well as the interests of the Arctic Council member states and its permanent participants (PPs). Western academic, media, and think-tank commentary on East Asian nations' applications are also assessed, as are the anticipated implications for the future of the Arctic Council and circumpolar governance more generally. Despite concerns that Asian state involvement in the Arctic Council may dilute the power of the member states and PPs, the authors argue that denying Asian states observer status — which would force them to pursue Arctic discussions in other fora — risks undermining the Arctic Council's place as the premier forum for high-level discussion on regional issues.

The papers presented at the Whitehorse workshop and the intensive conversation and debate that followed at the Waterloo workshop brought to the forefront the fundamental importance of East Asian engagement in the Arctic. Although the level of involvement is comparatively small — China, Japan and South Korea are much more heavily invested in Africa than they will be in the Arctic for the next half century — a new pattern has been established. Most importantly, the East Asian nations want to be part of the scientific research, regional planning and economic development activity in the Arctic. They clearly see in the North some of the crucial warning signs about global warming, offset by the possibility that the Arctic holds the raw materials needed to sustain industrial development in East Asia. Twenty years ago, only a handful of East Asian scientists and occasional tourists could be

Introduction

∞∞∞

seen in the Arctic; now, state-owned companies, regular Arctic tours for East Asian visitors, major research groups, and extensive Arctic profile-building operations can be seen across the North.

It is not clear, however, that the Arctic states or the Arctic peoples are either aware of the level of East Asian interest or fully prepared for their engagement. There are suspicions about the motives of their external agenda, particularly regarding their resource aspirations in the Far North and their insistence on being part of the Arctic Council and other northern diplomatic and political organizations. In a real and substantial way, most northerners do not see China, South Korea and Japan as truly Northern nations, with other than self-interested commitments to the region. Reconciling East Asian aspirations, which are part of the three countries' global strategies for environmental management and resource planning, with the desire of the Arctic states to regulate the circumpolar world themselves and in their collective interests, represents a major political and diplomatic challenge.

This collection, and the two meetings that led to the publication of this book, represent the launch, rather than the conclusion, of an ongoing, international collaboration on the future of East Asia in the Arctic; these issues will not soon disappear. East Asian interest in the region is real and sustainable. The search for governance structures and consultative processes that respect indigenous, circumpolar and global interests in the Arctic is well underway. What is clear is that the Arctic now has a significant East Asian component. The shape, nature and intensity of East Asian engagement in the Arctic is much less clear. Therefore, close monitoring, international collaboration and continued research will be essential if the shared, but far from similar, interests of East Asia and the Arctic are to be reconciled.

Kimie Hara, Renison University College, University of Waterloo

Ken Coates, Johnson-Shoyama Graduate School of Public Policy, University of Saskatchewan

1

Forces for Change in the Arctic: Reflections on a Region in Transition

///

Ken Coates
••••••••••••

INTRODUCTION

The first European maps of the Arctic were fanciful drawings, filled with monsters and strange lands. At this point, when Europeans had yet to venture into the region, they saw the area as mysterious, in a dangerous and exciting way. It took many generations for explorers and adventurers to reach into the vast expanses of the Far North, discovering endless miles of ice and rock, tiny numbers of indigenous inhabitants, and few of the resources that drew the colonial powers to Asia, Africa, North America and South America. The Arctic was destined to be the final frontier, the last place on earth to feel the forces of settlement and development by non-indigenous peoples.[1]

The latest maps of the Arctic are far more accurate, enhanced by satellite imagery and depicting a region in the midst of a fast-moving, human-induced climatic change. Northerners like the maps that put the North Pole at the centre — the so-called "polar projections" — and that identify the new geopolitical realities of the circumpolar world. These maps reveal a new world of disputed international

---

1 For an overview of the development of the Far North, see Grant (2010) and K. Coates et al. (2008).

boundaries, rapidly retreating sea ice and related climate changes, and outlines of areas of high resource potential. The maps could not be more different — from the mysteries and unknowns of the past to the confusion and uncertainties of the present. All of these maps speak to the unique character of the Arctic, inhabited by very few people, almost all of those indigenous to the area. It is an area that remains largely unknown and unexperienced by most of the world, and existing primarily in the world of the imagination.[2]

The past quarter century has brought remarkable changes to the Arctic. Not since the immediate post-World War II world, when the imperatives of the Cold War brought the US and Union of Soviet Socialist Republic (USSR) militaries into the Far North, has the region faced such pressures. While the development of early warning systems and military bases brought change and dislocation across the Arctic, particularly in Alaska and the Russian Far North, greater transformations remained in the offing. The 1960s and 1970s provided a trial run for the twenty-first century, beginning with oil and gas exploration and development in Alaska and the Beaufort Sea in the 1960s and 1970s, and accelerating through efforts to navigate the Northwest Passage (NWP), particularly by the SS *Manhattan* in 1969.[3] These activities increased media attention to the North, alternately demonstrating the economic potential of the Far North (the Prudhoe Bay oil field in Alaska)[4] and also the difficulties associated with capitalizing on the possibilities of the Arctic (Canadian oil and gas exploration and the attempts to navigate the NWP).[5]

East Asia's engagement with the Arctic represents a new phase in the development of the region, one marked by international intrigue, diplomatic posturing, careful negotiations, occasional military blustering and grandiose economic plans. As the impact of Asia's economic and political interests is beginning to be felt in the Far North, it helps to reflect on the forces of change that are transforming the Arctic and that have elevated the Far North from a marginalized, largely ignored region,

---

2   There is a vast literature on the contemporary North. For three very different perspectives on the region, see Emmerson (2010), Smith (2011) and Byers (2010).

3   For an insightful account of this now-little-known event, see Coen (2012).

4   For an excellent account of this important development, see P. Coates (1993).

5   See K. Coates and Powell (1989). It is interesting to reflect on this book 25 years later, and to realize how much more has been accomplished than expected, how much has changed on the legal, political and constitutional fronts, how indigenous socio-economic challenges are much the same and how little non-Arctic attitudes about the region have changed.

to one that is a primary focus for international development pressures and high-level geopolitics. The forces are not listed in priority order, but they are designed to provide an indication of the myriad and interconnected influences that are shaping politics and policy in the region.

CLIMATE CHANGE

The rapid shifts in the global environment are, almost all analysts agree, most noticeable in the Arctic. The impacts are both dramatic and obvious: the declining size of the sea ice, changing weather patterns, warmer winters, the melting of old ice, changes to permafrost, shifting patterns of animal, plant, insect and bird populations, and countless other changes. Monitoring and responding to climate change in the Arctic has become a global priority, except where it really counts — in the adaptation of lifestyles and consumptive patterns to reduce human-driven environmental change. The likely melting of the permafrost stands out as a potentially vital ecological transition for the Arctic and the world, with the very real possibility of introducing life-altering dynamics into the global ecosystem.

UNTAPPED RESOURCE POTENTIAL

From the sixteenth-century voyages of Martin Frobisher through to the present, the Arctic has attracted the interest of resource developers. Most often, the Arctic has disappointed its promoters, with the resources proving illusory, technically difficult to extract, expensive to develop or unmarketable to the broader world. With extremely high estimates about the Arctic's oil and natural gas reserves, growing global demand for minerals and energy, and with increasing discoveries of mineral deposits that can be productively exploited, the time may well have come to develop Arctic resources on a broad and sustained scale. It is obvious that the resource companies of the world and resource-hungry nations are fixated on the possibilities of the Arctic, although the plans (outside of the Norway-Russia oil fields) largely focused on a multi-generational timeline.

THE EMPOWERMENT OF INDIGENOUS PEOPLES

Forty years ago, indigenous peoples had few rights and powers in the Northern nations. Starting with the Alaska Native Claims Settlement Act in 1971, indigenous communities and organizations began to accumulate great political power, autonomy and financial resources, including a significantly greater role in regional resource planning. The expansion of indigenous authority started with the creation of the Inuit Circumpolar Conference, the signing of major land claims agreements across much of the North American Arctic and the creation of permanent membership seats for indigenous groups within the Arctic Council. The movement toward indigenous empowerment was capped by the creation of Nunavut as an Inuit-controlled jurisdiction in the Canadian North and the success of the autonomy movement in Greenland. To a greater degree than almost anywhere in the world, indigenous peoples have a powerful role to play in the socio-economic and political transformation of the Arctic. This does not hold in Russia, however, where there have been substantial constraints placed on Aboriginal political organizations.

THE DEVELOPMENT OF CIRCUMPOLAR CONNECTIONS AND MINDSETS

In an effort that started with the Inuit, through the creation of the Inuit Circumpolar Conference and that now extends to education (the University of the Arctic), sports (the Arctic Winter Games), regional politics and administration (the Arctic Council and many other organizations, activities and strategies), the circumpolar world has come together in a remarkable and mutually beneficial manner. Indeed, there are few, if any, international zones in the world that have developed a collaborative, open and proactive intraregional mindset. Circumpolar peoples know, particularly as a result of climate change and resource developments, that they share a common future. They have the political structures and personal and professional connections to operationalize this circumpolar identity.

CONFLICTING MODELS OF APPLYING RESOURCE RENTS

Even if forecasts about Arctic resources are only partially true, the region will generate many billions of dollars in resource revenues for regional and national governments in the coming decades. The degree to which these resource rents are captured for northern, as opposed to for national or corporate, purposes is likely to be central to the future of the Arctic. In most countries, Arctic resources are seen as national in scope and utility. Nonetheless, new models of resource development and revenue sharing have emerged. These include the creation of heritage funds (Alaska), national endowments (Norway), indirect regional benefits (Sweden and

Finland), indigenous revenue sharing (Nunavut and modern treaty areas in northern Canada) and regional autonomy (Greenland). To the degree that these models permit regional, economic and social development, and improve indigenous well-being, resource development could be the trigger that brings regional population up to First World standards in terms of well-being or happiness. Alternately, if the patterns of the past are maintained or return, they could further enrich southern populations and entrench northern poverty.

INNOVATIONS IN NORTHERN GOVERNANCE

The Arctic has emerged as one of the most innovative geopolitical regions in the world. The innovations range from experiments in transregional governance, like the Arctic Council, to the entrenchment of indigenous autonomy and authority through modern land claim deals. The prominence of indigenous peoples in northern regions has, legitimately, given them more of a say in regional development than is the norm elsewhere in the world, and they have been using this effectively. New developments in the co-management of resources, revenue sharing, self-government, north-centred education, the promotion of mixed economies and other such measures have drawn global attention. The emergence of indigenous-controlled development corporations — directed by beneficiaries and not regional public governments, and with hundreds of millions of dollars in total assets — has the potential to transform the region economically and socially.

THE REALITY OF ARCTIC POVERTY

Northern places are, in the main, quite poor, particularly among the indigenous communities. In most jurisdictions, the social and economic development and well-being of indigenous communities lags well behind both regional non-indigenous populations and national standards. Indeed, the non-indigenous populations in the North are typically well off, largely due to employment with government or the resource sectors. Many of the best paid workers in the region, those working on oil rigs and in isolated mines, typically work on a fly-in/fly-out basis, taking their money (and social costs) south. In some cases — and northern Canada stands out as an egregious example — the situations facing indigenous peoples are quite dire, marked by high rates of violence, low life expectancy, substance abuse and unemployment. In others, with northern Norway having much better social outcomes, governments have mobilized regional resource wealth to ensure improved opportunities for indigenous peoples and communities. Overall, fanciful visions of massive Arctic resource wealth stand in stark and unacceptable contrast to the reality of indigenous poverty.

ARCTIC BOUNDARIES

The Arctic is the focus for the most significant drawing of international boundaries in recent decades. While the question of the official lines of demarcation related to continental shelves and underwater zones of national responsibility has been around for some time, the prospect of Arctic resource wealth, particularly offshore oil and gas, has given the issue great urgency. The application of the United Nations Convention on the Law of the Sea, which will resolve the matter through scientific, rather than military intervention, has given the world a peaceful path to the resolution of the issue, one that stands in sharp contrast to the growing controversies over minor islands in East Asia. That Norway and Russia settled their boundary disputes without controversy speaks to the likelihood of a peaceful and collaborative resolution of the border issue, despite the bellicose statements from Canada and Russia. Ironically, the most intense boundary issue relates to competing Canadian and US claims in the Beaufort Sea, bringing two great neighbours into conflict over a potentially resource-rich piece of underwater territory.

THE COLLAPSE OF THE USSR AND THE RUSSIAN WILD CARD

Even with the demise of the former USSR, Russia is still the largest country in the world. In a stunning series of developments, the Russian North has been transformed. These changes range from massive out-migration from Arctic towns and cities, which has hollowed out once-thriving communities, to the establishment of new local governments across the vast northland. Indigenous peoples have had their political rights circumscribed in recent years, and Arctic militarization and resource development has accelerated. Russia has wrapped itself in an Arctic mantle as a sign of its determination to re-emerge as a world power, after several decades of atrophy. Russia is a true Arctic wild card. Some North American analysts worry about its military and territorial ambitions; environmentalists are understandably concerned that its approach to development is harmful and unsustainable; supporters of indigenous rights worry about recent constraints on indigenous organizations. At the same time, Russia has stunning resource potential, which creates great opportunities for regional and national development. No one really knows Russia's trajectory or circumpolar impact in the coming years, but it is unlikely to be minor. Furthermore, the country's assertive behaviour in the Ukraine and Crimea has raised Western fears of a return to Russian aggression and, if nothing else, potential internal disputes within the country.

THE MILITARIZATION OF THE ARCTIC

The Arctic matters, particularly to Russia, Canada and the United States. All three countries have invested substantial emotional and political energy to declarations of determination to protect Arctic interests. Canadian Prime Minister Stephen Harper's famous phrase, "Use it or lose it," with regard to the Arctic is only one of numerous political pronouncements, from Harper and Russian President Vladimir Putin in particular, about national interests in the North. The Government of Russia has invested substantially in Arctic defence and militarization, increasing pressure on the United States and Canada to follow suit. While the practical effects of Arctic militarization have been comparatively small, the attention given to this issue emphasizes the importance that the northern countries apply to the region and raises the rhetoric, if not the stakes, in circumpolar affairs.

EMERGING MODELS OF RESOURCE EXTRACTION

It was not so long ago that the development of Arctic resources brought whole towns, with large, nonindigenous populations and significant infrastructure investments, into the North. Many politicians saw these developments as being the foundation for a new regional order. That model is now largely moribund. In its place, oil and gas companies and mining firms have resorted increasingly to fly-in/ fly-out operations. This method of operation leaves the costs of looking after families (schools, hospitals) in the south, limits corporate commitment to northern locales (camps can be closed down much more quickly than towns), and makes it easier to recruit workers. The mobile workforce lessens demands on northern governments and allows them to focus their efforts — and their money — on improving living conditions for the long-term residents, primarily Aboriginal, of the Far North.

THE GLOBALIZATION OF ARCTIC SCIENCE AND TECHNOLOGY

Arctic science and technology has long been international in scope, marked by the sharing of ideas and the minimal resources scientists could bring to bear on northern problems. Over the past quarter century, scientists from around the world have entered the field, with research groups from across Europe, Asia and around the world joining in the collective effort to better understand the Arctic, to gauge the impact of climate change and to develop strategies for responding to both the urgent environmental questions and resource opportunities. The global effort has been marked, as well, by cooperation and partnership, ranging from the sharing of equipment, including icebreakers, to collaborative research projects.

The world used to be interested in the Arctic conceptually. Now the scientific community is gathering together to learn more about this fascinating region and to prepare the North for the anticipated changes. Importantly, very little of this scientific and technological effort is being applied to the needs and aspirations of northern residents. Instead, major investments in the biological and geological sciences are helping the broader world understand how Arctic climate change will affect people outside the Far North, and comparatively little effort is being devoted to producing solutions that work for the people in the Arctic.

THE SOUTHERN IMPERATIVE IN CONTEMPORARY ARCTIC SOCIETY

Global protestations about admiration for northern life and indigenous populations, and concern about the region's well-being and future belie a systematic lack of personal international interest in going to the Arctic. Each year, the few hardy (and generally wealthy) souls who head to the Arctic as tourists are vastly outnumbered by millions of sunseekers heading to southern Europe, the Caribbean, Southeast Asia, the Pacific Islands or Mexico. Part of the rationale is cost: the expense of travelling to the Far North far exceeds trips to many tropical locations. The other reality is that modern society is cold averse. Holidays focus on warm areas, as does recreational activity generally (with the exception of skiing, widely regarded to be a declining industry). The Scandinavians, Russians and other northern peoples have adapted well to the North, but even in those nations, the patterns of out-migration, flight from cold weather and limited attachment to the North are strong. The harsh winters — on which climate change is actually having a relatively small impact to date — are tough and very expensive to overcome. Modern society is not well-conditioned to accept hardship. Even the northern resource projects typically offer impressive living conditions for their mobile workers. The lack of real interest in the North — and in cold, winter, snow and ice — is potentially significant, as contemporary northern and temperate-zone citizens get more distant from lives on the land.

THE CULTURE OF CONSULTATION

Northern politics do not work like they used to. Only a few decades ago, national and southern governments made and imposed decisions. Major projects were launched with little or no regional engagement. A series of conflicts in the 1960s and 1970s — over the proposed use of nuclear weapons to create a harbour in Alaska, the planned construction of the Alta dam in northern Norway, and the hotly debated Mackenzie Valley Pipeline in northern Canada — changed the regional political environment. Indigenous and northern people demanded to be heard. And they were. Western democracies now have structures in place to ensure consultations with northern and indigenous stakeholders, which is often extensive, time-consuming and costly. Southern governments can cajole and promote, but they have a much harder time, outside of Russia, imposing their will on northerners. The culture of consultation should produce more region-friendly solutions; developments across the North show that engaging with communities does not stop resource activity and can often turn development projects toward much greater regional benefit.

THE INTERNATIONALIZATION OF THE ARCTIC

Only two decades ago, the Arctic had developed one of the most impressive intraregional models of cooperation and engagement, exemplified by the Arctic Council. Collaboration efforts started by the Inuit spread to other indigenous groups, and then to regional public governments and national governments. Contacts at the levels of commerce, sports, culture and public affairs brought circumpolar peoples together in ways that seemed highly unlikely as late as the 1970s. Just as the circumpolar institutions and organizations were solidifying their roles and authority, however, the combination of climate change, border issues and natural resource potential drew global interests to the Arctic. What was once a marginalized zone had come into international prominence. Outsiders clambered for a place on the

Arctic Council, if only as permanent observers.[6] Governments from China to the European Union declared a strong interest in northern resource development, and insisted on the right to be at the table during Arctic discussions. The Arctic has, in less than a generation, been transformed from an emerging political region into a zone of international contention, a state of affairs that is not likely to be reversed. This transition is critical, for the North is still focused on solidifying intraregional connections, while other parts of the world, foremost among them East Asian countries, are trying to work their way into a game where the rules are still under development.

CONCLUDING THOUGHTS

There are other major forces at play in the region, ranging from the very real threat of the elimination of Arctic languages and cultures by mass media and popular culture to the equally real prospects for underseas mining in the Arctic Ocean. The list above, however, provides a good indication of the recent transformation of the geopolitics of the Arctic, the impressive array of interests in the region, and the complexity and interconnection of the forces of change in the Far North. In such a rare situation, where global interest is focusing on a vast area with a small resident population, the intricacies and imperatives shift quickly — and often profoundly. The Arctic is no longer mysterious, but its future is truly uncertain. Research on the North has accelerated dramatically; there are likely more North Americans studying Arctic shipping than there are Arctic-ready ships. The fate of the region, and particularly the vulnerable Arctic ecosystem and the small, widely dispersed indigenous populations, will likely be decided by a series of political, diplomatic, economic and legal agreements over the coming two decades. No one can claim that the Arctic is irrelevant any more. No one, however, can say with certainty how the coming years will unfold.

This is the environment into which East Asian countries are now moving. China, Japan and South Korea have been relatively minor players to date, although their interest in the North is expanding rapidly, in line with East Asia's growing need for natural resources. The three nations are leading with their Arctic scientists, much as North America and Europe did for generations. The companies are not far behind, making major investments in the region and planning for even greater ones in the near future. East Asian diplomats have become much more active in Arctic affairs,

---

6   The story of the emergence of the Arctic Council is well told in English (2013).

and have pushed hard to get a regular position on the Arctic Council. East Asia is coming to the Arctic. The Far North, to put it simply, is not ready for the active and sustained presence of Japan, China and South Korea at present, much as East Asia has not yet shown a strong familiarity with the nuances and historical patterns of Arctic development. The coming years promise to be exciting, indeed.

WORKS CITED

Byers, Michael. 2010. *Who Owns the Arctic?: Understanding Sovereignty Disputes in the North.* Vancouver: Douglas and McIntyre.

Coates, Ken, Whitney Lackenbauer, William Morrison and Greg Poelzer. 2008. *Arctic Front: Defending Canada in the Far North.* Toronto: Thomas Allen.

Coates, Ken, and Judith Powell. 1989. *The Modern North People, Politics and the Rejection of Colonialism.* Toronto: Lorimer.

Coates, Peter. 1993. *The Trans-Alaska Pipeline Controversy.* Fairbanks: University of Alaska Press.

Coen, Ross. 2012. *Breaking Ice for Arctic Oil: The Epic Voyage of the SS Manhattan Through the Northwest Passage.* Fairbanks: University of Alaska Press.

Emmerson, Charles. 2010. *The Future History of the Arctic.* New York: PublicAffairs.

English, John. 2013. *Ice and Water: Politics, Peoples and the Arctic Council.* Toronto: Allen Lane.

Grant, Shelagh. 2010. *Polar Imperative: A History of Arctic Sovereignty in North America.* Vancouver: UBC Press.

Smith, Laurence. 2011. *The World in 2050: Four Forces Shaping Civilization's Northern Future.* New York: Plume.

2

The Process of Formulating Japan's Arctic Policy: From Involvement to Engagement

///

Fujio Ohnishi

INTRODUCTION

Although Japan has been involved in a number of activities in the Arctic since the end of the Cold War, the Japanese government has not yet made its Arctic policy official. In recent years, however, as the impact of climate change on the Arctic has become increasingly apparent, the Japanese government has begun to define its role and interests in the Arctic at the ministerial level. This is partly because the rapidly melting ice in the Arctic, caused by global warming, affects not only the Arctic Ocean and its surrounding ecosystem, but also causes the sea level to rise on a global scale, altering the earth's climate system — issues that are of concern for Japan (Arctic Monitoring and Assessment Programme [AMAP] 2011, 11). According to the Japan Agency for Marine-Earth Science and Technology (JAMSTEC), the latest research reveals that the retreat of sea ice is related to colder winter temperatures in Japan (JAMSTEC 2012). Of further concern to Japan, the melting ice in the Arctic Ocean means the area is rapidly globalizing as it becomes more and more integrated into the market economy. Globalization brings new global players into the Arctic, thus effecting an increase of marine activities in the region.

This chapter summarizes the three milestones of Japan's involvement in the Arctic and examines the process of formulating Japan's Arctic interests at the ministerial level. Then, it discusses opportunities and challenges for Japan in the Arctic. Finally, the paper concludes with three considerations, which could help inform the Japanese government's formulation of its Arctic policy.

THREE MILESTONES IN JAPAN'S ARCTIC INVOLVEMENT

There are three milestones in the involvement of Japan in the Arctic. The first marked involvement dates back to the Svalbard Treaty signed in 1920. As one of the 14 high contracting parties to the treaty, Japan holds certain legal rights and obligations, including rights of fishing and hunting in the territories and the territorial waters (article 2), liberty of access and entry (article 3), the establishment of an international meteorological station (article 5) and the same treatment (of nationals of the signatory countries) with the nationals of Norway, "with regard to methods of acquisition, enjoyment and exercise of the right of ownership of property, including mineral rights, in the territories specified in article 1" (article 7). In practice, these rights are difficult to execute unilaterally, but they can be executed in accordance with the relevant Norwegian jurisdiction.

Recently, some conflicts have been renewed among signatory parties as to the interpretation of the Svalbard Treaty's applicability regarding the exclusive economic zone (EEZ) and continental shelf around Svalbard. The Japanese Ministry of Foreign Affairs (MoFA) had not formulated its position toward the treaty; however, present and future developments in terms of resource exploitation and shipping in the Arctic will increase the area's strategic importance for Japan (Ohnishi 2012, 338).

Japan's second important involvement in the Arctic is in the field of science. Japan has engaged in polar science for more than half a century. This long-standing interest has naturally prompted research in the Arctic. The 1987 Murmansk speech by then Soviet Union President Mikhail Gorbachev changed the political atmosphere of international relations in the Arctic, suggesting, as one of six concrete proposals, the coordination of scientific research in the Arctic, which led to a dramatically increased interest regarding Arctic research. This increased interest resulted in the establishment of the International Arctic Science Committee (IASC), an active and major non-governmental organization promoting Arctic research. The establishment of the IASC, in turn, affected Japanese researchers in natural science. The Japanese government founded the National Institute of Polar Research (NIPR), an inter-university research institute in 1973, which in turn established the Arctic Environment Research Center (AERC) in 1990. The AERC opened a research station at Ny- Ålesund on Svalbard in 1991, in collaboration with the Norwegian Polar Research Institute. Joining the IASC from 1991, the NIPR began to engage in a variety of national and international research activities in the Arctic. While the NIPR focused on terrestrial fields of research, JAMSTEC began marine research in collaboration with the United States. JAMSTEC conducted its first research cruise with the oceanographic research vessel *Mirai* in 1998. Since then, invaluable observational studies have resulted from more than 10 Arctic expeditions by JAMSTEC.

A third important involvement in the Arctic was also given impetus by Gorbachev's proposal regarding the opening of the Northern Sea Route (NSR). "To examine all the possibilities of the NSR, an international commercial sea lane, Japan's then-named Ship and Ocean Foundation (now called the [Ocean Policy Research Foundation] OPRF), aided by the Nippon Foundation, in collaboration with partners from Norway and Russia, carried out the [International Northern Sea Route Program] INSROP from 1993 to 1999" (OPRF 2013). The INSROP was an international project of close collaboration among the partner countries, with 390 participating researchers from 14 countries "pursuing the multidisciplinary study of the NSR" (ibid.). Phase 1 of the INSROP was carried out from 1993 to 1995, and phase 2 from 1997 to 1998 (ibid.). In connection with the INSROP, an experimental voyage via the NSR was performed with the *Kandalaksha*, a Russian ice-breaking cargo vessel, from Yokohama, Japan to Kirkenes, Norway (ibid). During the trip, an on-board research team, composed of 18 experts and specialists from Japan, Russia and Canada, made various observations and measurements, affording them a good opportunity to deepen their understanding of natural conditions and ship performance through the NSR (ibid.). In advance of the establishment of the Arctic Regional Hydrographic Commission in 2010, the INSROP pioneered charting of the shipping route in the Arctic.

THE PROCESS OF FORMULATING JAPAN'S ARCTIC INTERESTS

The impact of climate change on the Arctic and the speed at which the ice has been melting in summer seasons have been repeatedly reported by media in Japan. An incident that caused some alarm was Russia planting its national flag on the seabed of the North Pole in August 2007. One of Japan's national newspapers reported the event as the beginning of a "resource race" (Komaki and Mizuno 2007). In short, the impact of climate change, causing rapid ice melting, also affected the Japanese policy-making community, which began looking more carefully at the Arctic.

Several government ministries began making their agendas relevant to Arctic development. Intensive efforts were prompted by the Ministry of Education, Culture, Sports, Science and Technology (MEXT). Faced with the increasing effects of climate change in the Arctic Ocean and their potential impact on Arctic terrestrial environments — as already observed in the repeated breaking of records of the minimum extent of the Arctic ice cap — the MEXT revitalized its Arctic research programs. For example, in May 2011, the Japan Consortium for Arctic Environmental Research was founded as a platform for coordinating the Arctic research activities of Japan. In June 2011, in the course of a governmental initiative for facilitating green innovation and environmentally friendly technologies, the MEXT also initiated the Green Network of Excellence, under which the five-year Arctic Climate Change Research Project was funded, managed by the NIPR and JAMSTEC.

One can also see efforts by the MoFA. In line with increasing prospects for the Arctic Council as the most relevant body for Arctic governance, in April 2009, Japan's then Senior Vice Minister for Foreign Affairs Seiko Hashimoto attended the Antarctic Treaty-Arctic Council Joint Meeting in Washington, DC, officially announcing Japan's application for permanent observer status in the Arctic Council. Since then, the Japanese government has been attending Arctic Council meetings as an ad hoc observer. In line with its efforts, the MoFA established the Arctic Task Force in September 2010 to help identify Japanese interests in the Arctic. Through several bilateral meetings, the Japanese government requested the support of Arctic states for the approval of Japan's application for permanent observer status to the Arctic Council. On November 6, 2012, Japan's former Senior Vice Minister for Foreign Affairs Shuji Kira attended a meeting between the Arctic Council's Swedish chair and the council's observers and ad hoc observers in Stockholm, Sweden. In his statement, Vice Minister Kira asserted that Japan deserved permanent observer status because of its active contribution to the activities under the Arctic Council, and assured the council that Japan would respect the sovereignty of the member states, their sovereign rights and jurisdiction (Kira 2012). A more recent effort by the MoFA is the appointment of Masuo Nishibayashi, ambassador of cultural exchange, to be concurrently appointed in charge of Arctic affairs (MoFA 2013). As a result of these efforts, Japan was admitted as an observer to the Arctic Council's 8th Ministerial Meeting in Kiruna, Sweden. At the meeting, Nishibayashi said that the melting Arctic ice opened opportunities in the region for both researchers and businesses, which increased the awareness of Japanese people (Pedersen 2013).

Owing mainly to the potential impact of the opening of the NSR as a commercially viable shipping route between East Asia and Europe, in August 2012, the Ministry of Land, Infrastructure and Tourism (MLIT) set up a board in order to examine the route's feasibility and logistics for Japanese shipping companies, including ports in the northern part of Japan. The MLIT gathers relevant information through its internal and external channels. The National Institute for Defense Studies (NIDS) also conducted work in this area. In its annual report, the NIDS explains that Japan cannot stand outside future Arctic development, and recommends that Japan build reliable relationships with the Arctic states (NIDS 2011, 83–85). Additionally, in July 2012, a non-partisan group of parliamentarians on Arctic security was formed. The chair of the group, Shinzo Abe, has now become Japan's prime minister.

In line with the government's activation of policy formulation toward the Arctic, discussions are also underway in the private sector. The OPRF — a private think tank known for organizing INSROP and for its major role in the Basic Act on Ocean Policy in July 2007 — contributes significantly to studies on the Arctic and in helping to formulate policy recommendations. As part of its efforts in this context, the OPRF launched the Arctic Conference Japan in 2010, with experts in international law, security, science, shipbuilding, shipping and climate change. Over the past two years, conference members have continued to meet to establish a unified view of multi-faceted Arctic issues and to address Japan's Arctic policy and strategy in order to meet the interests of Japan and the world. In its proposals released on April 25, 2012, the Arctic Conference Japan urged the government to: establish a task force as a "playmaker" to design Japan's Arctic policy; engage actively in Arctic Ocean management; be actively involved in the environmental protection of the Arctic Ocean; reinforce involvement in Arctic natural resources development; bolster Arctic research; promptly respond to logistical changes by the opening of Arctic seaways; design a new security program in response to the opening of the Arctic seaways; contribute to the establishment of order in the Arctic Ocean; and establish a framework for Japan-Russia dialogue on Arctic issues (Arctic Conference Japan 2012, 1–9).

In addition, the Japan Institute of International Affairs (JIIA), founded in 1959 as a private, non-partisan policy think tank focused on foreign affairs and security issues, organized a research project called "Arctic Governance and Japan's Foreign Strategy," which was funded by the MoFA in 2012 as one of its international affairs research/recommendation projects. The JIIA study group released its final report in March 2013, in which the following six recommendations were made to the government:

- "Japan's financial means and technology should be utilized in the area of resource exploration and development to build win-win relationships with Coastal States" (Asari 2013, 3).

- "In the area of marine transportation, appropriate application of the [United Nations Convention on the Law of the Sea] should be ensured on the basis of the principles of the right of innocent passage (in the territorial waters of Coastal States) or freedom of navigation (in the waters beyond the territorial waters of Coastal States) on Arctic shipping routes" (ibid., 4).

- "On the security front, the Japan-US cooperation should be further strengthened, taking into account implications for the strategic environment if power projections in the Arctic Ocean become easier" (ibid., 7).

- "Fully taking into consideration the delicate environment of the Arctic Ocean, Japan should harness its expertise and technology to play a leading role in the area of environmental preservation" (ibid., 8).

- "Active diplomacy should be pursued so that governance founded on a peaceful and stable international order [can] be ensured in the Arctic Ocean" (ibid., 10).

- "The Japanese government's Arctic policy structure should be reinforced" (ibid., 11).

OPPORTUNITIES AND CHALLENGES FOR JAPAN IN THE ICE-MELTING ARCTIC

OPENING ARCTIC SHIPPING ROUTES

There are three distinct realms of opportunity for Japan in the ice-melting Arctic. The first and most beneficial opportunity lies in the opening of Arctic shipping routes. The NSR — also called the Northeast Passage — is more beneficial for Japanese shipping companies than the Northwest Passage, as the trip using the NSR is about 40 percent shorter than the 11,500-nautical-mile haul through the Suez from Hamburg to Yokohama. The number of commercial ships passing through the NSR has increased radically since 2010. In 2012, 46 vessels passed through the

NSR. For example, the liquefied natural gas (LNG) tanker *Ob River*, chartered by Russia's Gazprom Group, arrived at the Japanese LNG terminal with liquefied gas from Norway in December 2012, which was the first transit through the NSR made by the LNG tanker.

This trend, however, poses challenges. Japanese shipping companies have not operated transport through the NSR yet. The main reason is that it is economically less viable due to the fees that Russia sets, based on the current cargo flow (Arctic Council 2009, 117). Moreover, as a Tokyo shipping company's planning expert (who wished to remain anonymous) explained in a personal interview, reserving ice-class ships only for the summer season is an unendurable burden for shipping companies that are competing for cost performance in the global market.[1] Uncertain, intermittent weather forecasting and the lack of reporting of icy ocean conditions also pose serious hazards for Arctic shipping (Emmerson and Lahn 2012, 23).

The key to making NSR transits more economically viable lies in efforts both for correcting the disparity between the Russian regulations and globally accepted international rules and standards, and for improving weather forecasting technology, including the reporting of ice conditions. In this regard, the ongoing work for preparing the Polar Code under the International Maritime Organization is crucial.

OIL AND GAS

The second opportunity is in the development of oil and gas fields. Since 1989, the Japan Oil, Gas and Metals National Corporation (JOGMEC) — formerly known as Japan National Oil Corporation — has been a member of the Kalaallit Nunaat Marine Seismic (KANUMAS) project, "a regional seismic program, including new data acquisition and preliminary studies for hydrocarbon potential near offshore Greenland" (JOGMEC 2012).[2] "In December 2011, the Bureau of Minerals and Petroleum...of the Government of Greenland announced the opening of the licensing rounds in the Greenland Sea, offshore Northeast Greenland" (ibid.). In an attempt to participate in the rounds, Greenland Petroleum Exploration Co., Ltd. was established (ibid.).

---

1   Personal communication, July 31, 2012.

2   According to JOGMEC (2012), "The KANUMAS project has been sponsored by the KANUMAS Group, comprising Statoil, BP, ExxonMobil, Chevron, Shell, JOGMEC and NUNAOIL A/S (National Oil Company of Greenland). In return, each member of the KANUMAS Group was granted a special preferential position to be activated when a call for tenders for exploration and exploitation licenses is issued for the area concerned."

Since the Great East Japan Earthquake in March 2011, the demand for oil and gas as alternatives to nuclear power plants has increased in Japan because the government suspended all 54 reactors, which accounted for 31 percent of the country's energy supplies. According to one estimate, crude oil imports were 4.38 million barrels per day in 2012 and will exceed 4.2 million barrels per day in 2013 (Nagatomi et al. 2012). Japan's LNG import is estimated at 87.6 million tons in 2012 and will increase to 88.7 million tons in 2013 (ibid.).

However, there are also complications in this category. Technological difficulties as a result of harsh Arctic weather make mining and exploitation difficult obstacles for investing in oil and gas. Furthermore, disputes — over maritime borders between the United States and Canada, the dominion over Hans Island and the interpretation of the Svalbard Treaty — also negatively affect the potential for the development of oil and gas in the Arctic, as does the delimitation of the continental shelf adjacent to the North Pole.

FISHERIES IN THE CENTRAL ARCTIC OCEAN

The third opportunity comes with potential fisheries in the Central Arctic Ocean (CAO). The warming sea temperature in the Arctic Ocean may cause the migration of fish stocks northward. Currently, there is no regional fishery management agreement covering the CAO where the high sea intersects with the EEZs of coastal states. In order to realize potential fisheries, data about fish stocks in the CAO must be obtained to facilitate sustainable management. Although this is not a straightforward task, and there is no evidence about the wealth of fish stocks in the CAO, the prospect for possible fisheries in this area provides incentives for invigorating the Japanese fishing industry.

CONCLUSION

The ice-melting Arctic is producing many global issues, such as the escalation of global warming, a rise of sea levels and a drastic overall impact on the global climate. It is crucial for Japan to deal with these issues through the facilitation of Arctic research. At the same time, however, the changing Arctic environment offers the potential to invigorate the Japanese economy. This circumstance encourages the Japanese government to formulate its Arctic policy with a long-term perspective focusing on both opportunities and challenges (Ohnishi 2013, 46–48). Toward the formulation of such an Arctic policy, the following three considerations are beneficial.

The first consideration concerns the relationship between scientific findings and economic interests. As this chapter shows, since the beginning of the 1990s, the Japanese scientific community has devoted efforts toward a better understanding of the Arctic environment and the impact of climate change. However, this research has been conducted without being connected to the potential economic interests that it holds for Japanese society. When the government formulates its Arctic policy, the data and knowledge obtained from scientific research should be strategically used for planning and promoting the long-term perspectives on the economic benefits that Japan can draw from the Arctic.

The second consideration should be a close investigation of the regional order in the Arctic and its possible linkages with East Asian countries. As the Arctic Ocean is integrated with the global market, non-Arctic East Asian states such as China, South Korea and Japan will advance their commitments in the Arctic, thus becoming more involved in Arctic issues. This means that international relations in the Arctic will affect those in East Asia. The government needs to pay attention to this linked side effect between the Arctic and East Asia.

The third consideration is about the attitude of the government toward indigenous people in the Arctic. Indigenous people are substantial stakeholders in Arctic affairs and hold informal but significant influence on decisions made by regional institutions and governments in the Arctic. Their influence will be more apparent under the Canadian chairmanship of the Arctic Council. Thus, the Japanese government should make diplomatic efforts not only toward the Arctic states but also toward subnational actors such as indigenous groups in the Arctic.

WORKS CITED

AMAP. 2011. "Snow, Water, Ice and Permafrost in the Arctic [SWIPA] Executive Summary." AMAP. www.amap.no/documents/doc/swipa-2011-executive-summary-snow-water-ice-and-permafrost-in-the-arctic/744.

Arctic Conference Japan. 2012. *Policy Proposals: Actions and Measures Japan Is to Take with a View to Ensuring Sustainable Use of the Arctic Ocean.* OPRF.

Arctic Council. 2009. *Arctic Marine Shipping Assessment 2009 Report.* Arctic Council, April. www.pame.is/images/stories/AMSA_2009_Report/AMSA_2009_Report_2nd_print.pdf.

Asari, Hidecki. 2013. "Chapter 8: Recommendations for Japan's Diplomacy 'Arctic Governance and Japan's Diplomatic Strategy' Project." JIIA. www2.jiia.or.jp/en/pdf/research/2012_arctic_governance/08e-recommendations.pdf.

Emmerson, Charles and Glada Lahn. 2012. *Arctic Opening: Opportunity and Risk in the High North*. London: Lloyd's and Chatham House. www.lloyds.com/~/media/Files/News%20and%20Insight/360%20Risk%20Insight/Arctic_Risk_Report_20120412.pdf.

Gorbachev, Mikhail. 1987. Untitled speech given at the Ceremonial Meeting on the Occasion of the Presentation of the Order of Lenin and the Gold Star Medal to the City of Murmansk.

JAMSTEC. 2012. "Sea-Ice Variability in the Barents Sea Brings Arctic Warm and Continental Cold: Clues to Coldness in Japanese Winter." Press release, February 1. www.jamstec.go.jp/e/about/press_release/20120201/.

JOGMEC. 2012. "JOGMEC Provides Equity Financing for Petroleum Exploration Offshore Greenland." Press release, February 29. www.jogmec.go.jp/english/news/release/release0086.html.

Kira, Shuji. 2012. "Statement by Parliamentary Senior Vice-Minister for Foreign Affairs of Japan Mr. Shuji Kira." Speech given at the meeting between the Swedish Chairmanship of the Arctic Council and Observers/Ad-hoc Observers, Stockholm, Sweden, November 6. www.arctic-council.org/index.php/en/about/documents/category/392-observer-meeting-stockholm-6-nov-2012?download=1508:japan-statement.

Komaki, Akiyoshi and Takaaki Mizuno. 2007. "Momentarily." [In Japanese.] *Asahi Shinbun*, August 22.

MoFA. 2013. "Appointment of Ambassador in Charge of Arctic Affairs." Press release, March 19. www.mofa.go.jp/press/release/press6e_000002.html.

Nagatomi, Yu, Toshiaki Hachiuma, Masayuki Kako, Takayuki Yoshioka, Hidenori Suzuki, Akira Tanagisawa and Kochichi Ito. 2012. "Short-term Energy Supply and Demand Outlook: Analysis on Scenario through FY2013 — Summary." PowerPoint presentation delivered at the Institute of Energy Economics Japan's 411th Forum on Research Work, Tokyo, December 21. http://eneken.ieej.or.jp/data/4672.pdf.

NIDS. 2011. *East Asian Strategic Review 2011*. NIDS.

Ohnishi, Fujio. 2012. "Comments on Chapter 6: Japanese Perspective." In *The Arctic in World Affairs: A North Pacific Dialogue on Arctic Marine Issues*, edited by Oran R. Young, Jong Deog Kim and Yoon Hyung Kim, 337–346. Seoul: Korea Maritime Institute and East-West Center.

———. 2013. "Climate Change and the Arctic Issues: Broadened Economic Possibilities and Challenges for Japanese Diplomacy." [In Japanese.] *Intelligence Report* 59: 34–49.

OPRF. 2013. "Examples of Major Studies and Research and Development Implemented in the Past: INSROP." OPRF. www.sof.or.jp/en/activities/index6_1.php.

Pedersen, Torbjøn. 2013. "After Dinner, the Arctic Council Held a Less Exclusive Forum." [In Norwegian.] *Aftenposten*, May 16. http://eavis.aftenposten.no/aftenposten/87637/archive/demo/?page=16.

3

China and the Arctic: China's Interests and Participation in the Region

///

Kai Sun
· · · · · · · · ·

INTRODUCTION

In the past, the Arctic has only been the interest of natural scientists in China focusing on polar research and world travellers; however, things have changed in the past two decades. Since that time, the Arctic has been getting increased attention from Chinese media, social scientists and government officials for a number of reasons, including the increasing international attention surrounding the melting of the Arctic ice caps and the changes that this is expected to bring in both geopolitical and geo-economic terms.

China's interest and participation in Arctic affairs has been growing with the melting of Arctic sea ice, which has come as a result of global climate change. This interest and participation in Arctic affairs has caught a lot of international attention, and even suspicion about China's intentions as an "outsider" joining the Arctic. In this chapter, the recent surge of China's Arctic interests, including academic research interests by social and natural scientists, business interests and political interests (mainly manifested by the open discussion of several Chinese officials on Arctic issues) are discussed. It also discusses China's interest and participation

◇◇◇◇◇◇◇◇◇◇◇◇◇

in the Arctic, and finally, the challenges and possibilities for China's future Arctic participation are discussed.

CHINA'S ARCTIC INTEREST

China's interest in the Arctic has grown in the past two decades, and this interest is only expected to increase in coming decades. China's primary interests in the Arctic are not only in "real-world" practice, which includes the economic interests and business opportunities of a changing Arctic, but also in academia, with more research projects on Arctic social and natural sciences, and more publications in academic journals.

In recent years, there has been an increase in Chinese writings on Arctic affairs from the social science perspective. To some degree, this academic interest also reflects the Chinese government's growing interest in Arctic issues. David Wright (2011a) summarizes Chinese academic writers on this topic, citing several prominent authors who are vocal about Arctic studies in China: Guo Peiqing and Liu Huirong from the Ocean University of China, who write on Arctic political and legal issues; Lu Junyuan from Suzhou University, who writes on Arctic international relations; Li Zhenfu from Dalian Maritime University, who writes on Arctic passages; and several other researchers in Shanghai who are studying Arctic governance.

The rise of China's academic interest in Arctic affairs is also shown through its institutional building in the past two to three years. For example, in 2010, Ocean University of China founded the Research Institute of Polar Law and Politics, which is one of the first institutes dedicated to polar social science research. There are also polar research institutes at Shanghai Jiao Tong University, Fudan University and Wuhan University. China's national social science research fund, managed by the National Planning Office of Philosophy and Social Science (NPOPSS), is the highest level of funding agencies in the country. Its suggested project topics are usually regarded as the barometer of China's governmental focus. Both Arctic studies and "Russia's Arctic Policy and Its Regional Impacts" are among the funding agency's 2012 suggested project topics, and Arctic studies is also among the fund's suggested project topics in 2013 (NPOPSS 2011; 2012). China's State Oceanic Administration is another major source of funding, with a Polar Strategic Fund set up in 2006 that provides funds for natural science and social science polar research projects. In recent years, the funded projects include more research from social science disciplines. In June 2013, the First China-Nordic Arctic Cooperation Symposium was held in Shanghai with sponsorship from the Polar Research Institute of China (PRIC) and China's State Oceanic Administration (China Daily 2013). The symposium was attended by more than 70 practitioners and scholars, and as a result, a China-Nordic Arctic research centre will be established. The research centre will cover studies on Arctic climate change and its impacts, as well as policy and legislation related to the Arctic.

The melting of the Arctic and the opening of Arctic passages and resources have also attracted quite a lot of interest among Chinese businessmen. The most significant headline-maker is billionaire Huang Nubo, a Chinese real estate developer, and his ongoing investment plan in Iceland. Huang's investment in Iceland — the purchase of a 300 km^2 area in Iceland for a tourist resort, including a luxury tourist centre with a golf course, villas and other attractions — was first announced in September 2011 (Mei 2012). The original plan has met with difficulties from the Icelandic Parliament and was changed from a land purchase into a land rental agreement for 99 years' development. Huang was expected to sign the contract in October 2012 (ibid.); however, this changed plan was thwarted again by Icelandic officials in late 2012 (Fontaine 2012).

As Wright (2011a) states, "China is quite aware of the U.S. Geological Survey's estimates that '25% of the world's undiscovered hydrocarbon resources are found there, along with 9% of the world's coal and other economically critical minerals.'" So property development opportunities, such as that envisioned by Huang Nubo, are but one kind of opportunity that the opening Arctic can offer to Chinese companies. Beyond tourism, there are significant opportunities to develop Arctic resources in partnership with companies from Arctic countries. China's state-run oil companies are pioneering in this regard, joining the bids for Arctic resource development and investing strategically in Arctic resources.

ARCTIC CAPACITY BUILDING

As the old Chinese proverb goes, "capacity decides the place," and China is fully aware of this in the Arctic play. Thus, strong and robust capacity in Arctic research and other issues is a must, in order to gain a place and to contribute to good Arctic governance. Polar research capacity is key to any polar expedition, and China is enhancing its Arctic capacity building, which it emphasizes at high-level conferences on polar research. Chen Lianzeng, deputy director of the State Oceanic Administration, emphasized this in the 14th Meeting of the Chinese Advisory Committee for Polar Research. At the meeting, Deputy Director Chen's emphasis was on better coordination and planning of polar research, practical implementation of polar research findings, and enhanced education and professional training for polar works (Chinese Arctic and Antarctic Administration 2012). ✐

Yellow River Station, China's first and only Arctic scientific research base, was established on Svalbard, Norway in 2004. China has conducted five Arctic expeditions to date, with the first and second scientific research expeditions carried out in 1999 and 2003, before the research station was built. The third and fourth expeditions were conducted in 2008 and 2010. The fifth — and most well-known expedition — occurred in summer 2012. In this expedition, China's only operating icebreaking research ship, the *Xue Long* ("Snow Dragon") travelled 18,500 nautical miles, including about 5,370 nautical miles in the Arctic ice zone. This was the first time that a Chinese vessel had made a round-trip, high-latitude voyage across the Arctic, reaching a latitude as high as N87°40' (*Science and Technology Daily* 2012). China is planning its sixth Arctic expedition, and "an advanced new icebreaking research vessel to meet the increased need of polar scientific research" is being built in collaboration with a Finnish company (Embassy of Finland 2012). The new icebreaker is capable of breaking ice up to 1.5 m thick, with a tonnage of 8,000, will have a cruising capacity of 20,000 nautical miles, and can work in water for up to 60 days with a top speed of 15 knots. It is scheduled for use in 2014 (Xinhua News Agency 2012a).

Though China is a signatory to the Svalbard Treaty, it is a latecomer to Arctic research, and research in this field does not get much attention within China. There is a great gap between the international research capacity for studying Arctic issues and China's research level in the field, in both natural and social sciences. Thus, international cooperation is an important way for China to enhance its Arctic research capacity. It is doing so by joining international research organizations and conducting joint Arctic research expeditions. China joined the International Arctic Science Committee in 1996, becoming the organization's sixteenth member country. In 2005, China hosted the Arctic Science Summit Week and initiated and organized the Pacific Arctic Group; that same year, China was admitted to the Ny-Ålesund Science Managers Committee. Through these international platforms, Chinese scientists have more access to keep up with international Arctic research communications and information, and have the opportunity to participate in cutting-edge research with other scientists from abroad. China also joined and actively participated in the activities of the International Polar Year (IPY) 2007-2008. That year, Chinese scientists proposed 16 Arctic research projects to the IPY, and one of them, Project PANDA, was accepted as one of the IPY's core research projects. Project PANDA "is a multi-goal research plan including deep ice coring at Dome A, the highest location on the Antarctic ice sheet, and a study of the interactions of the ocean-ice shelf-ice sheet system from Pridz Bay to Dome A via the Amery

Ice Shelf" (Xinhua News Agency 2007). Although Project PANDA is an Antarctic project, it shows China's enhanced polar research capacities and its aspirations for international cooperation in polar research. Through active participation in IPY activities, China also aims to enhance public education on polar affairs, thus increasing the general public's awareness of polar issues.

As compared to Antarctic research expeditions, funding for Arctic research is relatively small. Funding for China's Arctic research expeditions comes from different sources: the National Development and Reform Commission, which is mainly responsible for providing funds for infrastructure building; the Ministry of Finance, which is mainly responsible for the cost of implementing the polar research expeditions; the National Science Fund, which funds Arctic research projects; and the Ministry of Science and Technology, which provides funding for regular observations. There is neither special nor regular funding for polar research in any of the aforementioned ministries, so China's polar expeditions suffer from a lack of adequate and stable funding.

CHINA'S ARCTIC DIPLOMACY

There is no doubt that China would like to participate more actively in Arctic affairs. With China's increased interest in the Arctic, it is engaging in more bilateral and multilateral relations with Arctic counties. China is not an Arctic country, so international cooperation is the only way for China to join the Arctic play. With respect to the legal order of the Arctic, the Chinese government's position is that the current system of international law of the sea provides a sound legal foundation for the settlement of Arctic affairs covering the basic problems of Arctic affairs, including maritime delimitation, marine environmental protection, navigation and scientific research.

In a 2010 statement on the website of the Chinese Foreign Ministry, Hu Zhengyue, then assistant minister of foreign affairs, said that "recognizing and respecting each other's rights constitutes the legal basis for cooperation between Arctic and non-Arctic states. In accordance with the United Nations Convention on the Law of the Sea [UNCLOS] and other relevant international laws, Arctic states have sovereign rights and jurisdiction in their respective areas in the Arctic region, while non-Arctic states also enjoy rights of scientific research and navigation. To develop a partnership of cooperation, Arctic and non-Arctic states should, first and foremost, recognize and respect each other's rights under the international law" (cited in Zhu 2011). The principle of international cooperation was also emphasized by Zhao Jun (2013), Chinese ambassador to Norway, in a speech he delivered at the Arctic Frontiers conference held in Tromsø, Norway, in January 2013. He said that "China respects the sovereignty, sovereignty rights and jurisdiction of the Arctic states, attaches importance to Arctic scientific research and environmental protection, and supports the principles and objectives of the Arctic Council…China's Arctic research could not have been done without cooperation from other Arctic countries. China is hoping to continue enhancing its cooperation on Arctic scientific research with the Arctic countries, and to share the findings of the scientific research, so as to contribute to peace, stability and sustainable development of the Arctic region" (ibid.).

China is practising this through multilateral and bilateral diplomacies, and on Arctic research expeditions, China is open to international cooperation with scientists from other nations. Four scientists — from Russia, South Korea and Japan — joined China's 1999 Arctic research expedition; 13 foreign scientists — from the United States, Canada, Japan, South Korea, Finland, Russia, among other nations — joined China's 2003 Arctic research expedition; 11 foreign scientists joined the 2008 Arctic research expedition; and eight foreign scientists joined the 2010 Arctic research expedition (Qu et al. 2011). Chinese scientists have also joined foreign Arctic research expeditions and have started exchange and cooperation programs with Arctic research centres around the globe, including the University of Alaska, the University of Washington, the International Arctic Research Center and the Korea Maritime Institute.

As for bilateral relations, China is conducting Arctic diplomacy and discussing cooperation for Arctic issues with all eight Arctic countries. Although the United States is a reluctant superpower in Arctic affairs (Huebert 2009), it remains a very influential player in Arctic affairs. Indeed, Arctic issues have been a priority of the high-level US-China Strategic and Economic Dialogue since the third round in 2011, and were listed again in the fourth-round dialogue in 2012. Moreover, Canada is a major Arctic player. During Canadian Prime Minister Stephen Harper's visit to China in February 2012, China's interests in Arctic issues were among the topics for discussion (Payton 2012). In May 2013, Canada assumed a two-year term as chair of the Arctic Council; China is expected to apply for formal observer status during Canada's term.

The most prominent display of China's efforts at Arctic diplomacy is with the Nordic countries. Chinese President Hu Jintao visited Denmark in June 2012, marking the first visit by a Chinese head of state since the two countries established diplomatic ties 62 years ago. The Arctic was not a major topic during the visit, but a good relationship with Denmark is a must in galvanizing support for China's future application to the Arctic Council. In April of that same year, Chinese Prime Minister

Wen Jiabao visited Iceland and Sweden, which was also the first visit by a Chinese premier to both countries in decades. The visits by top Chinese leaders not only shows the increased importance of these Nordic countries on China's diplomatic relations list, but also demonstrates expanded bilateral cooperation in economic and academic fields. The visit to Iceland was quite fruitful, with a total of six agreements and declarations being signed during the visit — two of which are directly related to Arctic development. A framework agreement will strengthen the countries' bilateral Arctic cooperation, while a memorandum of understanding in marine and polar science and technology will enhance research cooperation (Staalesen 2012). The China-Nordic Arctic Research Center, housed within the PRIC in Shanghai, is China's first joint research centre dedicated to social studies of Arctic issues. According to Zhang Xia, director of the strategic studies office at the PRIC, the new centre will push forward international cooperation in Arctic Studies between China and all the Nordic countries (Xinhua News Agency 2012b).

WHY CHINA LOOKS NORTH: THE ARCTIC AND CHINA

China is joining the Arctic play for three reasons: out of environmental concern (as a "near Arctic state," China may be impacted by Arctic climate change, necessitating research); economic opportunities, as the opening of Arctic passages offers great financial opportunity; and better Arctic governance.

ARCTIC ENVIRONMENTAL CHANGES AND CHINA

China is located in the northern hemisphere, with its far north close to N50° latitude, and thus defines itself as a "near Arctic state." According to a report by the Intergovernmental Panel on Climate Change, global warming in the Arctic is accelerating at a rate two times faster than the rest of the world, and environmental changes there negatively impact the rest of the world, especially countries in the northern hemisphere, so China is concerned with the impacts that such warming might have on it (cited in Xinhua News Agency 2012c). And it seems that China is experiencing some climate change impacts; for example, some scientists say the early 2013 cold weather and snowstorm in China are related to environmental changes and sea ice loss in the Arctic. As China relies heavily on agricultural production, a warming Arctic is also expected to impact that sector of the economy. As Chen Lianzeng, deputy head of China's State Oceanic Administration has said, "As the largest developing country located in the Northern Hemisphere, the climatic and environmental changes in the Arctic will have a profound effect on the climate and environment in China, and directly relate to Chinese industry, agriculture and people's living. Therefore, the conduct of scientific research and expectation on the Arctic has significant meaning to China and its sustainable development" (cited in Zhang 2010).

ARCTIC PASSAGES AND CHINA

As the largest exporter and second-largest importer of global shipped goods, China relies heavily on sea lanes. The prospect of opening Arctic passages is the most attractive reason for China's coming to the Arctic. The benefits of the Arctic passages are fourfold:

- The shortened distance. Arctic passages are nearly 2,000–3,500 nautical miles shorter than the customary sea routes from Chinese coastal ports to the east coast of North America, and reduce the length of customary routes from ports north of Shanghai to the ports of western Europe, the North Sea and the Baltic Sea by 25 to 55 percent.

- The reduced cost. By using the Arctic passages, it is estimated that the cost of Chinese international trade will be reduced by US$53.3 billion to US$127.4 billion yearly.

- The commercial use of Arctic passages will put China much closer to Arctic resources and make its use of them more feasible.

- The ports in northern China will benefit enormously from the opening of Arctic passages, because a greater volume of goods will be transported through these ports. According to Guo Peiqing, associate professor of polar politics and law at the Ocean University of China, Arctic passages "will change the structure of global trade. It may well bring about the emergence of a new, circumpolar super-economic belt made up of Russia, North America and Northern Europe" (*Maritime Magazine* 2010).

ARCTIC RESOURCES AND CHINA

As one of the world's fastest-growing and biggest developing countries, there is no doubt that China needs more energy and resources for its future development, and a large part of these will be imported from abroad. The Arctic contains up to 30 percent of the world's undiscovered gas and about 13 percent of the world's undiscovered oil resources. The region also contains large amounts of chromium, coal, copper, diamonds, gold, lead, manganese, nickel, rare earths, silver, titanium, tungsten and zinc. China is diversifying its energy sources, and the opening of the Arctic offers more possibility of providing resources. Commentators agree that Arctic minerals are China's new strategic target (Erickson and Collins 2012). There is no doubt that for China, gaining access to Arctic resources — which, according to estimates are mostly located within the exclusive economic zones of Arctic coastal states — will require cooperation with the Arctic countries to gain access to those resources. Chinese companies are seeking opportunities both with Russian oil tycoons in developing Russia oil in the Arctic region, and with Canadian oil companies.

CHINA IN THE ARCTIC: RESOURCE GUZZLER OR RESPONSIBLE STAKEHOLDER?

China's primary reasons and intentions for coming to the Arctic are interpreted differently by foreign commentators and scholars than by their Chinese counterparts, including government officials. Generally speaking, the international interpretation of China's coming to the Arctic falls in one of two extremes: it is either an opportunity, or it is a threat. Media commentators and "hardcore realist" scholars are more prone to the latter categorization; more liberal scholars tend to be more inclusive and see China's coming to the Arctic as an opportunity for improving good governance in the Arctic. _Really?_

Those who uphold the "threat" mentality raise concerns about the possibility of China's sovereign claims over certain parts of the Arctic. Secondly, they voice apprehensions that China's state-sponsored strategic investment in the Arctic might bring about a new "gold rush" to the Arctic region. Some of these worries are overstated, misinterpreted and wrongly cited. There was, for example, a wrongly cited hawkish argument by Chinese Rear Admiral Yin Zhuo about China's would-be policy on Arctic affairs. In an article by Gordon C. Chang (2010), which appeared in *The Diplomat*, Admiral Yin was quoted as saying that "The Arctic belongs to all the people around the world as no nation has sovereignty over it." The original source, however, reads that "Yin Zhuo said, according to UNCLOS, north pole and the surrounding areas, does not belong to any one country, but to all the people in the world" (Luo 2010). In fact, as no country has provided enough proof of extended continental shelf to the point of the North Pole, the area surrounding the North Pole is considered international commons, a view shared by Paul Berkman and Oran Young (2009).

Chinese commentator Li Zhenfu writes that "the possibility of [China's] open declarations of sovereignty over the Arctic and Arctic sea routes, as well as territorial claims cannot be eliminated" (cited in Wright 2011a). Sentiments such as these have stirred a kind of fury from foreign writers such as David Wright (2011b), who states that "we must stand up to China's increasing claim to Arctic." In fact, making any such sovereignty claims in the Arctic is by no means China's official intention in joining the Arctic play. In his later writings, it should be noted that Li Zhenfu is more conservative and rational. *An apologist*

More liberal writers and scholars see China's interest in the Arctic as legitimate and reasonable, and they would like to "listen to the voices of non-Arctic states" (Young 2012); some even see China's coming to the Arctic as an opportunity (Lasserre 2010). If we look at what China is doing in the Arctic, there is no doubt that the alarmists are no more than exaggerating and analyzing issues through an old Cold War or "China Threat" mentality.

While it is true that China's official position on Arctic issues seldom mentions Arctic resources, there is no doubt that the accessibility of such rich resources will be a bonus for China, as it is developing so quickly. That said, China is following the rules and regulations set by Arctic countries and international agreements. For new and emerging rules governing international practices, China, along with other non-Arctic countries, is eager to weigh in its influence, but only through following the already-established rules, and solely for the purpose of good Arctic governance.

As for the Arctic Council, China (along with five other countries) was granted observer status at the council's eighth ministerial meeting in May 2013. This move demonstrates the council's acceptance of China's contribution to good governance in the Arctic. The next question for China, then, is what can it contribute to the work of the Arctic Council as an observer? According to the Arctic Council's Senior Arctic Officials' (SAO) Report to Ministers, as an observer state, China will attend Arctic Council meetings, will have better access to information and greater opportunity to have its voice heard (SAO 2011, 50-51). The primary privileges for permanent observers are sitting in on the conferences, and receiving documents and other information in advance of the meetings (ibid.). Under the authorization of the chair, observers may make speeches, present written statements, submit relevant documents and take part in the activities of the Arctic Council's working groups (ibid.). Observer states may also get the opportunity to exchange ideas with representatives from Arctic states at the ministerial meeting (ibid.). According to Shin Mang-ho, director general of international legal affairs of South Korea's foreign ministry, non-Arctic states regard the observer status as "a more secure position so

[they] can watch how the meetings go, and discuss cooperation with stakeholders afterward" (quoted in Shin 2012). The observer status is primarily symbolic, but more substantial work should follow, such as China's enhanced research in Arctic issues, and possibly a white paper on China's Arctic policy.

It is good that China has joined the Arctic Council as an observer, but there are other platforms for China to join in Arctic affairs, including international organizations such as the International Maritime Organization (IMO), which is formulating rules for navigating in the ice-covered region in the Arctic. China can, and is expected, to play a more active role in helping the IMO shape navigation regulations. Other international platforms, such as the United Nations Framework Convention on Climate Change are also good venues for China to play a more active role, since a new and updated climate change regime is under discussion, and such forums necessarily include discussion about the Arctic.

CONCLUSION

China is keeping a close eye on the Arctic's development, and increasingly participating in Arctic issues. It has legitimate and natural rights for its presence in the Arctic. The main purpose of China's Arctic presence in the past two decades was to conduct scientific research on climate change and its potential impacts, especially for China. With the melting of the Arctic, and with Arctic passages and resources becoming more accessible, it is also logical for China to look to the Arctic for economic opportunities.

Although there are some radical Chinese scholars whose writings have caused some international academics and media commentators concern, the Chinese government's official standpoint is clear in its acknowledgement of the interests, rights and sovereignty of Arctic countries in the region. China is fully aware that only through international cooperation with Arctic countries and countries of common interest can it realize its interests in the Arctic. Thus, being a responsible stakeholder in the Arctic and a law-abiding user of Arctic passages and resources will be the only way forward. Because of China's current and potential contributions to regional and global issues in the Arctic, it is also beneficial for Arctic countries to include China in the Arctic play for better governance outcomes for the Arctic region.

WORKS CITED

Berkman, Paul and Oran Young. 2009. "Governance and Environmental Change in the Arctic Ocean." *Science* 324: 339-40.

Chang, Gordon C. 2010. "China's Arctic Play." *The Diplomat*, March 9. http://thediplomat.com/2010/03/09/china%E2%80%99s-arctic-play/.

China Daily. 2013. "China to Build Research Center for Arctic Region." [In Chinese.] China Daily, June 6. www.china.org.cn/china/2013-06/06/content_ 29042380.htm.

Chinese Arctic and Antarctic Administration. 2012. "Chinese Polar Expedition of the Advisory Committee at Its 14th Meeting Held in Beijing." Chinese Arctic and Antarctic Administration, October 15.

Embassy of Finland. 2012. "Aker Arctic to Design the First Chinese Polar Research Icebreaker." Embassy of Finland press release, July 31. www.finland.cn/ public/default.aspx?contentid=254552&nodeid=35178&contentlan=2&cultu re=en-US.

Erickson, Andrew and Gabe Collins. 2012. "China's New Strategic Target: Arctic Minerals." *The Wall Street Journal* China Real Time Report, January 18. http://blogs.wsj.com/chinarealtime/2012/01/18/china%E2%80%99s-new-strategic-target-arctic-minerals/.

Fontaine, Paul. 2012. "Huang Nubo 'Angry and Annoyed.'" *The Reykjavik Grapevine*, December 3. http://grapevine.is/Home/ReadArticle/Huang-Nubo-Angry-And-Annoyed.

Huebert, Rob. 2009. "United States Arctic Policy: The Reluctant Arctic Power." School of Public Policy Briefing Papers 2 (2).

Lasserre, Frédéric. 2010. "China and the Arctic: Threat or Cooperation Potential for Canada?" Canadian International Council China Papers No. 11, June. www.opencanada.org/wp-content/uploads/2011/05/China-and-the-Arctic-Frederic-Lasserre.pdf.

Luo, Jianwen. 2010. "Rear Admiral: China Cannot Be Absent in Developing the Arctic." [In Chinese.] China News Online, March 5. www.chinanews.com/gn/ news/2010/03-05/2154039.shtml.

Maritime Magazine. 2010. "China Eyes Arctic Resources and Shipping Potential." *Maritime Magazine*, November 18. www.maritimemag.com/index. php?option=com_content&view=article&id=94:china-eyes-arctic-resources-and-shipping-potential&catid=4:news&Itemid=6.

Mei, Jia. 2012. "Zhongkun Set to Rent Icelandic Land for Tourism." [In Chinese.] China Daily, October 16. www.chinadaily.com.cn/bizchina/2012-10/16/content_15820413.htm.

NPOPSS. 2011. "2012 National Social Science Fund Project Reporting Announcement." [In Chinese.] NPOPSS, December 12. www.npopss-cn.gov.cn/GB/219469/16575773.html.

———. 2012. "2013 Annual National Social Science Fund Guide." [In Chinese.] NPOPSS, December 27. www.npopss-cn.gov.cn/n/2012/1227/c219473-20030485.html.

Payton, Laura. 2012. "7 Big Topics for Harper's China Trip (Including Pandas)." CBC News, February 3. www.cbc.ca/news/world/story/2012/02/03/pol-stephen-harper-china-trip.html.

Qu, Tanzhou et al., eds. 2011. Research on Arctic Issues. [In Chinese.] Beijing: Ocean Press.

SAO. 2011. Senior Arctic Officials Report to Ministers. Arctic Council SAO, May.

Science and Technology Daily. 2012. "The Return of China's Fifth Arctic Expedition." [In Chinese.] September 28. www.stdaily.com/stdaily/content/2012-09/28/content_523865.htm.

Shin, Hyon-hee. 2012. "S. Korea Seeks Bigger Role in Arctic." Asia News Network, May 16. www.asianewsnet.net/news-30743.html.

Staalesen, Atle. 2012. "China Strengthens Arctic Cooperation with Iceland." Barents Observer, April 24. http://barentsobserver.com/en/arctic/china-strengthens-arctic-cooperation-iceland.

Wright, David. 2011a. "The Dragon Eyes the Top of the World: Arctic Policy Debate and Discussion in China." China Maritime Study 8, August. www.usnwc.edu/Research---Gaming/China-Maritime-Studies-Institute/Publications/documents/China-Maritime-Study-8_The-Dragon-Eyes-the-Top-of-.pdf.

———. 2011b. "We Must Stand Up to China's Increasing Claim to Arctic." Calgary Herald, March 8. www2.canada.com/news/must+stand+china+increasing+claim+arctic/4400687/story.html?id=4400687.

Xinhua News Agency. 2007. "China Participates in International Polar Year for the 1st Time." [In Chinese.] Xinhua News Agency, March 2. www.china.org.cn/english/international/201310.htm.

———. 2012a. "China's New Icebreaker Scheduled for Use in 2014." [In Chinese.] Xinhua News Agency, April 9. www.china.org.cn/china/2012-04/09/content_25092246.htm.

———. 2012b. "China-Nordic Cooperation in Arctic Research Center Will Be Located in Shanghai." [In Chinese.] Xinhua News Agency, August 18. http://news.xinhuanet.com/tech/2012-08/18/c_123599688.htm.

———. 2012c. "Fifth Arctic Expedition Looking for Our Climate Change "Comment." [In Chinese.] Xinhua News Agency, September 13. http://news.xinhuanet.com/tech/2012-09/13/c_123710722_2.htm.

Young, Oran R. 2012. "Arctic Stewardship: Maintaining Regional Resilience in an Era of Global Change." *Ethics & International Affairs* 26 (4): 407–420. doi:10.1017/S0892679412000585.

Zhang, Jiansong. 2010. "Chen Lianzeng: Arctic Expedition for Sustainable Development Is of Great Significance." Xinhua News Agency, June 25. www.gov.cn/jrzg/2010-06/25/content_1637741.htm.

Zhao, Jun. 2013. "China and the High North." Speech given at the Arctic Frontiers Conference, Tromsø, Norway, January 21. http://archive.arcticfrontiers.com/index.php?option=com_docman&task=doc_download&gid=713&Itemid=516.

Zhu, Lijiang. 2011. "Chinese Practice in Public International Law: 2010 (II)." *Chinese Journal of International Law* 10 (4): 883–95. doi:10.1093/chinesejil/jmr046.

4

Arctic Prospects and Challenges from a Korean Perspective

//

Young Kil Park
··················

INTRODUCTION

South Korea's interest in the Arctic reached a peak on May 15, 2013, when the country obtained permanent observer status in the Arctic Council. The country's interest in the Arctic began in the 2000s, following reports of new sea routes created by accelerated thawing in the Arctic due to increasing temperatures.

Most South Korean Arctic-related activities have been limited to scientific research, but hopes are high that admission to permanent observer status in the Arctic Council will boost South Korea's economic growth. However, the reality is that considering various challenges facing the country, including the difficult question of when the Arctic Ocean will be deemed "sufficiently" thawed for sea routes, there may be few tangible results for quite some time.

This chapter examines South Korea's interests and involvement in the Arctic, and analyzes its current and future challenges. It summarizes the Arctic-related activities the country has pursued so far; examines specific interests in the fields of science, sea routes and hydrocarbon resources, fishing and governance; and, finally, evaluates the challenges ahead.

SOUTH KOREA'S INTERESTS AND INVOLVEMENT IN THE ARCTIC

SCIENTIFIC RESEARCH IN THE ARCTIC

South Korea became involved in polar region scientific research when it joined the Antarctic Treaty in November 1986.[1] In February 1988, the King Sejong Research Station was established in Antarctica. A research department dedicated to the polar regions at the Korea Ocean Research and Development Institute (KORDI), now the Korea Institute of Ocean Science and Technology (KIOST), has been active since 1987, but it mainly focused on the Antarctic — rather than Arctic — environment.

The establishment of the Arctic Council in 1996 increased South Korea's interest in Arctic research, and the country began conducting joint research with Japan. In June 1999, two scientists conducted marine research with the Geological Survey of Japan. The following month, South Korea dispatched two researchers to the Chinese icebreaker *Xue Long* ("Snow Dragon") to explore the Bering and Chukchi Seas. In August 2000, scientists conducted marine research with the Arctic and Antarctic Research Institute and with the head research organization of the Ministry of Natural Resources and Environment of Russia.

It wasn't until 2001 that South Korea laid the foundation for independent research. The Korea Arctic Scientific Committee was established in October 2001. In April 2002, Korea joined the International Arctic Science Committee (IASC). That same month, the Dasan Station was founded in the Svalbard Islands, Norway.[2] In April 2004, the Polar Research Center at KORDI was expanded to form the Korea Polar Research Institute (KOPRI).[3] Independent research capacity was finally achieved when the Korean icebreaker *Araon* was built in November 2009.[4] The *Araon*

---

1   Korea became an Antarctic Treaty Consultative Party in October 1989.

2   See http://eng.kopri.re.kr/home_e/contents/e_3210000/view.cms.

3   KOPRI categorized South Korea's entry into the Arctic Ocean through scientific research in three phases. The first phase started around 2000, the second when Dasan Station was established and the third when South Korea conducted joint research with other countries (Kim 2012, 60).

4   The *Araon* weighs 7,487 tons with a length of 111 m and depth of 9.9 m. The icebreaker can accommodate 85 passengers and can navigate waters for up to 70 days, with a top speed of three knots, breaking ice as thick as 1 m.

conducts annual research activities in Antarctica from October to April, and in the
Arctic Ocean between July and August.

OPENING OF A NEW ARCTIC ROUTE

Since 1951, Arctic temperatures have increased about twice as fast as those in the
rest of the world. In summer 2012, the amount of sea ice in the Arctic reached new
lows (NASA 2012). The rapid thawing of the sea ice is troubling — but it also offers
economic possibilities through new Arctic sea routes.

South Korean research on Arctic sea routes began only recently. A brief study
was conducted on the Arctic sea route in 2003, but it failed to gain attention (Choi
and Cho 2003, 96). As a result of growing interest in the Arctic, however, the Korea
Maritime Institute (KMI) recently published two papers: "A Strategic Overview of
Development of the Arctic Ocean"[5] and "Shipping and Port Condition Changes and
Throughout Prospects with Opening of the Northern Sea Route."[6]

Currently, a ship trying to reach northern Europe from Northeast Asia must travel
through the East and South China Seas, the Strait of Malacca and the Suez Canal.
The Northern Sea Route (NSR) above Russia offers a drastically shorter route.
Currently, the NSR is free of ice for about two months each year, and the ice-free
season is expected to grow longer as temperatures rise. In three years, the Arctic
Ocean could be ice-free during the summer months (Park 2013). According to one
estimate, the NSR could become entirely navigable year-round by 2037 (Cho 2013).

A KMI research paper suggested that this would reduce the travel distance by
40 percent, cutting the time by a maximum of 10 days and reducing fuel costs by
25 percent (Lee, Song and Oh 2011). In addition, using the NSR will allow ships to
avoid the Strait of Malacca, the Strait of Hormuz and the Suez Canal, which have
heavy traffic. Lastly, the NSR is currently free of piracy, unlike, for example, the
Gulf of Aden.

Korea's first use of the NSR occurred in July 2009, when two cargo ships departed
from Ulsan, South Korea, and arrived in Rotterdam, the Netherlands, via the Bering
Sea and the Arctic Ocean (Kramer and Revkin 2009). In 2010, four vessels made
the journey; this number increased to 34 in 2011 (*The Economist* 2012). In 2012,
46 ships traversed the NSR (Milne 2013) — and as many as 10 ships came to and

---

5   See Hwang, Eom and Heo (2010).

6   See Lee, Song and Oh (2011).

from South Korea. As of September 11, 2013, the Russian NSR Administration has granted some 495 ships permission to travel through the NSR.[7]

South Korean shipping companies began planning trial navigations to the Arctic in 2011, but were unable to follow through. With support from the Ministry of Oceans and Fisheries (MOF) through cuts in wharfage, *Stena Polaris*, a naphtha-laden freighter operated by Korean logistics company Hyundai Glovis, completed Korea's first commercial freight voyage via the Arctic Ocean on October 22, 2013, after taking 35 days to make the journey from the Ust-Luga port of Russia to the Gwangyang port of Korea (*Yonhap News* 2013a).

TRANSFORMING BUSAN PORT INTO A LOGISTICS-ORIENTED HUB PORT

As of 2011, South Korea's Busan Port ranked fifth in the world in terms of cargo, after Shanghai, Singapore, Hong Kong and Shenzhen (World Shipping Council 2013). Increased usage of the NSR will shift the centre of logistics to Northeast Asia — and Busan stands to benefit immensely due to its geographical location. According to a KMI report, the current container traffic between Asia and Europe amounts to 26 million 20-foot equivalent units (TEU), and this is expected to increase four- to sixfold by 2030; out of this figure, more than 85 million tons of cargo is predicted to travel via the NSR (Lee 2012, 82). If the NSR is actively used, the Singapore and Hong Kong ports will likely see less traffic.

POTENTIAL PARTICIPATION IN HYDROCARBON RESOURCE DEVELOPMENT AND EXPLOITATION

Another major area of interest is Arctic resource development. The US Geological Survey announced in 2008 that the Arctic holds 13 percent of the world's oil (90 billion barrels) reserves and 30 percent of its natural gas reserves (47 trillion m^3) (US Geological Survey 2008). The economic value of the untouched oil and gas in the Arctic is said to be worth US$13.6 trillion, while the value of other minerals in the Arctic Ocean such as iron ore, nickel and copper is expected to reach US$1.5 to US$2 trillion.

South Korea does not produce oil, either on land or in the sea. In addition, the country relies heavily on imports for most minerals, such as iron ore. As of 2010, South Korea imported 870 million barrels of oil, 82 percent of which came from the Middle East (*Yonhap News* 2011). Thus, diversifying the oil import

---

7   See www.nsra.ru/en/razresheniya/.

lines is crucial to its energy security. In addition, the KMI estimated that about US$1 billion in annual transportation costs would be saved if Arctic oil replaced just 10 percent of the oil imported from the Middle East (Lee 2012, 78).

South Korea hopes to increase direct participation in the development and import of Arctic hydrocarbon resources. So far, the country's track record in joint resource development has been very modest. The Korea Gas Corporation (KOGAS) pursued the development of the mining fields at West Cutbank and Horn River in British Columbia, Canada, by sharing equal stakes with the Canada-based Encana in 2010. In 2011, KOGAS acquired a 20 percent stake in the Umiak gas field in the Arctic. Unfortunately, a boom in shale gas production in North America drove prices down, suspending the development of the West Cutbank and Umiak field (*Money Today* 2013a).

BOOSTING THE SHIPPING AND OFFSHORE PLATFORM INDUSTRIES

Increased traffic in the NSR is expected to greatly benefit South Korea's shipbuilding industry. Arctic navigation requires special vessels, such as icebreakers, container ships with icebreaking capability, icebreaking tankers and fuel ships transporting liquefied natural gas, all of which sell for high prices. South Korean shipbuilders — among the world's top manufacturers — have been busy obtaining orders for such ships. Daewoo Shipbuilding & Marine Engineering,[8] STX Offshore and Shipbuilding Company, Hyundai Heavy Industries,[9] and Samsung Heavy Industries have recently received orders for such vessels. In sum, the South Korean shipbuilding industry is enjoying a great boon from the opening of the NSR.

In addition, South Korea's offshore platform industry is expected to take off as a result of hydrocarbon development in the Arctic. Although it is difficult to predict the increase in demand for offshore platforms, the KMI estimates that US$9 billion worth of additional orders will be placed by 2020 (Lee 2012, 78).[10]

---

8   See, for example, *Money Today* (2013b).

9   See, for example, *Chosun Ilbo* (2011).

10   The volume of orders in the global offshore platform market reached US$48.6 billion from January to August 2012. Among them, Brazil took up 36.8 percent, South Korea 27 percent and China 13.1 percent. Cho Sang-rae, head of the Society of Naval Architects of Korea, estimated the offshore platform market would outgrow the shipping industry by 2030, worth about US$450 billion (*Yonhap News* 2013b).

ENTERING INTO THE ARCTIC FISHERIES INDUSTRY

Currently, fishing is not a major industry in the Arctic Ocean. Fishers operate in some areas for about six months (April to September). However, with continuous thawing of the ice, the fishing industry is expected to grow gradually. Cheung et al. (2010, 32) estimate that between 2005 and 2055, the maximum catch in the exclusive economic zone of Arctic coastal states will increase by 45 percent in Norway, 27 percent in Greenland, 25 percent in the United States, 21 percent in Russia, 20 percent in Iceland and five percent in Canada.

South Korea's high-sea fishing industry currently operates in the Sea of Okhotsk and the Bering Sea, but has yet to venture into the Arctic Ocean. According to an industry expert, successful entry into the Arctic Ocean by the South Korean fishing industry requires strong government support — a grant for trial operations and crew training, along with information on geography and the weather (Song 2012a; 2012b, 32).

INCREASING PARTICIPATION IN ARCTIC GOVERNANCE

South Korea's participation in Arctic governance began when it applied for ad hoc observer status in the Arctic Council in 2008. As commercial interests in the Arctic route and resources grew, South Korea sought more active participation.

South Korea has approached Arctic governance in two ways: by becoming a permanent observer in the Arctic Council and by entering into bilateral agreements with Arctic nations. The council, which began as an intergovernmental consulting body to address regional Arctic issues, has now established a permanent secretariat and adopted legally binding agreements.[11] Recognizing the council's gradual transformation into an "international organization," South Korea lobbied for permanent observer status. On May 15, 2013, South Korea was admitted as a permanent observer. South Korea's new status allows it to observe all Arctic Council meetings and participate in the projects of the six working-level committees. It can also suggest and finance new projects.

South Korea's bilateral efforts are mainly focused on Russia since it is geographically close and occupies most of the coast along the NSR. In October 2010, the two countries signed the Agreement on Maritime Transport, and agreed to

---

11   For example, in 2011, the Arctic Council decided to establish a secretariat in Tromsø, Norway, which was completed in 2013. It also adopted the Arctic Search and Rescue Agreement in 2011, and the Agreement on Cooperation on Marine Oil Pollution Preparedness and Response in the Arctic in May 2013.

construct a gas pipeline via North Korea in 2012. On July 9, 2013, at the thirteenth meeting of the Korea-Russia Joint Council on Economy, Science and Technology, the two also signed a memorandum of understanding (MOU) for bilateral cooperation in port development.

In addition, former South Korean President Lee Myung-bak visited Denmark (Greenland) and Norway for the first time in September 2012 to strengthen cooperative relations (An 2012). Four MOUs concerning energy and resource cooperation in Greenland were signed. The South Korean government also joined the Svalbard Treaty on September 7, 2012.[12]

SOUTH KOREA AS A PERMANENT OBSERVER IN THE ARCTIC COUNCIL: PROSPECTS AND CHALLENGES

FUTURE PROSPECTS

Forging and Maintaining Good Relations with Arctic Council Members and Permanent Participants

Although South Korea, Japan and China were recently granted observer status in the Arctic Council, the applications were met with some wariness.[13] Some apprehension is understandable as the council is primarily a regional organization that deals with regional issues — in fact, the council has still not formulated a comprehensive plan that incorporates the interests of non-Arctic entities (Manicom and Lackenbauer 2013, 2). Assertive scholarship by some scholars, urging China to make claims to the Arctic Ocean, has contributed to the unease (ibid., 1),[14] as have the ongoing maritime and territorial disputes in the East and South China Seas.

On the whole, however, the Arctic states welcome the new observer nations, as they add considerable financial and scientific capacity to the council's working groups (ibid., 5). In addition, as a condition for admission as observers, these countries have accepted the Arctic states' "sovereignty, sovereign rights and jurisdiction in the Arctic" and recognized the Law of the Sea as the legal foundation for Arctic management (Arctic Council 2011).

---

12   Officially known as the Treaty Regulating the Status of Spitsbergen and Conferring the Sovereignty on Norway, the treaty was adopted on February 9, 1920 in Paris and took effect on August 14, 1925.

13   See, for example, Byers (2011) and Wright (2011).

14   There is even a widespread misperception that China claims a portion of the Arctic Ocean.

South Korea, in particular, enjoys good bilateral relations with the Arctic states, as evidenced by the many Arctic-related bilateral agreements. The country must continue to ride this current of goodwill. In addition, South Korea must be careful not to marginalize the indigenous permanent participants (PPs) of the council. If South Korea is serious about participating in the council, it should forge constructive relationships with the PPs, perhaps by working on the Sustainable Development Working Group (Manicom and Lackenbauer 2013, 5).

A Comprehensive Arctic Strategy — South Korea's Pan-Government Arctic Development Plan

South Korea seeks to leverage its permanent observer status to gain a foothold for entering the Arctic Ocean. To this end, it recently announced a comprehensive Arctic strategy, the details of which are to be revealed later this year (Yoon 2013).

Efforts to create a comprehensive Arctic strategy began last year during the first Policy Forum for an Arctic Strategy, held on September 7, 2012. In his presentation "The Direction of the Arctic Policy," Young-Jin Yeon, the Land, Infrastructure and Transport Ministry's marine policy director, proposed developing a mid-to-long-term Arctic plan and business model, stronger "bipolar" research capacity, and coordination of polar region policies to form a basis for future Arctic policies (Yeon 2012, 18–21). In November 2012, the ministry announced measures to modernize polar region policies, which included the pursuit of bipolar policies, the formation of a new government department for the polar regions, and a pan-governmental council to coordinate the policies of different departments. At the end of 2012, a bill for the promotion of polar activities was sent to the National Assembly.[15] The bill proposes systematic government support for various scientific activities related to the polar regions. It also stipulates the separation of KOPRI from KIOST, a move that was somewhat controversial.

After the new administration (led by President Park Geun-hye) took office in February 2013, the MOF was reinstated. With the MOF taking the lead, the government has been developing an Arctic policy master plan. On June 24, 2013, the MOF held the second Policy Forum for an Arctic Strategy, where it announced

---

15   The bill is currently pending. The bill was submitted by the ruling Saenuri Party's leader Hwang Woo-yea on behalf of other lawmakers on November 19, 2012 and introduced to the National Assembly's Agriculture, Food, Rural Affairs, Oceans, and Fisheries Committee on June 18, 2013. See http://likms. assembly.go.kr/bill/jsp/BillDetail.jsp?bill_id=PRC_D1J2J1X1M1Y9J1R0T1Q7U0W5O8W2C4.

the Pan-Government Arctic Development Plan. The MOF provided an outline of the plan and stated that details would be revealed later this year.

The plan consists of four parts. First, it calls for greater international cooperation in the Arctic, including plans for more vigorous participation in the Arctic Council and other organizations, as well as bilateral cooperation with Arctic nations. Second, it supports more active scientific research, including plans for improving research infrastructure, climate change research capacity and joint studies. Third, it attempts to identify an Arctic business model, which will include measures for stronger cooperation with Arctic nations in maritime transportation and port development, including development of the Arctic route, and in the areas of shipbuilding, offshore platforms, energy and resources, along with measures to enter the Arctic fisheries industry. Fourth, it seeks to establish legal institutions, including new laws to support Arctic activities, and form an Arctic information centre.

CHALLENGES AHEAD

Limitations as a Permanent Observer

An observer of the Arctic Council has no voting rights and a very limited voice. The primary role of observers is to observe the work of the council and participate in the various working groups. Despite these limitations, South Korea can still represent opinions of non-Arctic nations, particularly East Asian countries. Building close cooperative relations with other observers that share similar interests with South Korea, such as China and Japan, will be important. In addition, South Korea must not be solely focused on commercial aspects of the Arctic, but must also address global concerns, such as the protection of the Arctic environment and indigenous peoples.

Challenges Facing Scientific Research in the Arctic

In contrast to South Korea, which did not begin scientific research in the Arctic until the 1990s, Japan started scientific research in polar regions about 50 years ago. Japan established the National Institute of Polar Research in 1973 and built a research station in the Svalbard Islands in 1991. Japan also joined IASC in 1991 and conducted various national and international studies in the Arctic (Ohnishi 2013, 9). Nevertheless, South Korea has made significant strides since the 2000s by establishing research infrastructure and actively conducting research, and South Korean scientists are currently conducting a broad range of research activities.

There are, however, some challenges facing South Korea's research in the Arctic. First, current research infrastructure is insufficient. The Dasan Station leases half of a fairly small two-storey building where researchers only stay for limited periods of time for specific projects. The station also lacks certain research equipment. In Antarctica, by contrast, there are many researchers stationed at the multi-purpose Sejong Station in 18 buildings. The Jang Bogo Station, another research base close to the South Pole, is scheduled to be constructed by 2014. Second, South Korea has only one icebreaker, *Araon*, which is mobilized in Antarctica for most of the year, hindering research activities in the Arctic. Lastly, unlike Antarctic research, which is conducted on the basis of a five-year plan in compliance with the Act on Antarctic Activities and the Protection of Antarctic Environment, Arctic research activities do not enjoy legal support.

It is clear that South Korea still focuses primarily on Antarctica for scientific research and lacks mid-term plans or legal support for Arctic projects. Fortunately, a major part of the Pan-Government Arctic Development Plan focuses on strengthening Korea's scientific research activities in the Arctic by improving infrastructure and research capacity, so changes may be coming soon.

Limitations on Using the NSR

To gain a competitive edge over the traditional sea route, the Arctic route must meet various challenges (Lee 2013, 48-49). The first challenge is preventing environmental degradation in the Arctic Ocean. The International Maritime Organization published guidelines on this matter,[16] but the effectiveness of the measures needs further review. The second issue is reducing Russia's expensive icebreaking and piloting fees. To this end, a compromise between Northeast Asian countries and Russia should be reached. The third problem is finding a balance in the cargo traffic between the Far East (namely, North and East Asia) and Europe. As of 2011, the total volume of containers transported between the Far East and Europe was about 20 million TEU. Out of this, about 14 million TEU were transported from the Far East to Europe, while just six million TEU travelled the other way (Gardiner 2012, 21). If ships make round trips, the balance in cargo traffic translates into lower transportation costs. Fourth, there are too few safe ports for services on the Russian coast along the NSR. To meet this challenge, Russia must modernize its ports and harbours. Additional challenges include the lack of a comprehensive

---

16   See International Maritime Organization (2010).

shipping management system and sea route information. Until these challenges are met, the traditional sea route will remain dominant.

Balancing South Korea's Economic Goals with Environmental Concerns

South Korea's interest in the Arctic largely stems from the belief that the region is vital for securing the country's future economic growth. This view, however, is too narrowly focused on commercial gains. Opening the Arctic presupposes rising temperatures around the globe, which may result in a global catastrophe if not controlled. Therefore, a balance must be struck between pursuing commercial interests and protecting the Arctic environment and combatting rising temperatures. China has been accused of placing its national economic goals before environmental commitments;[17] South Korea should take measures to avoid similar criticism.

Preparing in Advance for Geopolitical Changes in East Asia following the Opening of Arctic Routes

The East Sea (Sea of Japan) is expected to play a much larger role 20 to 30 years from now when the Arctic route is freely navigable. Currently, the East Sea functions mostly as fishing grounds; however, it could become a logistics hub when the Arctic route opens up.

Accordingly, ports such as Busan and Ulsan in South Korea, Najin and Sonbong in North Korea and Vladivostok in Russia are likely to see increased traffic. China, which does not share the East Sea with the other countries, has already acquired rights to develop and operate ports in North Korea's Najin and Sonbong for the next 50 years. The two Koreas, Japan and Russia may have to compete more fiercely in the East Sea given China's involvement.

Based on these assumptions, the following policies can be taken into consideration. First, a road map should be established to streamline and expand infrastructure in ports such as Busan. Second, the rising military and strategic value of the East Sea should be taken into consideration along with its increasing economic value. Third, a strategic plan connecting the East Sea, the Sea of Okhotsk and the Arctic Ocean needs to be developed. Fourth, a regional integration approach should be taken to connect inland areas close to the East Sea, such as the Russian Far East, Northeastern China and Mongolia. Fifth, changes in the roles of Dokdo and Ullengdo, South Korea's small islands in the East Sea, should be noted. Dokdo, which is currently

---

17 See, for example, Brady (2012, 11).

under the effective control of South Korea, is at the centre of a major diplomatic discord with Japan, as the latter also claims sovereignty over the islet. It is doubtful whether the same territorial conflict will continue for the next 20 to 30 years.

CONCLUSION

South Korea has made significant strides in entering the Arctic Ocean, but many serious challenges must be addressed before the Arctic can become the source of economic prosperity recently portrayed by the local media. Until then, the traditional sea routes will remain dominant; thus, South Korea must not neglect its current trade routes and energy security scheme. The government's Pan-Government Arctic Development Plan will be fully revealed later this year, and the future success of Korea's Arctic endeavours will rely to a great extent upon the execution of that plan.

WORKS CITED

An, Myungok. 2012. "President Lee Steps into the Arctic Circle for South Korea's Arctic Initiative." Korea.net, September 17. www.korea.net/NewsFocus/Policies/view?articleId=102568.

Arctic Council. 2011. "Observers." www.arctic-council.org/index.php/en/about-us/arctic-council/observers.

Brady, Anne-Marie. 2012. "Polar Stakes: China's Polar Activities as a Benchmark for Intentions." *China Brief* 12 (14).

Byers, Michael. 2011. "Asian Juggernaut Eyes Our 'Golden' Waterways." *The Globe and Mail*, August 29.

Cheung, William, Vicky Lam, Jorge Sarmiento, Kelly Kearney, Reg Watson, Dirk Zeller and Daniel Pauly. 2010. "Large-scale Redistribution of Maximum Fisheries Catch Potential in the Global Ocean Climate Change." *Global Change Biology* 16 (1): 24–35. doi:10.1111/j.1365-2486.2009.01995.

Cho, Tae-yul. 2013. "The Arctic, New Silk Road of the 21st Century." *Korea Focus*, May 21. www.koreafocus.or.kr/design3/Politics/view.asp?volume_id=139&content_id=104785&category=A.

Choi, Kyung-Sik and Seong-Cheol Cho. 2003. "The Northern Sea Route and Operation of Icebreaking Cargo Ships." [In Korean.] *Journal of the Korean Society of Ocean Engineers* 17 (6).

Chosun Ilbo. 2011. "Hyundai Heavy Develops World's Largest Ice Breaker." [In Korean.] August 24. http://biz.chosun.com/site/data/html_dir/2011/08/24/2011082400900.html.

Gardiner, Nigel. 2012. *Container Market 2012/13 - Annual Review and Forecast: Incorporating the Container Forecaster—3Q12.* London: Drewry Maritime Research.

Hwang, Jin-Hoe, Sun-Hee Eom and So-Young Heo. 2010. "A Strategic Overview of Development of the Arctic Ocean." [In Korean.] Seoul: KMI.

International Maritime Organization. 2010. "Guidelines for Ships Operating in Polar Waters." Res. A. 1024 (26).

Kim, Ye-Dong. 2012. "Science and Technology Promotion to Enter the Arctic." Presentation for the 1st Joint Policy Forum for Establishing Arctic Ocean Strategies, September, Seoul.

Kramer, Andrew E. and Andrew C. Revkin. 2009. "Arctic Shortcut Beckons Shippers as Ice Thaws." *The New York Times*, September 11. www.nytimes.com/2009/09/11/science/earth/11passage.html?scp=1&sq=Beluga%20Kramer&st=cse&_r=0.

Lee, Sung-Woo. 2012. "Potential and Protect of the Arctic Use." Presentation for the 1st Joint Policy Forum for Establishing Arctic Ocean Strategies, September, Seoul.

———— 2013. "Potential Arctic Shipping." In *The Arctic in World Affairs: A North Pacific Dialogue on Arctic Marine Issues*, edited by Oran R. Young, Jong Deog Kim and Yoon Hyung Kim. Seoul: KMI Press.

Lee, Sung-Woo, Ju-Mi Song and Yeon-Sun Oh. 2011. "Shipping and Port Condition Changes and Throughout Prospects with Opening of the Northern Sea Route." [In Korean.] Seoul: KMI.

Manicom, James and P. Whitney Lackenbauer. 2013. "East Asian States, the Arctic Council and International Relations in the Arctic." CIGI Policy Brief No. 26. April.

Milne, Richard. 2013. "Arctic Shipping Set for Record as Sea Ice Melts." *The Financial Times*, July 21. www.ft.com/cms/s/0/c947b810-f06a-11e2-929c-00144feabdc0.html#axzz2eWkIrm00.

Money Today. 2013a. "KOGAS Hit Hard by U.S. Shale Gas." [In Korean.] *Money Today*, May 30.

————. 2013b. "DSME Signs Maximum $5 billion Deal. What Technology Contributed to the Yamal Windfall?" [In Korean.] *Money Today*, July 7.

NASA. 2012. "Arctic Sea Ice Shrinks to New Low in Satellite Era." August 27.

Ohnishi, Fujio. 2013. "Japan and the Arctic: Prospects for Japan's Role in Globalizing Arctic Politics." Paper presented at the East Asia-Arctic Relations: Boundary, Security and International Politics workshop, Whitehorse, March 2.

Park, Kyunghee. 2013. "South Korea's Bet on Arctic Shipping Lanes." *Bloomberg Businessweek*, August 22. www.businessweek.com/articles/2013-08-22/south-koreas-bet-on-arctic-shipping-lanes.

Song, K. S. 2012a. "Participation in the Arctic Fisheries Resource Development."
Presentation for the 1st Joint Policy Forum for Establishing Arctic Ocean
Strategies, September, Seoul.

——— 2012b. "Promoting Science and Technology to Enter the Arctic Ocean."
Presentation for the 1st Joint Policy Forum for Establishing Arctic Ocean
Strategies, September. Seoul.

The Economist. 2012. "Banyan: Snow Dragons." *The Economist*, September 1.

US Geological Survey. 2008. "Circum-Arctic Resource Appraisal: Estimates of
Undiscovered Oil and Gas North of the Arctic Circle." USGS Fact Sheet 2008-
3049. Washington, DC.

World Shipping Council. 2013. "Top 50 World Container Ports." www.worldshipping.org/
about-the-industry/global-trade/top-50-world-container-ports.

Wright, David. 2011. "We Must Stand Up to China's Increasing Claim to Arctic."
The Calgary Herald, March 8.

Yeon, Young-Jin. 2012. "The Direction of the Arctic Policy." Presentation for the
first Policy Forum for an Arctic Strategy. September, Seoul.

Yonhap News. 2011. "Oil Import in South Korea." [In Korean.] *Yonhap News*, March 13.

———. 2013a. "Taking the First Step toward developing the Arctic Sea Route …
Opening 'Ocean Silk Road'." [In Korean.] *Yonhap News*, October 22.

——— 2013b. "China Starts to Catch up in Offshore Platforms, too…South Korea
Needs More Competitiveness." [In Korean.] *Yonhap News,* February 21.

Yoon, Sojung. 2013. "Korea Announces Comprehensive Arctic Policies." [In Korean.]
Korea.net, July 30. www.korea.net/NewsFocus/Policies/view?articleId=110561.

5

East Asia and the Arctic: Alaskan and American Perspectives

//

Jerry McBeath
• • • • • • • • • • • • • • • •

INTRODUCTION

The global competition for natural resources and diminishing sea ice have increased international interest in the Arctic, and East Asian nations have recently been involved in the charge. In particular, China, Japan and South Korea have become frequent visitors to the North, and they have visions of long-term participation in Arctic affairs.

This chapter asks how the state of Alaska, the only Arctic state of the United States, and the United States itself view East Asian involvement. Is there a distinctly Alaskan or American position on East Asian engagement? Is the participation of East Asia in Arctic development a political issue, or a matter of public debate?

To answer these questions, this paper treats the roles of Alaska and the United States in six substantive areas: US national strategy for the Arctic; oil and gas exploration and development; marine transportation; fisheries; investment; and governance. In each area, the challenges and opportunities to the state and nation are examined; then consideration is given, in this respect, to whether Alaskan and US attitudes toward East Asian participation are welcoming or hostile.

◇◇◇◇◇◇◇◇◇◇◇◇◇

The global position of the United States is different from that of other Arctic states, and Alaska stands in a different relationship regarding its federation than do other federal states in the Arctic. The United States occupies a unique position in the international system, because it is currently the only superpower. Superpowers worry about threats to their status and tend to neglect peaceful regions like the Arctic. Global hegemons tend to treat rising powers with suspicion and regard them as threats. China is a rising power,[1] and for this reason, US reactions to China's behaviour in the Arctic may appear rigid and inhospitable. On the other hand, the United States has military alliances with Japan and South Korea and friendly relations with both. Alaska's relationship with its federal union is different from that of provinces/republics in the other federal nations of the Arctic (Canada and Russia). The US federal system is more centralized than that of Canada, and Alaska is the only Arctic state among America's 50 subnational governments. Alaska is also the second-newest US state and is quite sparsely populated (740,000 residents in 2013). Many Alaskan policy makers believe that the federal government stands in the way of its development through stringent controls on natural resource management and stifling regulations covering each aspect of economic development.

In 2014, Alaska's strategies toward Arctic development have evolved. In 2010, the Alaska state legislature established the Alaska Northern Waters Task Force (ANWTF), which identified needs in several areas, such as oil and gas development, indigenous issues, infrastructure development, fisheries and influence on federal Arctic policy (ANWTF 2012). The ANWTF also recommended the creation of the Alaska Arctic Policy Commission to develop a comprehensive Arctic strategy. The state legislature established the commission in 2012, which began deliberations in March 2013.

In the sections that follow, the ANWTF's report and recommendations are mentioned, specifically regarding the need for Alaska's more aggressive engagement in the Arctic. In this context, comments on the mood of Alaska and US policy makers on East Asian involvement in the Arctic are added where available, but first, the US national strategy is examined.

---

1   On this point, see Jakobson and Peng (2012), which assesses China's Arctic activities in the context of overall foreign policy objectives, and finds that it safeguards its national interest in economic development (including seeking access to shorter shipping routes and means to enhance food and resource security). Underlying this is an objective to attract respect as a major power (ibid., 20). However, the United States may have been motivated by the "China threat" thesis, when in 2005, it strongly objected to China National Offshore Oil Corporation's attempt to purchase Unocal. For a discussion of China's strategy in the Arctic, and particularly its status quo and revisionist dimensions, see Rainwater (2012) and Kraska (2011).

Figure 1: Travel Regions of Alaska

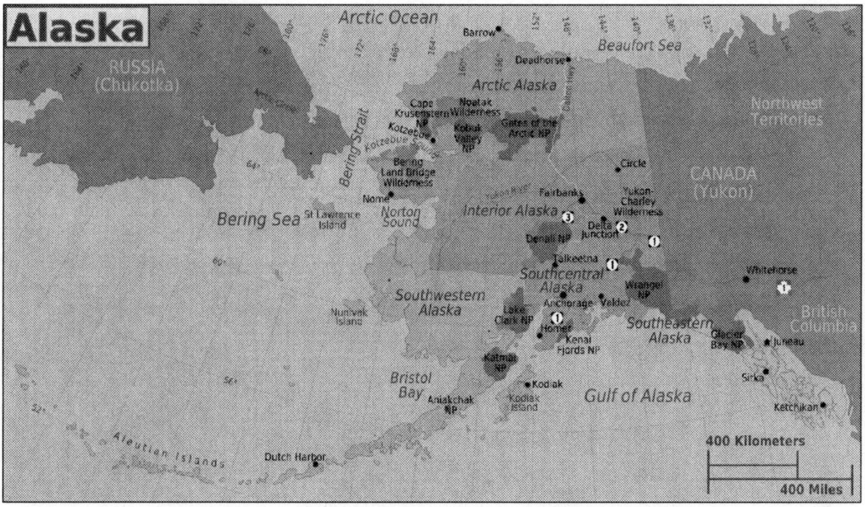

Source: Wikimedia Commons. (Image by Peter Fitzgerald.)

US NATIONAL STRATEGY FOR THE ARCTIC

It is noteworthy that the United States was the last of the "Arctic 8" to issue a statement on its goals and objectives for the Arctic region.[2] The strategy announced by President Obama in May 2013 is predictably general and vague. It focuses on US security interests,[3] emphasizing "responsible Arctic region stewardship" and strengthened engagement with international organizations (The White House 2013 2). The details of the strategy are outlined in the subsections below.

US SECURITY INTERESTS

In general, the strategy describes the priority of protecting the US people, territory and natural resources through a "combination of independent action, bilateral initiatives and multilateral cooperation" (ibid., 6). Four specific efforts are mentioned:

2 The eight nations comprising the Arctic region are: the United States, Canada, Russia, Iceland, Norway, Sweden, Finland and Denmark (Greenland).

3 For a full discussion of US national security interests in the Arctic, see Department of Defense (2011).

- The US federal government's continued development of Arctic infrastructure and improvement of strategic capabilities through cooperative work with "the State of Alaska, local and tribal authorities, as well as public and private actor partners" (ibid.). This section includes "the capacity to respond to natural or man-made disasters" (ibid.)

- Increased "Arctic domain awareness" (ibid.). This section addresses the limited knowledge of Americans about both the Arctic and rapid climate change, with the objective of improving understanding of conditions and circumstances potentially affecting US safety, security, environmental or commercial interests.

- Preserving Arctic region freedom of seas and airspace through enhanced national defence, law enforcement, navigation safety, marine environment response and search-and-rescue capabilities. Although the US Senate has yet to ratify the United Nations Convention on the Law of the Sea (UNCLOS), the strategy commits the United States to strategic partnerships in development of Arctic waterways management regimes and free flow of trade (ibid., 7).

- Finally, the search for energy security through a comprehensive ("all of the above") approach is emphasized, including the development of "renewables, expanding oil and gas production, and increasing efficiency" of use and conservation (ibid.).

RESPONSIBLE ARCTIC REGION STEWARDSHIP

This dimension of US strategy focuses on natural and human resource management and use. It includes: the protection of the Arctic environment and conservation of the region's resources; integrated management to balance economic development, environmental protection and cultural values; continued scientific research (on changes manifested in land/sea ice, biodiversity and permafrost), along with traditional knowledge in a holistic approach; and charting and mapping the Arctic region.

STRENGTHENED INTERNATIONAL COOPERATION

The strategy emphasizes four cooperative approaches that the United States should employ: forging bilateral and multilateral agreements with other Arctic states to promote prosperity, protect the environment and enhance security; working through the Arctic Council to advance US interests; ensuring US accession to UNCLOS; and cooperating with non-Arctic nations and non-state actors to advance common interests.

The strategy concludes by identifying the guiding principles that serve as the foundation of US Arctic engagement:

- safeguarding peace and stability in the region;

- using the best available information in decision making;

- pursuing innovative arrangements and new thinking on public-private and multinational partnerships; and

- consulting and coordinating with Alaska Natives, pursuant to tribal consultation policy.

OIL AND GAS EXPLORATION AND DEVELOPMENT

In a notable 2008 report, the US Geological Survey (USGS) estimated that 13 percent of the world's yet-to-be-discovered oil reserves and 30 percent of the undiscovered gas reserves are in the Arctic (USGS 2008a). The estimate includes some 90 billion barrels of oil, about 1,700 trillion ft^3 of natural gas and more than 40 billion barrels of natural gas liquids (USGS 2008b).

The USGS report estimates that most (84 percent) of the new deposits will be located offshore. According to a map created by the Department of the Interior (2010), approximately one-third of the estimated oil is expected to be found in the circum-Arctic region of Alaska and the Alaska Outer Continental Shelf (OCS). This means that Alaska will likely remain a vital part of Arctic oil and gas exploration and development activity, and that is good news for this highly natural-resource-dependent state, as approximately 85 percent of the state's general fund revenues are derived from production taxes, oil and gas royalties, and oil industry corporate income taxes.

Nearly 16 billion barrels of oil have been produced in Alaska since the discovery of oil on the North Slope in 1968, and most of this oil has been produced from wells in that area. Since the peak of production in 1988, when 2.1 million barrels of oil daily entered the pipeline and supplied about 25 percent of the total US oil production, oil from the legacy fields of Prudhoe Bay and Kuparuk has declined. Today, oil from these fields and from new wells in Alpine, Endicott and other sites has fallen to less than 600,000 barrels daily. Just over 100 wells have been drilled in the Arctic Ocean and the Bering Sea. The history of oil and gas development in Alaska has occurred largely onshore; the safety and environmental record of onshore production has been generally good, with no major spills (the largest, in 2006, was 270,000 gallons) or casualties (McBeath et al. 2008).

The decline of in-state oil production has increased interest in new exploration and development opportunities. The Trans-Alaska Pipeline System has carried oil from Prudhoe Bay to Valdez since 1977, but in 2013, it moved less than one-third of the average daily flow of the late 1980s. Declining throughput increases difficulty of oil flow through the pipeline, creating additional support for increasing oil production.

Some 16 percent of the Alaska population is Alaska Native, and these indigenous people have lived in the region sustainably for thousands of years. The majority of the North Slope population is Inupiat Eskimo, which has benefited economically from oil and gas development. Most Native Alaskans, however, differentiate onshore from offshore oil production, supporting the former and opposing the latter. Inupiat Eskimos believe emphatically that exploration for, and development of, OCS oil resources may endanger the bowhead whale population, which is both symbolically and actually vital for the survival of its whaling culture.

Nearly 700 gas wells have been drilled in Cook Inlet, supplying energy for most homes in south-central Alaska. There is a prospect for commercialization of natural gas produced from the North Slope and adjacent areas, which involves fewer environmental risks in terms of production, storage and transmission than crude oil. To date, however, this gas has been "stranded" on the North Slope, both because natural gas prices have fallen in recent years, reducing the incentives for production and transmission of expensive Alaska gas, and because the state, the company it has contracted with to build a pipeline to the Midwest (TransCanada Corporation) and the producers have failed to reach an agreement on production. The cost of such a pipeline — currently estimated to be between US$45 billion and US$65 billion — means that the decision will be made carefully and will require further negotiations between companies and the state over fiscal terms (Bohrer 2012).

The state of Alaska has a long-standing interest in exporting natural resource products, particularly oil and gas to East Asian nations. Since the early 1980s, for example, the Usibelli coal mine in Healy has been exporting coal to the Suneel corporation in South Korea (with a gap in exports in the early 2000s) and this contract is still in effect. The company also exports some coal to Taiwan. The Trans-Alaska Pipeline Authorization Act of 1973 required all petroleum from Alaska's North Slope to be sent to US refineries. Shortly after pipeline construction, however, state officials and congressional representatives sought to remove this restriction, believing the lowered transportation costs to Asia (as compared to shipping to refineries in California or Texas) would increase the state's take of production revenue. As a 1995 Cato Institute report noted:

> The natural market for North Slope oil is Japan, Korea, and northern East Asia, to which oil can be shipped for about 50 cents per barrel, but North Slope producers are required to use domestic tankers and market exclusively in the United States and its territories, a mandate that has often resulted in shipping costs of $5 per barrel. That price distortion has led to artificially low domestic prices for heavy crude on the West Coast, discouraging otherwise profitable exportation and production investments in Alaska and California. (Van Vactor 1995)

These export restrictions were lifted in 1996, toward the end of Frank Murkowski's tenure in the US Senate (he was the chief advocate for lifting the ban). From 1996 to 2004, the state exported 95.5 million barrels of crude oil (equal to 2.7 percent of Alaska production) to: South Korea, 46.2 million barrels; Japan, 24.5 million barrels; China, 16.5 million barrels; and Taiwan, 8.3 million barrels (US Energy Information Administration 2013). The economics of shipping have changed since that period of time, primarily because of the steep rise in oil prices, and in 2013, none of the North Slope production is exported outside the United States.

Japan and South Korea have high rates of dependence on imported oil and gas. China, once an oil exporter, has entered the global market for oil and gas purchases in the last decade, and now imports more than 50 percent of its oil and gas needs (Moyo 2012, 28). All three East Asian countries are already Alaska's major trading partners, and certainly the state welcomes increased trade with them. In 2012, Alaska's top trading partners were: China, at 29.1 percent of Alaska's total exports; Japan, at 17.2 percent of Alaska's total exports (dropping from its former first-place position in 2010, which it had held for more than a decade); and South Korea, at 15.0 percent of Alaska's total exports (US Census Bureau 2013). These countries also import large volumes of Alaska zinc, lead, copper, gold and even some rare earth elements (ibid.), and they are also a market for Alaska's coal and natural gas.

In fact, Alaska Governor Sean Parnell's latest proposal for moving stranded natural gas from the North Slope to market entails the production of liquefied natural gas (LNG) there and its ultimate trans-shipment to markets in East Asia. Parnell's second foreign trip since being elected to his first full term in 2010 was to Japan and South Korea, where he promoted Alaskan natural gas. Meeting with Japanese and South Korean officials, he remarked: "We look forward to capitalizing on the enormous potential that exists for Alaska's North Slope natural gas in our state and in Pacific Rim nations... This is a great opportunity to strengthen existing relationships and build new ones that will grow economic opportunity with Japan and South Korea" (Office of Governor Sean Parnell 2012).

The transportation route for Alaska's future shipments of natural gas to Asia is uncertain. The state has already committed to the construction of a large-diameter pipeline to move natural gas to the south, but it has devoted little attention to shipping natural gas on vessels across the Arctic Ocean. Reasons provided include shallow waters in Alaska near the Beaufort and Chukchi seas, and little interest of companies such as ExxonMobil, ConocoPhillips, BP and TransCanada Corporation, in backing the natural gas pipeline project to transport LNG via the Arctic Ocean (Burke 2013).

MARINE TRANSPORTATION

According to James Holmes (2012), the loss of perennial sea ice is likely to open Arctic waters to new shipping routes for part of each year sometime between 2035 and 2040, and East Asian nations would be major beneficiaries through a significant reduction in the time needed to move their goods to market. The Northern Sea Route, which passes along Russia's Arctic coast, would provide a direct route to northern Europe, while the Northwest Passage, which crosses the Canadian Arctic islands and the Alaska Arctic Ocean, would open up trade with the Atlantic coast of North America (Blunden 2012). Indeed, Arctic shipping could resolve the "Malacca dilemma," especially for China, but also for Japan and South Korea, as they import oil through this narrow chokepoint. There is, however, no certainty that a new global shipping route will be opened soon. According to polar shipping specialist Lawson Brigham, there is still too much ice blocking traffic, and the gains of a new trade route do not yet outweigh the costs (quoted in CBC News 2012; see Brigham 2011).

In 2012 alone, some 7,000 vessels operated in, or moved to, the Arctic for purposes of tourism, minerals mining, oil and gas exploration, military operations and other activities (ANWTF 2012, 14). Although search-and-rescue procedures have improved in the last two years (the United States reached agreement on search and rescue with the Arctic Council in 2011), other monitoring systems have not kept pace with increases in shipping and marine traffic. For example, vessel tracking and identification systems and pollution monitoring systems are insufficient, putting resources such as fisheries at increased risk.

The joint Alaska-US environmental regulatory regime in Alaska's Arctic waters is reasonably comprehensive and rigorous. Alaska's response to increased marine transport from East Asian nations would be apprehensive in the absence of new risk assessment and risk reduction options, such as those developed in response to the 2004 grounding and subsequent oil spill of the merchant vessel *Selendang Ayu*. The response to that disaster was a joint venture of the US Fish and Wildlife Foundation, the US Coast Guard and the Alaska Department of Environmental Conservation. A program for enhanced vessel monitoring and reporting, enhanced towing capabilities and increased coast guard cutters in the Aleutians, and installing additional towing systems have since been implemented (ANWTF 2012, 16).

Addressing the opportunities and challenges of burgeoning marine transportation at a conference in Norway, Alaska Lieutenant Governor Mead Treadwell said that the lessons of the 1989 Exxon Valdez oil spill needed to be applied, and marine shipping safety emphasized. In Treadwell's words, "Domestically, the United States regulates and monitors both tank and non-tank vessels to the hilt.... So do other Arctic states. But we have little say today about the environmental or human safety plans for the traffic that's sailing through Alaska's front yard in the Bering Strait" (quoted in Restino 2013). Nonetheless, the Arctic Council was successful in reaching consensus of the parties to the 2013 Arctic Marine Oil Pollution Preparedness and Response Agreement.

FISHERIES

Overfishing is a global condition that is especially pronounced in East Asian nations, but the North Pacific fishery is the most productive in the United States. Alaska's North Pacific Fishery Management region, the largest in ocean area, is regarded as the best-managed council. Alaska exports large volumes of fish products to the East Asian region, and this demand will continue to be strong. Indeed, demand may strengthen further, as some commercial fish species move into northern waters.

East Asian nations' seafood purchases figured in the recent change of Alaska's top trade partners. Formerly, Japan held the top position, primarily because of its purchases of fisheries products including king salmon, Alaska pollock and salmon roe. Then, as noted, China overtook Japan to become Alaska's largest trading partner in 2011. More than half of Chinese imports were seafood products. Overall, seafood composed half of Alaska's US$5 billion export economy. While the state ranks 42 of 50 states in terms of total exports, calculated on a per capita basis, Alaska is in the top 10.

However, good scientific information about changes in the population ecology of the 100 known species of fish in northern Alaska waters, their productivity parameters (rates of growth, recruitment and natural mortality) and the effects of fisheries on other fish species, marine mammals and seabirds are not well understood. Scientists lack data that could be used to estimate the biomass of potentially harvestable species. Without such information, it is not possible to develop estimates on potential sustainable fishery yields. For these reasons, the North Pacific Fishery Management Council approved a moratorium on commercial fishing north of the Bering Strait and included both the Chukchi and Beaufort Seas (North Pacific Fishery Management Council 2009). The council represents Alaska government agencies, Washington and Oregon fisheries' interests, and US fisheries-related agencies; the moratorium follows the precautionary principle, because based on limited available scientific evidence, it is not clear that fishing could continue without harm to existing fish populations, including resources used for subsistence.

In 2011, the Canadian federal government signed a memorandum of understanding with the Inuvialuit people of the western Arctic prohibiting the issuing of new commercial fishing licences in the adjacent Beaufort Sea until a management plan was devised. Meetings among the United States, Canada, Russia, Norway and Denmark, which began in April 2013, may lead to an international moratorium (Cheney 2013).

INVESTMENT IN INFRASTRUCTURE AND DEVELOPMENT PROJECTS

The engagement of East Asian nations with the Alaska-American Arctic will require a significant expansion of infrastructure. Oil, gas and mineral exploration and development will require construction of new roads, ports and harbours. The Alaska Department of Transportation and Public Facilities has conducted multiple studies of roads that can be used for industrial development (its "roads to resources" program), arctic ports and harbours studies, studies of needed airports and pipelines — as well as how the built environment will be affected by climate change.

To date, US federal funding has paid for the lion's share of new road, port and harbour construction, and this funding has been significantly reduced — a reduction of 20 percent to 30 percent for 2014 is anticipated — as federal deficits and debt have mounted. For the last decade, Alaska has enjoyed high budget surpluses in most years because of high oil prices. Healthy budgets have made possible capital budgets of US$3 billion annually in the last few years, but these will not continue into the future. Reduced oil production and the conservative Republicans' reduction in the progressivity of the Alaska petroleum production tax in 2013 will increase the need to attract substantial new sources of capital investment. It is clear that the US Arctic policy, signed by then President George W. Bush in 2009, and the US National Arctic Strategy of 2013 aim to improve the safety, security and reliability of transportation in the Arctic region. What is not clear, however, is whether, at either the state or federal level, long-term partnerships can be crafted easily with East Asian governments. This is more likely for mineral development projects.

The United States made a commitment to the Arctic Council's search-and-rescue response program in regions of the Arctic, which seems to necessitate a permanent base of the Coast Guard on the Alaska North Slope. At present, the most northern Coast Guard base in the United States is in Kodiak, which is more than 1,000 miles from Chukchi Sea drilling sites and from shipping lanes in the Bering Strait (ANWTF 2012, 19). This lack of a forward base influences the ability of Alaska and the United States to facilitate marine transportation (and of course, oil/gas and other mineral exploration and development) in the Arctic region.

The limited ability of Alaska and US interests to navigate areas with ice is another issue. The United States today has only one polar class icebreaker, the Coast Guard's *Healy*. Its other polar class icebreaker, the *Polar Star*, was under repair in Seattle and returned to service in late 2013. The *Polar Star*'s sister ship, the *Polar Sea*, was decommissioned in 2011 (ibid.). In contrast, Russia has a fleet of eight nuclear powered icebreakers, including a container ship, and a ninth is under construction — although its fleet serves a far larger population, resource and territorial base. China's merchant vessel the *Xue Long* ("Snow Dragon") receives good press for its frequent visits to the Arctic. It is the world's largest non-nuclear icebreaker; a second will join it in 2016. Both Japan and South Korea are adding icebreakers to their fleets (*Global Security* 2011).

GOVERNANCE

The United States has been a less serious participant in Arctic governance than the other Arctic states, but this condition is changing. Certainly, with the winding down of military engagements in Iraq and Afghanistan, the Arctic has gained attention as a future priority, indicated by its inclusion in the 2010 Quadrennial Defense Review. Yet, the United States is the only major maritime power and the only Arctic state that is not a party to UNCLOS, ratified by more than 160 nations. The US objection to the treaty — that it diminished national sovereignty — was resolved under President George H. W. Bush and finalized in the Clinton administration, and both Presidents G. W. Bush and Obama endorsed it for ratification, but it has been stalled in the Senate. The current Alaska US Senate delegation, composed of Senators Mark Begich and Lisa Murkowski, is working to persuade conservative colleagues to ratify UNCLOS. Senator Begich (2013) has said that, "Regrettably, a small number of Republican Senators — enough to deny the two-thirds majority needed for ratification — blocked a vote on this important treaty."

The signing of UNCLOS would be significant, because it extends OCS claims of nations to additional oil and gas reserves. Under treaty terms, nations can claim submerged lands and the resources of those lands (for example, minerals) if they can demonstrate that their continental margin extends beyond the 200-mile exclusive economic zone. The convention also secures open sea lanes (important to the United States in its dispute with Canada regarding the status of the Northwest Passage under international law) and corridors for submarine cables and pipelines (ANWTF 2012, 4).

A second area of improvement lies in the development of clarity regarding US Arctic policy. In 2009, President G. W. Bush adopted National Security Presidential Directive 66/Homeland Security Presidential Directive 25, which calls on the United States to:

- meet national security and homeland security needs relevant to the Arctic region;

- protect the Arctic environment and conserve its biological resources;

- ensure that natural resource management and economic development in the region are environmentally sustainable;

- strengthen institutions for cooperation among the eight Arctic nations (the United States, Canada, Denmark, Finland, Iceland, Norway, the Russian Federation, and Sweden);

- involve the Arctic's indigenous communities in decisions that affect them; and

- enhance scientific monitoring and research into local, regional, and global environmental issues. (The White House 2009, sec. 3)

President Obama signed an executive order establishing the first national policy for the stewardship of the ocean, the coasts and the Great Lakes (The White House Council on Environmental Quality 2010). This established the cabinet-level National Ocean Council and governance coordinating committee, and advanced national planning on Arctic issues. As noted above, in May 2013, the United States also formalized its national strategy on the Arctic.

Related to this clarification at the national level, in Alaska, the legislature has established the bipartisan 26-member Alaska Arctic Policy Commission and charged it with developing a comprehensive Arctic strategy by 2014. Together, these actions elevate the status of Arctic policy at the state and federal levels, and increase the likelihood that they will take into account the involvement of East Asian nations.

Finally, the United States now pays greater attention to the Arctic Council. Former Secretary of State Hillary Clinton was praised by the other Arctic states for her participation in the council's ministerial meetings and she was accompanied on one occasion by Secretary of the Interior Ken Salazar — a significant gesture, as it is rare for the interior secretary to attend international meetings. Newly appointed Secretary of State John Kerry attended the 2013 ministerial meetings in Sweden. Alaska's senior senator, Lisa Murkowski (2013), was the first US senator to attend a meeting of the Arctic Council, when she attended the Nuuk meeting in 2011.

The state of Alaska certainly emphasizes its international role. The ANWTF proposal reads, "The ANWTF Recommends that the Alaska State Legislature and the State of Alaska Support and Encourage Greater International Cooperation through the Arctic Council and Inuit Circumpolar Council-Alaska" (ANWTF 2012, 6). The state sends representatives to the Arctic Council meetings and to meetings of senior Arctic officials, and on this point, there is no significant difference whether governors are Republican or Democratic. Unlike a number of regional organizations, the Arctic Council has emphasized environmental security issues, which the Alaska task force endorsed (Ebinger and Zambetakis 2009).

At the 2013 ministerial meeting in Sweden, the Arctic Council expanded the number of permanent observer states. Before the meeting, the Alaska task force, which is composed of both federal and state representatives, commented, "The ANWTF also supports enlarging the number of non-Arctic nations that enjoy Observer status at the Arctic Council, however, not in such a way that would weaken the influence granted to the council's Permanent Participants" (ANWTF 2012, 7). The US State Department supported the applications of East Asian nations as well. The nations admitted as permanent observers are China, Japan, South Korea,

Singapore, India and Italy. The European Union was admitted technically, but remaining trade differences with Canada have delayed its formal admission.

CONCLUSION

There are few differences between the state of Alaska and the US federal government as to whether increasing East Asian involvement in the Arctic should be encouraged. Alaska, as a state exporting natural resources, and with relatively short transportation lines to East Asia, has already developed strong ties with this region, which it is willing to strengthen further.

There are important value differences between Alaska/America and China, and these are more of an impediment to friendly relations than the value differences between Alaska and Japan or South Korea, which are democratic nations. China remains an authoritarian power under the rule of a survivalist communist party, focused on economic development at whatever cost, and this is objectionable to many Alaskans and Americans.

This analysis also suggests that East Asian nations will benefit greatly from long-term involvement in the Arctic. They can gain access to natural resources they need to continue economic development and improve food security, and they may be able to reduce transportation costs by crossing Arctic waters. To expedite development, Alaska and the United States are no different from their Arctic neighbours: they welcome the expansion of East Asian nations' investment in their industry and infrastructure and their respect for the Arctic governance systems.

WORKS CITED

ANWTF. 2012. *Findings and Recommendations of the Alaska Northern Waters Task Force*. ANWTF, January. www.housemajority.org/coms/anw/pdfs/27/NWTF_Full_Report_Color.pdf.

Begich, Mark. 2013. "Law of the Sea Remains Critical for Alaska, Nation." *Homer Tribune*, January 16. http://homertribune.com/2013/01/law-of-the-sea-remains-critical-for-alaska-nation/.

Blunden, Margaret. 2012. "Geopolitics and the Northern Sea Route." *International Affairs* 88 (1): 115–129. doi:10.1111/j.1468-2346.2012.01060.x.

Bohrer, Becky. 2012. "Parnell Eyeing Ways to Further Advance Gas Line." *Alaska Journal of Commerce*, October 12.

Brigham, Lawson. 2011. "The Challenges and Security Issues of Arctic Marine Transport." In *Arctic Security in an Age of Climate Change*, edited by James Kraska. New York: Cambridge University Press.

Burke, Jill. 2013. "Alaska Watches as Canada Considers Shipping Tar Sands Oil Across Arctic Ocean." *Alaska Dispatch*, April 30. www.alaskadispatch.com/article/20130430/alaska-watches-canada-considers-shipping-tar-sands-oil-across-arctic-ocean.

CBC News. 2012. "Arctic Shipping Boom May Come with New Obstacles." Reprinted in *Alaska Dispatch*, April 28. www.alaskadispatch.com/article/arctic-shipping-boom-may-come-new-obstacles.

Cheney, Catherine. 2013. "Arctic Commercial Fishing Deal Would Set a Precedent." *World Politics Review*, April 24. www.worldpoliticsreview.com/trend-lines/12891/arctic-comm.

Department of Defense. 2011. *Report to Congress on Arctic Operations and the Northwest Passage OUSD (Policy)*. May. www.defense.gov/pubs/pdfs/tab_a_arctic_report_public.pdf.

Department of the Interior. 2010. "Estimated Undiscovered, Economically Recoverable Resources" Department of the Interior, July. www.doi.gov/whatwedo/energy/ocs/upload/UERR-map-2012-2017-80-NoYear-Note.pdf.

Ebinger, Charles K. and Evie Zambetakis. 2009. "The Geopolitics of Arctic Melt." *International Affairs* 85 (6): 1215–32. doi:10.1111/j.1468-2346.2009.00858.x.

Global Security. 2011. "World Wide Icebreakers — A List." *Global Security*, July 11.

Holmes, James. 2012. "Open Seas." *Foreign Policy*, October 29.

Jakobson, Linda and Jingchao Peng. 2012. "China's Arctic Aspirations." Stockholm International Peace Research Institute (SIPRI) Policy Paper No. 34, November.

Kraska, James. 2011. "The New Arctic Geography and U.S. Strategy." In *Arctic Security in an Age of Climate Change*, edited by James Kraska. New York: Cambridge University Press.

McBeath, Jerry, Matthew Berman, Jonathan Rosenberg and Mary F. Ehrlander. 2008. *The Political Economy of Oil in Alaska: Multinationals vs. the State*. Boulder, CO: Lynne Rienner Publishers.

Moyo, Dambisa. 2012. *Winner Take All: China's Race for Resources and What It Means for the World*. New York: Basic Books.

Murkowski, Lisa. 2013. Letter to Secretary of State John Kerry, February 8. www.murkowski.senate.gov/public/?a=Files.Serve&File_id=98dc20f7-8a9b-4728-936d-dcf418dd3229.

North Pacific Fishery Management Council. 2009. "Fishery Management Plan for Fish Resources of the Arctic Management Area." North Pacific Fishery Management Council, August. http://alaskafisheries.noaa.gov/npfmc/PDFdocuments/fmp/Arctic/ArcticFMP.pdf.

Office of Governor Sean Parnell. 2012. "Governor Promotes Alaska Gas in Pacific Rim." Press release, September 25. http://gov.alaska.gov/parnell/press-room/full-press-release.html?pr=6272.

Rainwater, Shiloh. 2012. "China's Arctic Strategy: Implications for Sino-Arctic Relations." Speech given at the 54th Annual Conference of the American Association for Chinese Studies, Atlanta, October.

Restino, Carey. 2013. "Treadwell Speaks of Obstacles to Burgeoning Arctic at Norway Conference." *Alaska Dispatch*, January 23. www.alaskadispatch.com/article/treadwell-speaks-obstacles-burgeoning-arctic-norway-conference.

US Census Bureau. 2013. "Total US Exports (Origin of Movement) via Alaska." State Exports for Alaska. www.census.gov/foreign-trade/statistics/state/data/ak.html.

US Energy Information Administration. 2013. "How Much Oil is Produced in Alaska and Where Does It Go?" US Energy Information Administration Frequently Asked Questions, July 3. www.eia.gov/tools/faqs/faq.cfm?id=35&t=6.

USGS. 2008a. "Circum-Arctic Resource Appraisal." USGS Energy Resources Program.

———. 2008b. "Circum-Arctic Resource Appraisal: Estimates of Undiscovered Oil and Gas North of the Arctic Circle." USGS Fact Sheet 2008-3049.

Van Vactor, Samuel A. 1995. "Time to End the Alaskan Oil Export Ban." Cato Policy Analysis No. 227, May 18. www.cato.org/pubs/pas/pa-227.html.

The White House. 2009. *National Security Presidential Directive 66/Homeland Security Presidential Directive 25*. The White House, January 9. www.fas.org/irp/offdocs/nspd/nspd-66.htm.

———. 2013. *National Strategy for the Arctic Region*. The White House, May. www.whitehouse.gov/sites/default/files/docs/nat_arctic_strategy.pdf.

The White House Council on Environmental Quality. 2010. *Final Recommendations of the Interagency Ocean Policy Task Force*. The White House Council on Environmental Quality, July 19. www.whitehouse.gov/files/documents/OPTF_FinalRecs.pdf.

6

Canada's Northern Strategy and East Asian Interests in the Arctic

//

P. Whitney Lackenbauer and James Manicom

The geopolitical importance of the Arctic and Canada's interests in it have never been greater. This is why our government has launched an ambitious Northern Agenda based on the timeless responsibility imposed by our national anthem, to keep the True North strong and free.

— Rt. Hon. Stephen Harper (2008)

China's every move evokes interest. The rise of a large power has throughout history caused jitters, and China is no exception. No one knows with certainty how China will use its power in the coming decades, despite the Chinese Government's assurances that its rise will be peaceful and that it seeks to promote a harmonious world. Now, even though the Arctic is not a foreign policy priority, China's growing interest in the region raises concern — even alarm — in the international community about China's intentions.

— Linda Jakobson and Jingchoa Peng (2012)

INTRODUCTION

Canadian political statements over the last decade make repeated reference to the centrality of the Arctic to Canada, and the growing international recognition that the Arctic plays a fundamental role in global systems. The Canadian Arctic comprises more than 40 percent of the country's land mass, 162,000 km of coastline and approximately one-quarter of the global Arctic. A torrent of recent commentaries point to the complex array of regional opportunities and challenges emerging in the face of rapid environmental change — and in anticipation of escalating rates of future change. Whether viewed as a barometer of global climate change, a scientific or resource frontier, a transit route to elsewhere, or a homeland, the Arctic has captured the attention of the world — from Sanikiluaq to Seoul, Tuktoyaktuk to Tokyo, Baker Lake to Beijing. Canada's historic and ongoing dilemma is how to balance sovereignty, security and stewardship in a manner that protects and projects national interests and values, promotes sustainable development and healthy communities, and facilitates circumpolar stability and cooperation.

The significance of the Arctic in Canadian political discourse has certainly grown since Stephen Harper became prime minister in 2006 and initially trumpeted the idea that "use it or lose it is the first principle of sovereignty." Canadians were inundated with brawny messages about resource development and the idea of Canada as an "Arctic superpower," aimed particularly at voters with deep-seated anxieties about Canada's potential loss of sovereignty. The ground had already been laid for this kind of rhetoric, with Canadian commentators mobilizing a cast of would-be challengers to Canada's Arctic "sovereignty":

- The United States was ostensibly seeking to undermine Canada's position about the Northwest Passage (NWP) forming part of its internal waters. This was coupled with Canada's supposed insecurity stemming from an outstanding boundary dispute in the Beaufort Sea (with its potential resource riches). In practical terms, however, the United States — Canada's primary trading partner and key ally — remains hard to sustain as an existential threat to Canada's territorial integrity or sovereignty.

- When Denmark sent naval ships to Hans Island, a tiny rock subject to competing claims with Canada, Canadian commentators quickly cast this quiet neighbour and North Atlantic Treaty Organization ally as a potential threat. University of Calgary political scientist Rob Huebert's (2005) memorable description that the Vikings had returned and might trigger larger doubts about Canada's claim to the entire Arctic Archipelago grabbed headlines for a short time, but reassuring diplomatic statements and the reality of the extent of the Hans Island dispute (which was confined to the insignificant rock itself) silenced the alarm.

• Russian explorer Artur Chilingarov's flag-planting exploit at the North Pole in 2007, coupled with Russia's military revitalization plans and resumption of strategic bomber flights in the Arctic, and the Putin-Medvedev regime's belligerent political rhetoric reassuring Russians that they would defend Russia's Arctic resources, created obvious conditions to resurrect the Russian bear as a potential Canadian adversary. Following the Ilulissat Declaration in May 2008, which committed Arctic states to peaceful dispute resolution, anxieties about regional conflict were quelled. Voices indicated that Canada and Russia actually had common, vested interests in circumpolar stability, which made the Russian threat seem less acute.[1]

Canada's official northern strategy and Arctic foreign policy statements have sent more positive signals about Canada's sovereign position and about opportunities for international cooperation in the circumpolar north. This dual messaging, emphasizing sovereignty, national security and national interests on the one hand, and international cooperation and stewardship on the other, reveals Canada's bifurcated mindset on Arctic issues. Despite the complexity of Canada's official position, it seems that Canadian interest in the Arctic cannot be sustained — at least in academic and media circles — without a threat narrative. The rising interest of so-called "new actors" in circumpolar affairs, particularly China and other East Asian states, offers renewed uncertainty and the possibility of a new threat narrative. Canadian commentators have been accordingly suspicious of East Asian intentions, despite Canada's positive bilateral relations with all three Northeast Asian states.

The basis for this Asia-in-the-Arctic alarmist rhetoric is speculative and imprecise, originating from (and largely reflective of) generalized discourses associated with the "rise of Asia" and Arctic change and sovereignty. Using *Canada's Northern Strategy* (Government of Canada 2009) and the *Statement on Canada's Arctic Foreign Policy* (SCAFP) (Department of Foreign Affairs and International Trade [DFAIT] 2010) as

---

1   On these themes in the Canadian context, see for example Griffiths (2003), Huebert (2003), Coates et al. (2008), Byers (2009), Griffiths, Huebert and Lackenbauer (2011), Lackenbauer (2010) and Dodds (2011). International overviews include Borgerson (2008), Zellen (2009), Emmerson (2010) and Landriault (2013).

filters, we suggest where East Asian states' Arctic interests may converge or diverge with those of Canada. There are considerable synergies between the interests of East Asian states and the Canadian Arctic agenda, making those Canadians who conceptualize Asian states as an Arctic threat seem especially narrow-minded — particularly given the scientific, environmental and resource development issues at play. The chapter ends with various messages that Canada may wish to emphasize in its interactions with Asian states to safeguard its national interests, promote sustainable development for the benefit of Northerners, and enhance cooperation and constructive dialogue in the circumpolar world. Canada should develop a clear message that clarifies its Arctic agenda, indicates opportunities for cooperation and collaboration, and corrects misconceptions about Canada's position on sovereignty and sovereign rights in the region.

CANADIAN PERSPECTIVES ON EAST ASIA'S INTERESTS IN THE ARCTIC

It is beyond the scope of this study to provide a robust interpretation of East Asian nations' strategies, commercial interests, scholarly literature and media commentary on the Arctic; other chapters in this book examine how China, Japan and South Korea view the Arctic. Rather than reiterating these points, this chapter analyzes how Canadian scholars and journalists infer motives into Chinese and other East Asian official statements and academic works.

Most Canadian attention on East Asian states' Arctic interests focuses on China. An Ekos Research (2011) report conducted for the Munk-Gordon Arctic Security Program is telling. According to the report, "respondents in each of the eight member states of the Arctic Council were presented with a list of countries and asked which one they would be *most* comfortable dealing with and which they would be *least* comfortable dealing with on Arctic issues....China was identified as the least desired partner by every nation except Russia" (ibid., xxii). Furthermore, Canadians expressed the lowest levels of support for including non-Arctic states in the Arctic Council and granting them "a say in Arctic affairs" (ibid., xxiv).

Although Canadians seem to view China's engagement in Arctic affairs with skepticism and even distaste, there is a striking lack of substantive discussion in academic and popular commentaries about *how* or *why* China constitutes a threat to Canada's Arctic interests. China has not unveiled an Arctic strategy, nor is there any official indication that it plans to do so. Accordingly, insight into why Canadians perceive China this way must come from more general data. A report commissioned by the Asia Pacific Foundation of Canada (2012, 3) confirms that "Canadians across the country are increasingly attuned to Asia and to Canada's place in the Asia Pacific region." This was particularly true of Northern Canada, where 57 percent of respondents reported that they paid more attention to Canada's relations with Asia in the previous year than they ever had in the past (ibid., 12, 16). Twelve percent of Canadians polled expressed "warm" (favourable) feelings toward China, while 29 percent indicated "cold" (unfavourable) ratings of China. This trend also fit with the generally favourable or "warm" feelings toward Western countries and unfavourable "cool" feelings to other Asian countries, except Japan (ibid., 3, 7).

According to the poll results, Canadians perceived that shifts in the international order placed China in an increasingly powerful position (ibid., 3). Two-thirds of Canadians polled believed that China's global influence would surpass that of the United States over the next decade. More than one-third of Canadian respondents described the United States as "in decline," while 42 percent perceived China as "growing" and 30 percent described it as "strong" (ibid., 4, 9, 26). Nonetheless, Canadians ranked China the "least favourable" overall. The leading factor was Canadians' perceptions of Chinese governance. Forty-five percent of respondents described China as authoritarian; 37 percent described it as "corrupt"; 34 percent as "threatening" (ibid., 9). Only four percent described China as "friendly" (ibid.). While five percent expressed a general feeling of admiration toward China, 22 percent said that they "disliked" the country (ibid.).

The poll found that Canadians tend to focus on economic relationships, and consider China to be important to Canada's prosperity. Accordingly, more than half of the respondents saw China's increasing economic power as more of an opportunity than a threat, perceiving opportunities for trade and investment and for diversification of global economic and political relationships (ibid., 14). A majority of Canadians (and 63 percent of Northerners) believed that "Canada must act now to take advantage of Asia's need for energy resources," but this did not extend to receptiveness for foreign ownership of Canadian resources by state-controlled companies (ibid., 29). A majority of Canadians, however, remain "unconvinced that the economic benefits of Asia's investment in Canada's energy sector outweigh concerns about foreign ownership of our natural resources" (ibid., 4-5). The Asia Pacific Foundation concluded that Canadians retain "a lingering hesitation and concern about Asia, particularly China" (ibid., 3). Although aware of the benefits of Asian foreign investment in Canada, the poll found that "fewer than one-in-five Canadians would be in favour of state-controlled companies from China...buying a controlling stake in a major Canadian company" (ibid.) It also noted a six-point increase in the proportion of Canadians worried about China's military power in the Asia Pacific region (ibid.).

These broader concerns about China's regional and global aspirations frame Canadian observers' interpretations of China's Arctic interests and agenda, which conform to a broader Western trend. Gang Chen, a researcher at the East Asian Institute, National University of Singapore, observes that:

> As an East Asian power that has neither Arctic coast nor the Arctic Council membership, China's open statement of not having a strategic agenda regarding the melting Arctic has been interpreted in dichotomous ways: some take it as a genuine expression from the Chinese government while others regard it as a tactic taken by the rising power to hide its real intention there due to its limited influence in the remote Arctic region. Such a divergence over whether China is following an Arctic strategy to secure its long-term economic interest or even geopolitical influence is analogical with, and to some extent, can be perceived as part of the early debates over whether China has a calculative grand strategy. (2012, 358-59)

This split in interpretation is clearly evident in Canadian commentary. On the one hand, alarmists — centred around what we label the "Calgary school" of David Wright and Rob Huebert — suggest that Canadians should be wary of East Asian states (particularly China) as revisionist actors with interests counter those of Canada. On the other hand, commentators such as Frédéric Lasserre suggest that Canada's national interests in the Arctic are generally compatible with those of East Asian countries and see opportunities for collaboration and mutual benefit.

University of Calgary historian David Wright is not an Arctic expert, but his linguistic skills have made him a leading commentator on what Chinese academics are writing about Arctic issues. His overarching message is that Canadians must recognize the attention that "astute and acutely observant geostrategic thinkers" in China have taken in the region (2011a, 1). Wright argues that "the Canadian Arctic has what China wants: natural resources and the possibility of a major new shipping route. China knows that Canadian control over these resources makes Canada a major international player, a country with natural resource wealth and geostrategic advantage befitting its sheer geographical size, but out of proportion with its relatively small population" (ibid.). He also notes that "there is at present quite a bit of room for discussion and debate in China over this issue, both in the halls of power in Beijing and, to a surprisingly open and public extent, in academic journals and popular news media" (Wright 2011b). While observing that Beijing has yet to formulate an official Arctic policy, he asserts that "what non-official observers are writing should worry Canadians" (ibid.). Amplifying the voices of the most aggressive Chinese analysts, Wright points to China's perceived entitlement to the resource riches of the Arctic as the world's most populous country, as well as its desire to see most of the Arctic basin remain "international territory [*sic*]" and to dilute Canada's sovereignty over the [NWP] to the point of "meaninglessness" (ibid.). Wright reinforces this concerned message in another study, recommending that:

> American policy makers should be aware that China's recent interest in Arctic affairs is not an evanescent fancy or a passing political fad but a serious, new, incipient policy direction. China is taking concrete diplomatic steps to ensure that it becomes a player in the Arctic game and eventually will have what it regards as its fair share of access to Arctic resources and sea routes. China has already committed substantial human, institutional, and naval resources to its Arctic interests and will continue to do so, likely at an accelerated rate, in the future. (2011c, 32)

This echoes University of Calgary political scientist Rob Huebert, who has signalled alarm about East Asia's Arctic intentions for more than a decade. As part of the "sovereignty on thinning ice" narrative that he developed in the early 2000s, Huebert has frequently cited the purportedly unannounced arrival of the Chinese research vessel *Xue Long* at Tuktoyaktuk in 1999 as an example of Canada's negligible control over activities in its Arctic, and the host of sovereignty-related challenges *potentially* posed by Asian states with their cutting-edge icebreaking capacity, insatiable appetites for resources (including water) and little vested interest in the status quo.[2]

As a regular fixture in the Canadian media on Arctic issues, Huebert has consistently framed twenty-first-century Arctic dynamics through a threat narrative. For example, in portending a "new Arctic age," Huebert (2008) stresses that the region is "on the verge of becoming a more complicated and crowded area" and Canadians had to know how "to meet many challenges." To control its Arctic, he asserts, Canada needs to act decisively to deal with "some of the challenges we know

---

2   See, for example, *The Globe and Mail* (2006).

about: Climate change, resource development, globalization (the South Koreans are entering the market to build ice-capable vessels, the Japanese are investing heavily in the study of Arctic gas hydrates off the coast of Canada, and China is going to become an Arctic player as well), Russia is on the rise again, and laws governing the maritime Arctic are in flux" (ibid.). Huebert continuously reiterates his concerns about East Asian interests in the region in his regular presentations and media statements. Commenting on the "real possibility" of future tension in the Arctic, Huebert (2012) emphasizes China's looming impact on Arctic security. "What we're seeing with the Chinese is that they've made it very clear that they want to be major players in the Arctic for reasons of transportation, natural resources, scientific research and strategic concerns," he notes (quoted in Yundt 2012). "They will be there. They're spending the money. Their navy is being modernized as we speak at a time when the American navy is facing huge budget cuts" (ibid.).

Other commentators have carried this line of argument to its logical conclusion. Victor Suthren (2006), the director general of the Canadian War Museum from 1986 to 1997, justified the need for naval investments by linking China and the Arctic:

> Canada's Arctic is melting into an ice-free major-ocean coastline that will provide the government of the day with the challenge of policing three busy ocean coasts; the extraordinary economic expansion of China is now being followed by heavy defence expenditures on developing a large and capable Chinese blue-water navy; and the vital seaborne trade that lies at the heart of Canadian economic well-being will see the flow of thousands of containers into our ports increase fivefold within our lifetimes. A seaborne terrorist attack on North America is increasingly a possibility.

The following year, Rear Admiral Tyrone Pile, the commander of Canada's Maritime Forces Pacific, told *The Calgary Herald* (2007) that the Chinese Navy would soon have twice as many submarines as the US Navy, leading the newspaper to speculate that China might project its power "as Great Britain and the U.S. once did." Pile indicated that China was aware that the NWP could soon be navigable and would "trim thousands of kilometres from Asia to Europe by bypassing the Panama Canal" (quoted in ibid.). This raised troubling questions: "how prepared is Canada to enforce its sovereignty claims in the region, if foreign ships, Chinese or otherwise, try to take advantage of this Arctic melting — without the formality of Ottawa's approval? What if those vessels are supported by their country's warships?" (ibid.).

The *Herald* editorial concluded that Canada had to achieve regional dominance in its northern waters to "deter a future Arctic sovereignty challenge" (ibid.).[3]

Huebert (2012, 1) recently declared that "China not only is interested in Arctic issues but is also actively developing the means to play an increasingly powerful position in the region. This has caught Canada off guard. Given the growing economic wealth and power of the new China, Canada needs to take into account Chinese interests in the Arctic." Perhaps because he is writing in his capacity as a board member of the Canadian Polar Commission, Huebert is rather tentative in his conclusions but intimates a growing complexity in the Sino-Canadian Arctic relationship:

> Very few people had even thought that such a relationship was likely or possible just a few years back. But China's determination to understand the changes that are now occurring in the Arctic, and to avail itself of the opportunities that may arise as a result, will increasingly challenge Canadian decision-makers. The Chinese are willing to approach their new arctic enterprises in a cooperative fashion; but they have made it equally clear that they will proceed regardless of the response from the other arctic states, including Canada. They are clearly making the expenditures to transform themselves into a major arctic power. This will bring opportunities for mutual gain, as Canada can benefit from working with the Chinese on a wide range of issues, but China is beginning to view the Arctic in a broader geo-political context, and on this level Canadian and Chinese interests may not always meet. (ibid., 6)

Predicting that China will "soon become much more powerful," Huebert urges that "Canada would be wise to start thinking much more seriously about this increasingly complex and interesting relationship" (ibid.).

Does this complexity portend divergent interests and conflict? Laval University geographer Frédéric Lasserre offers more optimistic appraisals of China's Arctic interests. Responding to scenarios positing China as a challenger to Canada's Arctic sovereignty, Lasserre (2010) refutes "prevailing assumptions in the general literature…that the Chinese government and Chinese shipping companies are merely waiting for the [NWP] to open up a bit more before launching full-scale service across Arctic Canadian waters between Asia and Europe." He finds no

---

3   See also Grant (2010a).

evidence that shipping companies' strategies seriously contemplated the NWP as an attractive deepwater transit route, or that China sought to claim territorial rights in the region. Consequently, Lasserre sees China's growing interest in Arctic affairs as "a good opportunity for Canada to voice its desire to foster cooperation in the region" and advance its interests through enhanced polar shipping regulations, scientific collaboration and adherence to international law (ibid.).[4]

Lasserre's message fits with European scholarly literature that also avoids alarmist rhetoric. Jakobson and Peng (2012) remark that while non-Chinese observers refer to China's "more assertive" Arctic actions, "China's Arctic policies are still in a nascent stage of formulation." They emphasize that "China has not published an Arctic strategy and is not expected to do so in the near- to medium-term" (ibid.). Nevertheless, in a low-key, pragmatic and measured way, Chinese officials have taken steps to investigate and "protect" China's regional interests, emphasizing the global impacts of the melting sea ice. Jakobson and Peng place the Chinese government's key interests in three broad categories: to strengthen its capacity to respond appropriately to the effects that climate change in the Arctic will have on food production and extreme weather in China; to secure access, at reasonable cost, to Arctic shipping routes; and to strengthen China's ability as a non-Arctic state to access Arctic resources and fishing waters.

These interests are reasonable, conform with international law and are compatible with Canada's foreign and domestic policy priorities, as long as non-Arctic actors respect Northerners' interests and Canadian sovereignty and sovereign rights. Most Canadians, however, are conditioned to conflate external interests in the Arctic with threats. This is tied to a long history of anxiety borne of sporadic national and political interests, economic underdevelopment in some regions and sectors of the northern economy, and chronic insecurity about "sovereignty" loss.

CANADA AND THE ARCTIC: A HISTORY OF VACILLATING INTEREST, DRIVEN BY CRISIS REACTION

Canada inherited its High Arctic from Great Britain in 1880, but governed these territories in, to borrow Canadian Prime Minister Louis St-Laurent's often-quoted quip, a "fit of absence of mind" until after World War II. The primary impetus for major development was the Cold War, which placed the Arctic at the centre

---

4   For another report eschewing fear mongering about Chinese Arctic interests, see Michael Byers, quoted in in Boswell (2010).

of superpower geopolitics and the US circumpolar security agenda in conflict with Canada's sovereignty. The United States largely dictated the pace of military modernization in Canada's North and the accompanying socio-economic, cultural and environmental impacts. Brief bursts of national interest in the Arctic followed perceived sovereignty challenges in 1969 and 1985, leading Canadian governments to clarify the country's sovereignty position and to promise investments in northern defences, but political attention faded when the threats did. Civilian projects in the Arctic were similarly episodic and incomplete. As a result, the Canadian Arctic remains an unfulfilled political and economic opportunity, despite major domestic achievements like the creation of the Inuit-majority territory of Nunavut in 1999.[5]

With the end of the Cold War, the official discourse in Canada on Arctic affairs shifted away from continental security and narrow sovereignty interests to emphasize circumpolar cooperation and broad definitions of security prioritizing human and environmental dimensions. Canada was an early champion of the Arctic Council and promoted the inclusion of Aboriginal permanent participants at the table. In 1997, a parliamentary committee recommended that Canada's relations focus on international Arctic cooperation through multilateral governance to address pressing "human security" and environmental challenges in the region. Environmentally sustainable human development was "the long-term foundation for assuring circumpolar security," Bill Graham, chair of the House of Commons Standing Committee on Foreign Affairs and International Trade, explained, "with priority being given to the well-being of Arctic peoples and to safeguarding northern habitants from intrusions which have impinged aggressively on them" (Government of Canada 1997). This message was summarized in a policy statement released by the Liberal government in June 2000, which promoted four main pillars: enhancing the security and prosperity of Canadians (especially Northerners and Aboriginal peoples); asserting and ensuring the preservation of Canada's Arctic sovereignty; establishing the circumpolar region as a vibrant geopolitical entity integrated into a rules-based international system; and promoting the human security of Northerners and the sustainable development of the Arctic (DFAIT 2000).

Early in the new millennium, climate change reports, vigorous academic and media debates, and hyperbolic rhetoric over boundary disputes like Hans Island and the status of the NWP raised acute concerns about Canadian sovereignty. Canada's International Policy Statement, released by Prime Minister Paul Martin's Liberal government in 2005, identified the Arctic as a priority area given "increased security

---

5   For recent general overviews, see Coates et al. (2008) and Grant (2010b).

threats, a changed distribution of global power, challenges to existing international institutions, and transformation of the global economy" (DFAIT 2005). The next two decades were anticipated to bring major challenges requiring investments in new military capabilities and creative diplomacy. "In addition to growing economic activity in the Arctic region, the effects of climate change are expected to open up our Arctic waters to commercial traffic by as early as 2015," the statement noted (ibid.). "These developments reinforce the need for Canada to monitor and control events in its sovereign territory, through new funding and new tools" (ibid., 3). Although the Liberal government fell before it could implement its vision, it had intertwined sovereignty and security in political rhetoric and strategic documents.

The Canadian North was a key component of the Conservatives' 2005 election platform, which played on the idea of an Arctic sovereignty "crisis" demanding decisive action. Stephen Harper (2005) promised that Canada would acquire the military capabilities necessary to defend its sovereignty against external threats:

> The single most important duty of the federal government is to protect and defend our national sovereignty....It's time to act to defend Canadian sovereignty. A Conservative government will make the military investments needed to secure our borders. You don't defend national sovereignty with flags, cheap election rhetoric, and advertising campaigns. You need forces on the ground, ships in the sea, and proper surveillance. And that will be the Conservative approach.

Harper's political message emphasized the need for Canadian action, with particular attention to conventional military forces, differentiating his government from the Liberals, whom he believed had swung the pendulum too far toward diplomacy and human development.

Beginning with the Ilulissat Declaration in May 2008, however, the Canadian government's official statements have adopted a more optimistic and less bellicose tone. In his Whitehorse speech on March 11, 2009, then Minister of Foreign Affairs Lawrence Cannon (2009) acknowledged that geological research and international law — not military clout — would resolve boundary disputes. He emphasized collaboration and cooperation, stating that "The depth and complexity of the challenges facing the Arctic are significant, and we recognize the importance of addressing many of these issues by working with our neighbours — through the Arctic Council, other multilateral institutions and our bilateral partnerships....

Strong Canadian leadership in the Arctic will continue to facilitate good international governance in the region" (ibid.).

CANADA'S NORTHERN STRATEGY AND ARCTIC FOREIGN POLICY: WHERE AND HOW EAST ASIA FITS

DFAIT released the SCAFP in August 2010, articulating Canada's international efforts pursuant to the *Northern Strategy*. This document emphasizes the importance of the Arctic in Canada's national identity and its role as an "Arctic power." The overall message mirrors the general strategy's language, outlining a vision for the Arctic as "a stable, rules-based region with clearly defined boundaries, dynamic economic growth and trade, vibrant Northern communities, and healthy and productive ecosystems" (Government of Canada 2009; 2013a). Implementing a vision that supports sovereignty, security and stewardship will entail ongoing discussions about how to balance the interests of the Arctic states, Northern peoples, non-Arctic states and organizations, development and transportation companies, and other groups with interests in the region.

The SCAFP provides a list of other priorities for international attention. The remainder of this chapter explores how these interact with East Asian interests in the Arctic, as understood by Canadian and other Western commentators.

SOVEREIGNTY: ENGAGING WITH NEIGHBOURS TO RESOLVE BOUNDARY ISSUES

Predictably, the first and foremost pillar of Canada's foreign policy in the SCAFP is "the exercise of our sovereignty over the Far North" (DFAIT 2010, 4). The statement highlights that "protecting national sovereignty, and the integrity of our borders, is the first and foremost responsibility of a national government. We are resolved to protect Canadian sovereignty throughout our Arctic" (9). The hardline security message that had figured prominently in earlier statements is muted and the tone of cooperation with circumpolar neighbours and Northerners is amplified. The SCAFP commits Canada to "seek to resolve boundary issues in the Arctic region, in accordance with international law" (6). While such disputes pose no acute sovereignty or security concerns to Canada, most commentators see them as a political liability.

While it is not a "boundary" dispute, Canada's legal position that the NWP constitutes internal waters is not universally accepted. The United States has taken a public position suggesting that the passage is an international strait (although it has never been used as such in functional terms), but most other countries have remained silent on the issue. Canadian commentators often assume that, given their interests as maritime nations, East Asian states would oppose Canada's position. Wright, for example, observes that "some Chinese scholars are carefully examining Canada's claims of historical sovereignty over the Arctic in general and the [NWP] in particular," indicating that "Beijing does not want to affirm the accuracy or appropriateness of Canada's historical claims" (2011a, 1-2). Although he concedes that "the small number of scholars in China who consider these claims in detail seem largely to end up sympathetic with, and supportive of," the Canadian position, he reiterates that "the Chinese government itself does not seem ready to affirm Canadian Arctic sovereignty" (ibid.). Wright suggests that "Canada needs to be on its guard against Chinese attempts to water down Canada's Arctic sovereignty and should strengthen cooperation with democratic Arctic states for the security and stability of the region" (ibid.).

Although some Canadian commentators point to Chinese scholarly statements that raise questions or doubts about Canada's legal position on the NWP, a closer appraisal suggests that the Chinese are often citing the work of these same Canadian scholars in making their case. Thus, there is a deeply flawed circular logic at work when Canadian commentators, such as Huebert, point out vulnerabilities in Canada's position, and then use East Asian commentators' reference to these potential vulnerabilities as proof that their concerns are warranted. Clearly, more careful analysis of the source(s) of East Asian analyses are required before drawing conclusions about their stance on Canada's legal position regarding its internal waters.

Contrary to hawkish perspectives circulated by the Calgary school and in the popular media, China is unlikely to challenge either Canada's position on the NWP or its straight baselines. China may have interest in Arctic shipping lanes, but its own interests as a coastal state — for example, its perspective on the Qiongzhou Strait — are virtually identical to Canada's perspective on the NWP. Furthermore, China (and indeed all East Asian states) has made straight baselines claims based on a liberal interpretation of article 7 of the United Nations Convention on the Law of the Sea (UNCLOS) and is therefore unlikely to challenge Canada's position — unless Canada were to join the United States in its comprehensive opposition to Asian states' maritime claims.[6]

---

6   On China's straight baseline claim, see Kim (1994, 899).

Conversations with Asian academics support this perspective and reinforce the probability that East Asian states will respect settled maritime claims in the Arctic. Furthermore, Chinese scholars emphasize that a central tenet of Chinese foreign policy is non-interference in other countries' internal affairs. Consistent with this principle, they indicate that China will not interfere in Arctic states' exercise of sovereignty or dispute the rights of coastal states to establish extended continental shelves. In the end, it is highly probable that Canada will assume jurisdiction over as much continental shelf as is permissible under UNCLOS and will settle overlaps with its Arctic neighbours through negotiation, regardless of Asian preferences. For their part, Asian states look forward to conducting research (in compliance with Arctic state jurisdictions) that supports resource exploitation in prospective areas such as the Beaufort Sea.[7]

As Yang Jian, vice president of the Shanghai Institutes for International Studies, explains in a commentary for the 2012 Arctic Yearbook, "For China, Arctic affairs can be divided into those of a regional nature and those of global implications. It has been China's position that the former should be properly resolved through negotiation between countries of the region. China respects the sovereignty and sovereign rights of Arctic countries, and hopes that they can collaborate with each other and peacefully resolve their disputes over territory and sovereignty" (Jian 2012a).

This reflects what Jakobson and Peng describe as the more "subdued" public messaging from Chinese Arctic scholars since 2011, which also fits with China's "preoccupation with staunchly defending its perceived rights in the South and East China seas" (2012 v-vi; 15-16). Similarly, as countries with extraneous baseline claims, Japan and South Korea are unlikely to criticize Canada's Arctic baselines. With regard to the status of the waters of the NWP, Canada may have more to fear from South Korean and Japanese perspectives than from those of the Chinese (Bateman and Schofield 2008).

SECURING INTERNATIONAL RECOGNITION FOR THE FULL EXTENT OF CANADA'S EXTENDED CONTINENTAL SHELF

Canada has made significant investments to ensure that it "secures international recognition for the full extent of its continental shelf" in the Arctic (DFAIT 2010, 7).

---

7   James Manicom, personal interview with Guo Peiqing, Qingdao, November 20, 2012.

UNCLOS defines the rights and responsibilities of states in using the oceans and lays out a process for determining maritime boundaries. Littoral countries are therefore mapping the Arctic to determine the extent of their claims. Canada ratified UNCLOS in November 2003 and had until December 2013 to submit evidence of its extended continental shelf claim beyond the existing 200-nautical-mile exclusive economic zone. To this end, the 2004 federal budget announced CDN$69 million for seabed surveying and mapping to establish the outer limits of Canada's continental shelves in the Arctic and Atlantic Oceans. In 2007, the Canadian government allocated another CDN$20 million to complete the mapping of its shelf to meet the deadline, and DFAIT officials were confident that claims would be submitted on schedule (Standing Senate Committee on Fisheries and Oceans 2008, 13). Where Canada has overlapping claims with its Arctic neighbours, it has promised to sort these out diplomatically. The other Arctic states made a similar pledge in the May 2008 Ilulissat Declaration.

No East Asian state has a claim to the Arctic shelf. Therefore, suspicions of territorial revisionism by China do not stand up to scrutiny. There is little evidence that Chinese leaders are considering claiming Arctic space. Alarmists point to Rear Admiral Yin Zhou's assertion in March 2010 that "the Arctic belongs to all the people around the world as no nation has sovereignty over it," as well as his comment that "China must play an indispensable role in Arctic exploration as we have one-fifth of the world's population" (quoted in Chang 2010). According to Gordon Chang, Yin actually said that "the current scramble for the sovereignty of the Arctic among some nations has encroached on many other countries' interests." Some commentators, including Chang, saw this as China abandoning its cautious approach to publicizing its Arctic views and "staking a claim" to the region in repudiation of the Arctic states' sovereignty (ibid.). Yin, however, was speaking in the context of China's broader maritime strategy and referring to the area in the central Arctic Ocean that is beyond national jurisdiction. International lawyer Aldo Chircop (2011, 14) notes that:

> China has spoken for the global commons in ways that no other major state has done in recent times. Clearly there is self-interest in reminding Arctic states that extended continental shelf claims, while permitted to coastal states under UNCLOS, should not trench on the international seabed area. In doing so, however, it is also playing the role of advocate for the common heritage of mankind and interests of developing countries, which no other Arctic state is doing. It has given itself a voice for developing

countries. Considering its substantial official development assistance in all developing regions, this is a role which many developing countries are likely to endorse.

Chinese leaders are likely aware that to claim Arctic space, they would need to conquer an Arctic coastal state. Given the players involved, this would likely lead to nuclear war — obviously negating any benefits of territorial acquisition through conquest, which is also outlawed by the UN Charter.

Furthermore, superficial comparisons between China's interests and behaviour in the East and South China Seas and in the Arctic basin fall short on various fronts. First, China's role and interests are different in both regions. While China has the interests of a maritime state in the Arctic, in East Asian seas its posture is closer to that of a coastal state, reflecting concerns about foreign vessels conducting activities close to shore and provoking calls for thicker coastal state jurisdiction over maritime areas (Greenfield 1992). China bases its sovereignty claims to the South and East China seas on disputed features like the Diaoyu, Spratly and Paracel Islands, on associated claims to maritime jurisdiction and on historic rights. China has no comparable footprint in the Arctic. Second, although much has been made of Chinese "assertiveness" in disputed maritime areas, China does not perceive its behaviour as assertive. Rather, Chinese analysts argue that China has reacted to provocations by rival claimants. For instance, tensions in 2012 over the Diaoyu Islands emerged as a consequence of Japan's purchase of the islands from their private owner, a move Beijing decried as illegal and invalid on the basis that the islands are Chinese. Similarly, Chinese assertiveness in the South China Sea is a reaction to perceived efforts by claimants to violate China's claimed jurisdiction by exploring for resources and permitting fishing in disputed waters (Goldstein 2011). By contrast, China's concerns in the Arctic relate to the possibility that coastal states' claims to extended continental shelves may erode the size of the "area" that is beyond coastal state jurisdiction. This is hardly analogous to regional disputes in Asia, in which China has a stronger vested interest.

The Arctic presents an opportunity for Canada and other Arctic states to engage East Asian states on questions of global maritime governance. China, Japan and South Korea have submitted claims to an extended continental shelf in the East China Sea and the Pacific, as have Denmark, Russia and Canada. Problematically, the Commission on the Limits of the Continental Shelf has not ruled on disputed aspects of these submissions, because each party has protested various aspects of the others' claims (United Nations 2013). Here, it seems that Canada, Denmark and Russia have an opportunity to set an example for East Asian states for resolving contested continental shelf claims.

ADDRESSING ARCTIC GOVERNANCE AND RELATED EMERGING ISSUES

Canada's sovereignty agenda also addresses Arctic governance and public safety issues (such as emergency response and search and rescue). The SCAFP notes that:

> Increasingly, the world is turning its attention northward, with many players far removed from the region itself seeking a role and in some cases calling into question the governance of the Arctic. While many of these players could have a contribution to make in the development of the North, Canada does not accept the premise that the Arctic requires a fundamentally new governance structure or legal framework. Nor does Canada accept that the Arctic nation states are unable to appropriately manage the North as it undergoes fundamental change. (DFAIT 2010, 8)

The statement reiterates that an extensive international legal framework applies to the Arctic Ocean, but that new challenges will emerge alongside increased shipping, tourism and economic development. Placing a clear priority on "regional solutions, supported by robust domestic legislation in Arctic states," Canada emphasizes collaboration with "other Arctic nations through the Arctic Council (the primary forum for collaboration among the eight Arctic states), with the five Arctic Ocean coastal states on issues of particular relevance to the Arctic Ocean, and bilaterally with key Arctic partners, particularly the United States" (ibid.).

Canada's official position indicates that it prefers a regional governance regime dominated by the Arctic states — a stance that may conflict with East Asian aspirations for a stake in regional governance. In response to the SCAFP, a *Toronto Star* (2010) editorial indicated that Ottawa "insists the Arctic Council eight are 'best placed to exercise leadership in the management of the region,' at a time when China and others are showing interest in the North. At root, Ottawa seems to be pushing for Arctic issues to be sorted out by as few interested players as possible, while keeping the rest of the world at a distance." East Asian commentators, however, insist that the Arctic Ocean cannot be considered the private and exclusive preserve of the Arctic coastal states. For example, Chinese Assistant Minister of Foreign Affairs Hu Zhenyue stated in June 2009 that "Arctic countries should protect the balance between the interests of states with shorelines in the Arctic Ocean and the shared interests of the international community" (quoted in Campbell 2012, 3). Some Chinese commentators, such as Li Zhenfu of Dalian Maritime University and Guo Peiqing from the School of Law and Political Science at the Ocean University of China, urge China to adopt a proactive campaign to protect its rights.[8] Other scholars preach restraint, suggesting that China should avoid provoking Arctic states by asserting views on topics such as resources and shipping. Indian political scientist Sanjay Chaturvedi (2012, 232) notes that "China's much pronounced official foreign policy stand on supporting state sovereignty in its classical-territorial sense could come in the way of articulating the vision of a more inclusive and democratic 'regional' (perhaps even global) governance for the circumpolar Arctic."

That East Asian commentators raise questions about the current Arctic governance regime and call for change should come as no surprise, given that Canadian commentators have raised serious questions about the capacity of existing arrangements to ensure regional security and stability. For example, Huebert (2009) suggests that the soft-law approach currently in place will prove ineffective in managing challenges related to climate change, resource development and increased shipping in the region. He has advocated strong regional institutions with legal powers and even an ambitious new Arctic treaty architecture modelled on the Antarctic Treaty — in obvious opposition to the Ilulissat Declaration (ibid.). Other Western commentators have avoided the treaty road while still suggesting that the current regime needs fundamental reform. The Arctic Governance Project — whose nine-member steering committee included Udloriak Hanson (then a policy analyst with Nunavut Tunngavik Incorporated [NTI]) and former Yukon Premier Tony Penikett — issued a report in April 2010 that declared the Arctic Council needed a "big makeover" because it had become outdated, owing to "cascades of change" in the region (Arctic Governance Project 2010). Although it did not envisage an Arctic Council with regulatory powers, the project team did recommend that the council expand its mandate and open its doors to more non-Arctic observers, including China (ibid.).

Much of the attention (and criticism) about Arctic governance over the last decade has been directed at the Arctic Council. Established in 1996 as a regional forum for circumpolar cooperation by the eight Arctic states, the council includes

---

8   In his review of China's Arctic interests for Defence Research and Development Canada, Christensen (2010) seems to have examined these authors and not the other side of the debate. His report "China in the Arctic: China's Interests and Activities in an Ice-Free Arctic" appears to be classified.

representatives from indigenous organizations (permanent participants [PPs]) and observers from non-Arctic states, intergovernmental and interparliamentary organizations, and non-governmental organizations. Efforts to increase the council's efficiency and effectiveness have not resolved all the issues,[9] and questions abound about its representativeness given rising global awareness of, and interests in, the region. Although the Arctic member states extended "permanent" observer status to China, Japan and South Korea (among other non-Arctic states and organizations) in May 2013, balancing the expectations of council observers, Arctic member states and PPs remains a challenge.

Canadian commentaries on East Asian interest in the Arctic Council deal almost exclusively with China. Our research indicates that the suggestion that China seeks to dominate the Arctic Council is flawed. Such an assessment is inconsistent with China's track record of behaviour in international institutions and with the nature of the council itself, given that it is clearly set up to privilege the Arctic member states and the PPs (Manicom and Lackenbauer 2013a; 2013b, 12–15). While most Chinese commentators and officials acknowledge that "Arctic countries, with a larger stake in Arctic-related issues, should play a more important role in Arctic affairs,"[10] this does not preclude East Asian states from taking a more active role in circumpolar governance. Given that China's official discourse now emphasizes support for the sovereignty and "legitimate" sovereign rights of Arctic states and observes that "Arctic cooperation has become more and more institutionalized and mature," Canada should view broader participation in the council as an opportunity to educate East Asian states on Arctic issues and enmesh them in the emerging regime (*Nunatsiaq News* 2013).

CREATING APPROPRIATE INTERNATIONAL CONDITIONS FOR SUSTAINABLE DEVELOPMENT

Other dimensions of the SCAFP reflect the interaction between domestic and international agendas in Canada's Northern strategy. Resource development — one of the primary catalysts for the surge in Arctic interest over the previous decade — is upheld as a main conduit to "unleashing the true potential of Canada's North" by "creating a dynamic, sustainable Northern economy and improving the social well-

9   See, for example, Koivurova and Molenaar (2009).

10   Chinese presentation to the Second Sino-Canadian Exchange on the Arctic, Halifax, June 25-26, 2012; identity withheld according to Chatham House rules.

being of Northerners" (DFAIT 2010). On a general level, this requires a framework of international cooperation in the Arctic region: it is unlikely that Canada can create "appropriate international conditions for sustainable development" (ibid.) in a region beset with intense competition and conflict.

The resource potential of the Arctic is huge. The Mackenzie region is estimated to hold upwards of 2.8 billion barrels of crude oil reserves and more than 60 trillion cubic feet of natural gas (Centre for Energy 2013). Further east, the Geological Survey of Canada estimates that the Sverdrup basin contains 4.3 billion barrels of oil and 79.8 trillion cubic feet of gas (Chandler 2008). Potentially exploitable minerals in the Canadian Arctic include iron ore, base metals and diamonds. Interest in Northern fisheries, tourism and freshwater may expand as global warming opens up easier access to the region. As a result, the notion that this treasure-laden frontier may hold the key to Canada's future prosperity has fired up the popular mind. Northern Canadians are excited by the opportunities offered by resource development. Concerns abound, however, about how Canada will facilitate development while protecting the ecosystem and sustaining communities and cultures.

Most attention relates to oil and gas development, given Canada's self-designation as an emerging clean energy superpower and the rising energy demands of Asian countries. Despite popular fears of a Chinese resource grab in the Arctic (and concomitant environmental impacts), this anxiety is irrational. Commercially viable Arctic hydrocarbon resources are either onshore or in waters well within national jurisdiction — a fact that most East Asian commentators acknowledge. Foreign participation will thus occur under Canadian law and at the pleasure of the Canadian government. Although China's record in other parts of the world suggests that it will prioritize resource development over environmental protection in polar regions as well (Brady 2012, 15), robust Canadian regulations and safeguards designed to avoid a Deepwater Horizon-type blowout should militate against rogue behaviour. China will also have a harder time moving into the Arctic than it has in acquiring its position in the oil sands: while it possesses the necessary capital, it lacks the experience and technological sophistication to develop unconventional oil reserves. In the Arctic, Chinese companies will be unable to proceed without Western technological support (Lasserre 2010, 7).

Some industry experts remain skeptical that international excitement over undiscovered oil and gas will translate into actual large-scale offshore development in the Canadian Arctic (Lindholt and Glomsrød 2012). Arctic operations are extremely expensive and Western oil companies currently operating in the region may welcome a Chinese partner to share the costs and risks. On the downside,

Canadian Arctic reserves have not yet been proven economically viable, and bringing them into production will take at least a decade. They may also fall prey to the sort of regulatory hurdles that plagued the Mackenzie Valley Pipeline, that Devon Energy experienced when working in the Canadian Beaufort or that Shell and other oil companies have experienced working in Alaska (Voutier et al. 2008, 105; Nelson 2010). Although East Asian states and companies will continue to monitor developments in the North American Arctic, initial industry moves suggest that their direct activities (at least in the short term) will concentrate on parts of the world where reserves are closer to production.

Another area of emphasis related to "sustainable development" involves Arctic shipping. East Asian interests in Arctic transit routes are an extension of broad trade concerns and the emergence of new polar shipping routes — either through the NWP, the Northern Sea Route (NSR) or even across the Arctic Ocean — will attract significant attention (Hong 2012). Repeating the findings of the 2009 Arctic Marine Shipping Assessment, however, Canada does not anticipate that the NWP will emerge as a viable, large-scale transit route in "the near term," given navigational challenges posed by unpredictable ice conditions. Accordingly, "other routes are likely to be more commercially viable" for the foreseeable future (DFAIT 2010; Arctic Council 2009). For example, South Korea's Ambassador to Norway, Byong-hyun Lee, explained in January 2013 that his country's particular interest "is in the [NSR] as an alternate shipping route between Asia and western Europe." He also notes that "the coming era of the Arctic seaway...also requires international cooperation to address technical and environment related matters in the Arctic Ocean" (quoted in *Nunatsiaq News* 2013).[11]

Canada's Arctic strategy also places high importance on the development of a mandatory polar code for shipping through the International Maritime Organization in recognition that the future governance of Arctic shipping will require an internationalist approach. While Arctic states have the right to exercise jurisdiction within their internal and territorial waters, their control does not extend into the polar basin (Smith and Stephenson 2013). It is clearly in Canada's interest to see uniform shipping standards for the region, given that it has spent more than two decades spearheading a group of countries, classification societies and industry experts that seek to implement a harmonious set of rules for the construction and operation of ships transiting ice-covered waters. These efforts have borne fruit in the *Guidelines for Ships Operating in Arctic Ice-Covered Waters*, which were adopted in 2002 and

---

11   For a similar perspective from Japan, see Tonami and Watters (2012).

updated to become the *Guidelines for Ships Operating in Polar Waters* in 2009. Canada and other Arctic states are now working to transform these guidelines into a mandatory polar code that will address certification, design, equipment systems, operations, environmental protection and training, providing an added layer of environmental protection and safety in the Arctic waters (Kikkert 2012, 319; 330).

Vessels bearing flags from around the world might eventually ply the Arctic waters, making international acceptance key to the implementation of a polar code. As major trading nations and ship builders, East Asian states' adherence will be integral to success. Providing that Asian shipping is not discriminated against or denied access to emerging sea routes without reasonable grounds, Asian interests are likely to accept international standards for vessels that embody a global approach to safety.

SEEKING TRADE AND INVESTMENT OPPORTUNITIES THAT BENEFIT NORTHERNERS AND ALL CANADIANS

In its narrative of a more prosperous North, the Canadian government emphasizes wealth and job creation through resource development. This will require foreign investment. Accordingly, Canada's official strategy promises to "seek trade and investment opportunities that benefit Northerners and all Canadians," particularly through enhanced ties with other Arctic states (DFAIT 2010). The government anticipates that "Northern commercial relationships can serve as conduits to expand trade and investment relations not only with our immediate Northern neighbours but also with other states such as those in central Asia and Eastern Europe" (ibid.).

Details are scant about how this might play out in practical terms. Asia is already the primary market for the growing Pangnirtung turbot fishery, bringing about CDN$400,000 to the local economy, with most product going directly to China (Vela 2013; Nobel 2012a). China is now Canada's second-largest trading partner (CDN$58 billion in 2010) after the United States. Although China's ambassador Zhang Junsai (2012) recently stated that "Canada should export much more to China other than wood, pulp, mineral resources" — particularly high-tech goods that cater to China's growing consumer class — it is likely that the North will continue to be a source of resources rather than industrial products. China wishes to enhance its cooperation in the energy and resource sectors, and state-owned Chinese companies have already invested billions of dollars in Alberta's oil sands. Chinese markets are also the driving force behind the proposed Northern Gateway pipeline currently under review by the National Energy Board, and tie into nascent proposals for an Arctic Gateway project (Moore 2012).[12] Some industry experts are skeptical, however, that international excitement over undiscovered oil and gas in the Arctic will translate into large-scale offshore development in the Canadian Arctic.[13]

Mining is another story. Economist Patricia Moore, a commodity specialist with Scotiabank, told the Nunavut Mining Symposium in April 2011 that she saw "no end" to the "tsunami" of Chinese money flowing into Canada's energy and mining sectors, with mining companies around the world "eyeing Nunavut with far more interest than before" (quoted in George 2011). MMG Limited, an Australian company that is 75 percent owned by Chinese state enterprise China Minmetals Corporation, plans two mines in Nunavut and several joint ventures between the Wuhan Iron and Steel (Group) Corporation and Century Iron Mines Corporation in northern Quebec. In Yukon, Yunnan Chihong Zinc & Germanium Co. Ltd. is involved in a joint venture proposal with Selwyn Resources to develop a lead and zinc project, and Jinduicheng Molybdenum Group Co. Ltd. and Northwest Nonferrous International Investment Company Ltd.'s Wolverine zinc and silver mine is already in operation. In the Raglan district in northern Quebec, Goldbrook Ventures Inc. has partnered with Jilin Jien Nickel Industry Co. to develop its nickel property in Nunavik (Munson 2012; George 2012). If resource prices remain high, mining companies from around the world — including Asia — will likely see opportunity in the Canadian North and will invest accordingly.

A final concern relates to Asian resource diplomacy and the effect it could have on Canadian governance. Chinese resource deals in the developing world have been characterized by the exchange of state aid dollars for exclusive access to resource production. These terms make Chinese national oil company (NOC) investment more appealing than that from international oil companies or from Western NOCs that do not engage in this kind of behaviour. Despite considerable infrastructure challenges in the North, however, there is reason to believe that Chinese investment will not include instruments of Chinese state power because of the strong rule of law in Canada. Accordingly, there is little chance that the negative side effects of Chinese resource investment found in Africa and other developing countries, including job loss due to labour disruption and associated social unrest due to growing resentment, will be repeated in a Canadian context.[14]

---

12   On the Arctic Gateway project, see PPM Public Policy Management (2010).

13   See, for example, Lindholt and Glomsrød (2012). Japan seems cool on resource development prospects in the Arctic more generally. See Tonami and Watters (2012, 98).

14   For concerns along these lines, see George (2011).

The Circumpolar Inuit Declaration on Resource Development Principles in Inuit Nunaat, signed in May 2011, lays out conditions for sustainable development (Inuit Circumpolar Council 2011a). Invoking the United Nations Declaration on the Rights of Indigenous Peoples and the Circumpolar Inuit Declaration on Sovereignty in the Arctic, the statement also emphasizes that "Inuit must be active and equal partners in policy-making and decision-making affecting Inuit Nunaat" (ibid.). Mary Simon, then president of Inuit Tapiriit Kanatami (ITK), put "the world...on notice that while Inuit look forward to new forms and levels of economic development, the use of resources in the Arctic must be conducted in a sustainable and environmentally responsible way, and must deliver direct and substantial benefits to Inuit" (Indian Country Today Media Network 2011). The declaration recognizes the importance of resource development, but it stresses that it must happen "at a rate sufficient to provide durable and diversified economic growth, but constrained enough to forestall environmental degradation and an overwhelming influx of outside labour" (Inuit Circumpolar Council 2011a). This may have an impact on the form and pace of development in Canada, given the shortage of skilled labour in the northern territories to fill the positions required in large-scale mining or oil and gas projects. Furthermore, in the declaration, Inuit insist that "all resource development must contribute actively and significantly to improving Inuit living standards and social conditions, and non-renewable resource development, in particular, must promote economic diversification through contributions to education and other forms of social development, physical infrastructure, and non-extractive industries" (ibid.). The declaration states that "Inuit welcome the opportunity to work in full partnership with resource developers, governments and local communities in the sustainable development of resources of Inuit Nunaat, including related policy making, to the long-lasting benefit of Inuit and with respect for baseline environmental and social responsibilities" (ibid.). The details of impact benefit agreements reached between Inuit groups and companies are not public, but these will be key mechanisms to ensuring that regional and local needs are addressed.

SUPPORTING INTERNATIONAL EFFORTS TO ADDRESS ARCTIC CLIMATE CHANGE

Al Gore's "inconvenient truth" rhetoric, Inuit activist Sheila Watt-Cloutier's passionate appeals and the Arctic Council's landmark Arctic Climate Impact Assessment report all served to catapult the Arctic to popular attention as the bellwether of global climate change. Although critics lament Canada's dismal track record on climate change,[15] the SCAFP insists that "Canada recognizes that climate change is a global challenge requiring a global solution" (DFAIT 2010). Canada's climate change strategy must be global in its aspirations for mitigation, while sensitive to the needs for local adaptation. It must contain on-the-ground capacity to monitor the physical, social, cultural and economic impacts of global warming in the Canadian Arctic, and support similar studies abroad.

East Asian states cite climate change as the key reason that the Arctic must be treated as an international space, given its impact on global processes. Joshua Ho (2011), a senior fellow at Nanyang Technological University in Singapore, notes that Asia is the most vulnerable continent to changing precipitation patterns, rising sea levels and extreme weather events. Ho cites another analysis, conducted by the Tyndall Centre for Climate Change Research at Oxford, which estimates that an increase of one metre in sea level by the end of this century will displace more than 100 million people and flood more than 900,000 km^2 of land in Asia. This will affect cities in China such as Guangzhou, Shanghai, Tianjin and Ningbo (ibid.). In this light, it is clear why Asian countries would want to take an active role in polar research, conduct Arctic studies and increase their involvement in international institutions and conferences (Campbell 2012, 3). According to the Intergovernmental Panel on Climate Change, increased flooding and the degradation of freshwater, fisheries and other resources will impact hundreds of millions of people (Chaturvedi 2012). Studies also indicate that the Arctic airstream generates extreme weather in China (Alexeeva and Lasserre 2012, 83).

Viewed through the lens of official statements, China's top two Arctic priorities are climate change and associated scientific research efforts. The Chinese public acknowledges climate change and concomitant consequences: a rise in sea level caused by the melting polar ice cap will affect China's coastline, displace millions of people and wreak untold economic damage and environmental disaster (Yang 2012). Furthermore, Jakobson and Peng (2012, 16) observe that Chinese commentators now prioritize climate change in their public agenda to generate a "new public narrative" designed to "circumvent the sensitivity of Arctic resources and sovereignty issues, and to calm outsiders' jitters about China as a rising power. Climate change cooperation provides China with opportunities to partner with other states on the Arctic agenda."

---

15   See, for example, Burck, Herwille and Krings (2013), who rank Canada worst of all Western countries and 58 of 61 countries surveyed.

South Korean Ambassador Lee also explained that his country sought permanent observer status to the Arctic Council pursuant to its commitment to fight climate change. Citing climate change as a "threat to humanity," he insisted that the Arctic needs a new model for development and envisaged Korea's interest in the region as aligned with "its endeavour towards global green growth" (quoted in *Nunatsiaq News* 2013). Given that international solutions to global warming demand buy-in from industrialized and industrializing countries, including the major East Asian states, there is an obvious congruence between Asian and Arctic state interests in this respect — although practical solutions are more elusive.[16]

STRENGTHENING ARCTIC SCIENCE AND THE LEGACY OF THE INTERNATIONAL POLAR YEAR

Science forms an important foundation for *Canada's Northern Strategy* across all four pillars and informs sound policy making. Canada's world-leading CDN$150 million investment in the International Polar Year (IPY) (2007–2009) provided momentum for a new national commitment to excellence in Arctic research (Struzik 2007; 2009). Furthermore, Arctic research initiatives emphasize Canada's international obligation to contribute to knowledge about the "nature, mechanisms and extent" of connections between the Arctic and the rest of the globe (Council of Canadian Academies 2008, 4). In 2007, as a signature deliverable of its strategy, the Canadian government committed to establish a new world-class Arctic research station. Slated to open in 2017, the Canadian High Arctic Research Station (CHARS) will be based in Cambridge Bay, Nunavut, serving as a science and technology hub in Canada's North, anchoring the existing network of scientific facilities across the region. Although CHARS is mandated to focus on national priorities aligned with the *Northern Strategy*, its solutions-driven programming is geared toward encouraging Canada to be innovative and to attract other countries to collaborate on its priorities (Government of Canada 2013b). This represents a significant national investment. On August 23, 2012, Stephen Harper committed CDN$142.4 million over six years for the construction, equipment and outfitting of CHARS, CDN$46.2 million over

---

16   Canada and other Arctic states will benefit from the support of East Asian states when addressing other pressing environmental issues through international standards, such as efforts to reduce mercury contamination. See Arctic Monitoring Assessment Programme (AMAP) Assessment (2011). On the human impacts, see Nobel (2012b).

six years for the CHARS science and technology program and CDN$26.5 million per year for the ongoing operation of the station starting in 2018-2019.

Rather than succumbing to media rhetoric about Canada's need to match East Asian states in a "polar icebreaker race" or accepting unfounded claims that China is outpacing its spending on Arctic research, Canada should shake its insecurity complex in the scientific domain (Ibbitson 2010). The federal government spent approximately CDN$152 million on Arctic science and technology in 2007-2008, made the largest national contribution to IPY (2007-2008), has invested CDN$85 million through its Arctic research infrastructure fund and invested more than CDN$113 million in the Network of Centres of Excellence ArcticNet program. Furthermore, the "impact factor" of Canadian Arctic scientific research is second only to that of the United States and is far higher than Asian research (Côté and Picard-Aitken 2009).

As a leader in Arctic science, Canada should pursue opportunities for enhanced research collaboration with East Asian scientists. South Korea and China each spend about CDN$60 million annually on polar research, and both have made heavy investments in icebreakers and research stations over the last decade. The Japanese government also "believes Japan can contribute to the sustainable development of the Arctic by providing scientific knowledge," Aki Tonami and Stewart Watters (2012) note. Without a physical footprint in the region, "it is critical for Japan to engage in international research and development in cooperation with littoral states to secure interests in the future" (ibid., 100). All three countries have established records in polar research and are members of the International Arctic Science Committee.

Science can serve as a conduit for international collaboration, influence and confidence building. Liu Huirong of the Oceanic University of China argues that an ongoing focus on climate change offers China the best opportunity for constructive engagement on Arctic issues, serving to raise issues related to biodiversity, shipping, fishery management and indigenous rights (quoted in Jakobson and Peng 2012, 16). According to Karen T. Litfin, the complexity of local-global linkages, "the problematic nature of sovereignty as a framework for addressing problems of global ecology," and the critical role of science in informing debates related to "planetary politics" make this an appropriate and shrewd approach for East Asian states to pursue (quoted in Chaturvedi 2012, 245). Chinese officials have indicated their country's desire to elevate track-two dialogues between academics on Arctic issues to track-one discussions, likely to seek a research agreement akin to China's with Iceland and Canada's with the United Kingdom (Jian 2012b). Zhang Junsai, China's ambassador to Canada, has stated explicitly that China hopes to form an Arctic scientific research team with Canada (Moore 2012).

ENCOURAGING A GREATER UNDERSTANDING OF THE HUMAN DIMENSION OF THE ARCTIC AND SUPPORTING INDIGENOUS PERMANENT PARTICIPANT ORGANIZATIONS

Canada is committed to "encourag[ing] a greater understanding of the human dimension of the Arctic to improve the lives of Northerners, particularly through the Arctic Council" and the Sustainable Development Working Group. Despite official assurances that the core of *Canada's Northern Strategy* is first and foremost about people, Northern indigenous groups have expressed concerns about their involvement in national and international decision making. Inuit representatives, for example, have suggested that the Canadian government agenda prioritizes investments in defence and resource development at the expense of environmental protection and improved social and economic conditions. They insist that sovereignty begins at home and that the primary challenges are domestic human security issues, requiring investments in infrastructure, education and health care.

Indigenous voices add to the complexity of the Canadian message projected to the rest of the world.[17] The Inuit Circumpolar Council (2011b) emphasizes that "the inextricable linkages between issues of sovereignty and sovereign rights in the Arctic and Inuit self-determination and other rights require states to accept the presence and role of Inuit as partners in the conduct of international relations in the Arctic." The declaration anticipates Inuit playing an active role in all deliberations on environmental security, sustainable development, militarization, shipping and socio-economic development. Senior officials, including Leona Aglukkaq, Canada's minister for the Arctic Council, insist that this is the government's foremost priority.

Some Canadian commentators have expressed concern that Asian decision makers do not have a well-developed understanding of the Arctic as a homeland as opposed to a resource or scientific frontier. Some even cited this lack of knowledge as a justification to deny the applications of China and other Asian states for observer status to the Arctic Council. The opposite argument is also sustainable — and arguably more advantageous to Canadian interests. In its role as chair of the Arctic Council from 2013 to 2015, Canada can demonstrate leadership by envisaging the

---

17   See, for example, Inuit Qaujisarvingat (2013).

council as a tool not only for inter-Arctic dialogue but for international education more generally.

In 2011, Kikkert noted concern amongst the Arctic Council's permanent participants that "if more actors continue to gain access to the Council, the organization will begin to lose its specialized status and regional identity to the harm of the indigenous peoples and circumpolar states" (8). Although some Inuit representatives have downplayed the prevalence of this fear, the SCAFP insists that "as interest by non-Arctic players in the work of the Council grows, [it] will work to ensure that the central role of the Permanent Participants is not diminished or diluted" (DFAIT 2010). Aglukkaq has also emphasized a "people-first" approach, indicating that the criteria for evaluating new observers must incorporate "the respect and support of indigenous peoples in the Arctic region" (quoted in Bell 2012).

East Asian officials insist that their countries have this respect and wish to learn more about how to support Aboriginal development efforts. In Chinese Ambassador to Norway Zhao Jun's words, China "respects the values, interests, culture and traditions of Arctic indigenous peoples and other Arctic inhabitants" and is open to exploring avenues for cooperation with northern peoples (quoted in *Nunatsiaq News* 2013). Similarly, Japan and South Korea have expressed a willingness to engage Northern indigenous groups. According to Parliamentary Senior Vice Minister of Foreign Affairs Shuji Kira (2012), "as regards the respect for values, interests, culture, and tradition of Arctic indigenous peoples, Japan is determined and eligible to address this matter in an appropriate way, based upon our own experiences with indigenous people living in Japan." Likewise, Korean researchers emphasize their track record of participation in the Arctic Council's Sustainable Development Working Group.[18] Some Canadian indigenous leaders, however, seem unconvinced that this is more than lip service. Terry Audla, president of ITK, warned an Ottawa conference in late January 2013 that the Arctic Council should be cautious about opening up observer status to applicants such as China that did not have a strong track record of respecting indigenous rights. This poses a dilemma to Inuit, Audla explained. Although their culture embraces dialogue and negotiation, "the council runs the risk of seeing its agenda being diluted or sidetracked by special interests" (quoted in Gregoire 2013).

The Inuit insist that they have rights rooted in indigenous use and occupancy, international law, land claims and self-government processes (Koivurova 2010).

---

18   James Manicom, personal interview with researcher at the Korean Polar Research Institute, Seoul, December 4, 2012.

They and other Northerners place a high policy priority on "recognition that an effective Arctic strategy requires a high and sustained level of inter-governmental and government-aboriginal cooperation" (ITK 2008, 12). For example, the Inuit sovereignty declaration, in asserting that "the foundation, projection and enjoyment of Arctic sovereignty and sovereign rights all require healthy and sustainable communities in the Arctic," stipulates that:

> In the pursuit of economic opportunities in a warming Arctic, states must act so as to: (1) put economic activity on a sustainable footing; (2) avoid harmful resource exploitation; (3) achieve standards of living for Inuit that meet national and international norms and minimums; and (4) deflect sudden and far-reaching demographic shifts that would overwhelm and marginalize indigenous peoples where we are rooted and have endured. (Inuit Circumpolar Council 2011b)

How East Asian scholars or officials perceive this declaration is unknown. Given recent indications that Canadian Inuit will use their legal rights recognized in land claims to disrupt resource exploration activities that they believe are prejudicial to their interests, and will sue the Canadian federal government for not implementing land claim provisions, it is probable that Inuit will hold the government responsible for protecting their interests.

CONCLUSIONS: MESSAGES CANADA
SHOULD SEND TO ASIAN STATES

> Through our Arctic foreign policy, we will deliver on the international dimension of our *Northern Strategy*. We will show leadership in demonstrating responsible stewardship while we build a region responsive to Canadian interests and values, secure in the knowledge that the North is our home and our destiny.

> Through our Arctic foreign policy, we are also sending a clear message: Canada is in control of its Arctic lands and waters and takes its stewardship role and responsibilities seriously. Canada continues to stand up for its interests in the Arctic. When positions or actions are taken by others that affect our national

interests, undermine the cooperative relationships we have built, or demonstrate a lack of sensitivity to the interests or perspectives of Arctic peoples or states, we respond.

Cooperation, diplomacy and respect for international law have always been Canada's preferred approach in the Arctic. At the same time, we will never waver in our commitment to protect our North.

— DFAIT (2010)

This strongly worded conclusion to the SCAFP summarizes the goals of Canada's foreign policy in the Arctic and emphasizes Canada's commitment to stand up for national and regional interests. With this in mind, Canadian leaders can support this cooperative and diplomatic strategy by communicating the following messages of inclusion, responsibility and respect to East Asian states:

- Canada respects international law. The country intends to delineate its extended continental shelf to the extent prescribed under UNCLOS. The Arctic Ocean *is* an ocean, and it is misguided for commentators to suggest that the sovereign rights accorded to coastal states everywhere else in the world should be denied to coastal states in the Arctic.

- Canada has no intention of dividing up the Arctic with the other Arctic coastal states and shutting out non-Arctic interests. Canada recognizes user state rights to the seas beyond national jurisdiction in the Arctic Ocean. Prime Minister Harper (2006) has already stated that Canada does not intend to invoke any "sector principle" claiming jurisdiction seabed up to the North Pole. At the same time, Canada expects East Asian states to play a constructive role in the development of robust international standards to activities occurring in Arctic waters.

- Canada welcomes Asian investment that will contribute to the exploration and exploitation of Arctic resources within Canada's jurisdiction. As the *Northern Strategy* emphasizes, Northerners must be the primary beneficiaries of this development. Simultaneously, Canada expects East Asian companies to act in accordance with domestic laws of Arctic states and international standards set out in the Arctic Council and elsewhere. These include special provisions for environmental protection given unique Arctic ecosystems.

- Canada should reiterate the findings of the 2009 Arctic Marine Shipping Assessment that the NWP is unlikely to become a viable, large-scale transit route in the near term. Canada will, however, continue to work with other states to develop a mandatory polar code that enhances Arctic marine safety and protects Arctic peoples and the environment.

- The general principle of respect for Northerners, including indigenous people of the Arctic, is foremost in Canada's national mindset. Anyone wishing to partner with Canada must be prepared to adhere to this philosophy and priority.

"The key foundation for any [international] collaboration will be acceptance of and respect for the perspectives and knowledge of Northerners and Arctic states' sovereignty," the Canadian government asserts in the SCAFP (DFAIT 2010). "As well, there must be recognition that the Arctic states remain best placed to exercise leadership in the management of the region" (ibid.). Leadership does not require exclusion, however, and Canada and the other Arctic states were wise to accept East Asian states' applications for observer status to the Arctic Council. Merely inviting them to observe proceedings at the council, however, is insufficient. Instead, Canada should develop a clear message that clarifies its Arctic agenda, indicates opportunities for cooperation and collaboration in science and economic development, and corrects misconceptions about Canada's position on sovereignty and sovereign rights in the Arctic.

WORKS CITED

Alexeeva, Olga and Frédéric Lasserre. 2012. "China & the Arctic," *Arctic Yearbook 2012.* www.arcticyearbook.com/images/Articles_2012/Alexeeva_and_Lassere.pdf.

AMAP. 2011. *AMAP Assessment 2011: Mercury in the Arctic.* www.amap.no/documents/doc/AMAP-Assessment-2011-Mercury-in-the-Arctic/90.

Arctic Council. 2009. *Arctic Marine Shipping Assessment 2009 Report.* Arctic Council Protection of the Arctic Marine Environment Working Group. www.pame.is/images/stories/AMSA_2009_Report/AMSA_2009_Report_2nd_print.pdf.

Arctic Governance Project. 2010. "Arctic Governance in an Era of Transformative Change: Critical Questions, Governance Principles, Ways Forward." The Arctic Governance Project, April. www.arcticgovernance.org/getfile.php/1219555.1529.wyaufxvxuc/AGP+Report+April+14+2010%5B1%5D.pdf.

Asia Pacific Foundation of Canada. 2012. *2012 National Opinion Poll: Canadian Views on Asia*. Asia Pacific Foundation of Canada, April. www.asiapacific.ca/sites/default/files/nop_2012_april25.pdf.

Bateman, Sam and Clive Schofield. 2008. "State Practice Regarding Straight Baselines in East Asia: Legal, Technical and Political Issues in a Changing World." Speech given at the Conference on Difficulties Implementing the Provisions of UNCLOS, Monaco, October 16.

Bell, Jim. 2012. "Aglukkaq Stresses 'People-first' Approach to Arctic Council." *Nunatsiaq News*, October 29.

Borgerson, Scott G. 2008. "Arctic Meltdown: The Economic and Security Implications of Global Warming." *Foreign Affairs* March/April: 63–77.

Boswell, Randy. 2010. "China Moves to Become Major Arctic Player." *Nunatsiaq News*, March 3.

Brady, Anne-Marie. 2012. "Polar Stakes: China's Polar Activities as a Benchmark for Intentions." *China Brief* 12/14.

Burck, Jan, Lukas Herwille and Laura Krings. 2013. *Climate Change Performance Index 2013*. Bonn: Germanwatch and Climate Action Network Europe.

Byers, Michael. 2009. *Who Owns the Arctic?* Vancouver: Douglas & McIntyre.

Campbell, Caitlin. 2012. "China and the Arctic: Objectives and Obstacles." US-China Economic and Security Review Commission Staff Research Report, April.

Cannon, Lawrence. 2009. "Notes for an Address by the Honourable Lawrence Cannon, Minister of Foreign Affairs, on Canada's Arctic Foreign Policy." Whitehorse, March 11. www.international.gc.ca/media/aff/speeches-discours/2009/386933.aspx?lang=en.

Centre for Energy. 2013. "Northwest Territories — Statistics." Centre for Energy Facts & Statistics. www.centreforenergy.ca/FactsStats/statistics.asp?template=5,13.

Chandler, Graham. 2008. "Really Stranded Gas." Up Here Business blog, June. http://gchandler.ehclients.com/index.php/graham/uphere2/really_stranded_gas/.

Chang, Gordon. 2010. "China's Arctic Play." *The Diplomat*, March 9. http://thediplomat.com/2010/03/09/china%E2%80%99s-arctic-play/?all=true.

Chaturvedi, Sanjay. 2012. "Geopolitical Transformations: 'Rising' Asia and the Future of the Arctic Council." In *The Arctic Council: Its Place in the Future of Arctic Governance*, edited by Thomas S. Axworthy, Timo Koivurova and Waliul Hasanat. Toronto: Munk-Gordon Arctic Security Program and the University of Lapland.

Chen, Gang. 2012. "China's Emerging Arctic Strategy." *The Polar Journal* 2 (2): 358–371. doi:10.1080/2154896X.2012.735039.

Chircop, Aldo. 2011. "The Emergence of China as a Polar-Capable State." *Canadian Naval Review* 7 (1).

Christensen, Kyle D. 2010. "China in the Arctic: Potential Developments Impacting China's Activities in an Ice-Free Arctic." Presented at the On Track Conference of Defence Associations Institute, November.

Coates, Ken, Whitney Lackenbauer, Bill Morrison and Greg Poelzer. 2008. *Arctic Front: Defending Canada in the Far North*. Toronto: Thomas Allen & Son Ltd.

Côté, Grégoire and Michelle Picard-Aitken. 2009. *Arctic Research in Canada: A Bibliometric Analysis*. Science-Metrix report to Indian and Northern Affairs Canada. www.science-metrix.com/pdf/SM_INAC_Bibliometrics_Arctic_Research.pdf.

Council of Canadian Academies. 2008. *Vision for the Canadian Arctic Research Initiative: Assessing the Opportunities*.

DFAIT. 2000. *The Northern Dimension of Canada's Foreign Policy.* http://dfait-aeci.canadiana.ca/view/ooe.b3651149E/5?r=0&s=1.

———. 2005. "Canada's International Policy Statement: A Role of Pride and Influence in the World." http://publications.gc.ca/site/eng/274692/publication.html.

———. 2010. *Statement on Canada's Arctic Foreign Policy: Exercising Sovereignty and Promoting Canada's Northern Strategy Abroad.* www.international.gc.ca/arctic-arctique/assets/pdfs/canada_arctic_foreign_policy-eng.pdf.

Dodds, Klaus. 2011. "We Are a Northern Country: Stephen Harper and the Canadian Arctic." *Polar Record* 47 (4): 371–4.

Ekos Research. 2011. *Rethinking the Top of the World: Arctic Security Public Opinion Survey.* Munk-Gordon Arctic Security Program, January. http://gordonfoundation.ca/publication/300.

Emmerson, Charles. 2010. *The Future History of the Arctic*. New York: PublicAffairs.

George, Jane. 2011. "The Global Mining Industry Arrives in Nunavut." *Nunatsiaq News*, April 6.

———. 2012. "Canadian Royalties Aims to Start Shipments from Nunavik Nickel in 2013." *Nunatsiaq News*, November 28. www.nunatsiaqonline.ca/stories/article/65674canadian_royalties_aims_to_ship_ore_from_nunavik_nickel_in_2014.

Goldstein, Lyle. 2011. "Chinese Naval Strategy in the South China Sea: An Abundance of Noise and Smoke, but Little Fire." *Contemporary Southeast Asia* 33 (3): 320–47.

Government of Canada. 1997. "Canada and the Circumpolar World: Meeting the
 Challenges of Cooperation into the Twenty-First Century." Report of the
 House of Commons Standing Committee on Foreign Affairs and International
 Trade, April.

———. 2009. *Canada's Northern Strategy: Our North, Our Heritage, Our
 Future.* Minister of Indian Affairs and Northern Development, July.
 www.northernstrategy.gc.ca/cns/cns.pdf.

———. 2013a. "Canada's Arctic Foreign Policy." Foreign Affairs, Trade and
 Development Canada. www.international.gc.ca/arctic-arctique/arctic_policy-
 canada-politique_arctique.aspx?lang=eng.

———. 2013b. "Canada High Arctic Research Station." Government of Canada
 Science website. www.science.gc.ca/default.asp?lang=En&n=74E65368-1.

Grant, Shelagh. 2010a. "Troubled Arctic Waters." *The Globe and Mail*, June 30.

———. 2010b. *Polar Imperative: A History of Arctic Sovereignty in North America.*
 Vancouver: Douglas & McIntyre.

Greenfield, Jeanette. 1992. *China's Practice in the Law of the Sea.* Oxford:
 Clarendon Press.

Gregoire, Lisa. 2013. "Arctic Council Should Be Cautious about New Observer
 Hopefuls." *Nunatsiaq News*, February 1.

Griffiths, Franklyn. 2003. "The Shipping News: Canada's Arctic Sovereignty
 Not on Thinning Ice." *International Journal* 58 (2): 257–82.

Griffiths, Franklyn, Rob Huebert and Whitney Lackenbauer. 2011. *Canada and the
 Changing Arctic: Sovereignty, Security and Stewardship.* Waterloo: Wilfrid
 Laurier University Press.

Harper, Stephen. 2005. "Harper Stands Up for Arctic Sovereignty." Speech in
 December 22. www.dennisbevington.ca/pdfs/en/2005/dec25-05_speech-
 harper.pdf.

———. 2006. "Securing Canadian Sovereignty in the Arctic." Speech in Iqaluit,
 August 12.

———. 2008. "Prime Minister Harper Announces the John G. Diefenbaker
 Icebreaker Project." Inuvik, August 28. http://pm.gc.ca/eng/news/2008/08/28/
 prime-minister-harper-announces-john-g-diefenbaker-icebreaker-project.

Ho, Joshua. 2011. "The Opening of the Northern Sea Route." *Maritime Affairs:
 Journal of the National Maritime Foundation of India* 7 (1): 106–20. doi:10.1
 080/09733159.2011.601062.

Hong, Nong. 2012. "The Melting Arctic and its Impact on China's Maritime
 Transport." *Research in Transportation Economics* 35 (1): 50–7.

Huebert, Rob. 2003. "The Shipping News Part II: How Canada's Arctic Sovereignty Is on Thinning Ice." *International Journal* 58 (3): 295–308.

———. 2005. "Return of the 'Vikings': The Canadian-Danish Dispute over Hans Island — New Challenges for the Control of the Canadian North." In *Breaking Ice: Renewable Resource and Ocean Management in the Canadian North*, edited by Fikret Berkes, Rob Huebert, Helen Fast, Micheline Manseau and Alan Diduck. Calgary: University of Calgary Press. 319–36.

———. 2008. "Canada Must Prepare for the New Arctic Age." *Edmonton Journal*, August 4.

———. 2009. "The Need for an Arctic Treaty: Growing from the United Nations Convention on the Law of the Sea." *Ocean Yearbook* 23.

———. 2012. "Canada and China in the Arctic: A Work in Progress." Meridian Newsletter. Fall/Winter 2011–Spring/Summer 2012. www.polarcom.gc.ca/uploads/Publications/Meridian%20FW2011-SS2012.pdf.

Ibbitson, John. 2010. "Stephen Harper's Frisky Northern Renaissance." *The Globe and Mail*, August 27.

Indian Country Today Media Network. 2011. "Circumpolar Agreement Affirms Inuit Development Rights." ICTMN, May 26. http://indiancountrytodaymedianetwork.com/article/circumpolar-agreement-affirms-inuit-development-rights-35848.

Inuit Circumpolar Council. 2011a. "A Circumpolar Inuit Declaration on Resource Development Principles in Inuit Nunaat." http://inuitcircumpolar.com/files/uploads/icc-files/Declaration_on_Resource_Development_A3_FINAL.pdf.

———. 2011b. "A Circumpolar Inuit Declaration on Sovereignty in the Arctic." www.itk.ca/sites/default/files/Declaration_12x18_Vice-Chairs_Signed.pdf.

Inuit Qaujisarvingat. 2013. *Nilliajut: Inuit Perspectives on Security, Patriotism and Sovereignty*. Ottawa: Inuit Tapiriit Kanatami. http://gordonfoundation.ca/sites/default/files/publications/NILLIAJUT_Inuit%20Perspectives%20on%20Security,%20Patriotism%20and%20Sovereignty.pdf.

ITK. 2008. "An Integrated Arctic Strategy." www.itk.ca/sites/default/files/Integrated-Arctic-Stratgey.pdf.

Jakobson, Linda and Jingchoa Peng. 2012. "China's Arctic Aspirations." Stockholm International Peace Research Institute [SIPRI] Policy Paper No. 34.

Jian, Yang. 2012a. "China and Arctic Affairs." 2012 Arctic Yearbook Commentary. www.arcticyearbook.com/index.php/commentaries/32-china-and-arctic-affairs.

————. 2012b. "China Has a Key Role in Safeguarding the Arctic." *China Daily*, June 29.

Kikkert, Peter. 2011. "Rising Above the Rhetoric: Northern Voices and the Strengthening of Canada's Capacity to Maintain a Stable Circumpolar World." *Northern Review* 33: 8.

————. 2012. "Promoting National Interests and Fostering Cooperation: Canada and the Development of a Polar Code." *Journal of Maritime Law and International Commerce* 43 (3).

Kim, Hyun-Soo. 1994. "The 1992 Chinese Territorial Sea Law in Light of the UN Convention." *International and Comparative Law Quarterly* 43 (4).

Kira, Shuji. 2012. Statement by Parliamentary Senior Vice-Minister for Foreign Affairs of Japan Shuji Kira, Meeting between the Swedish Chairmanship of the Arctic Council and Observers/Ad-hoc Observers, Stockholm, November 6.

Koivurova, Timo. 2010. "Sovereign States and Self-Determining Peoples: Carving Out a Place for Transnational Indigenous Peoples in a World of Sovereign States." *International Community Law Review* 12: 191–212.

Koivurova, Timo and Erik J. Molenaar. 2009. *International Governance and Regulation of the Marine Arctic: Overview and Gap Analysis.* Oslo: World Wildlife Foundation.

Lackenbauer, P. Whitney. 2010. "Mirror Images? Canada, Russia, and the Circumpolar World." *International Journal* 65 (4): 879–97.

Landriault, Mathieu. 2013. "La sécurité arctique 2000-2010 : Une décennie turbulente?" Unpublished Ph.D. dissertation, University of Ottawa.

Lasserre, Frédéric. 2010. "China and the Arctic: Threat or Cooperation Potential for Canada?" Canadian International Council China Papers No. 11, June. www.opencanada.org/wp-content/uploads/2011/05/China-and-the-Arctic-Frederic-Lasserre.pdf.

Lindholt, Lars and Solveig Glomsrød. 2012. "The Arctic: No Big Bonanza for the Global Petroleum Industry." *Energy Economics* 34: 1465–74.

Manicom, James and P. Whitney Lackenbauer. 2013a. "East Asian States, the Arctic Council and International Relations in the Arctic." CIGI Policy Brief No. 26, April.

————. 2013b. "The Chinese Pole." *Policy Options* 34 (4).

Moore, Lynn. 2012. "China Hopes to Settle Arctic Disputes by 'Peaceful Means': Ambassador." *Nunatsiaq News*, February 1. www.nunatsiaqonline.ca/stories/article/65674china_hopes_to_settle_arctic_disputes_by_peaceful_means_ambassador.

Munson, James. 2012. "China North: Canada's Resources and China's Arctic Long Game." *iPolitcs*, December 31. www.ipolitics.ca/2012/12/31/china-north-canadas-resources-and-chinas-arctic-long-game/.

Nelson, Kristen. 2010. "BP Delays Liberty Drilling to 2011, Citing Expected Plan Reviews." *Petroleum News*, July 11.

Nobel, Justin. 2012a. "Cold Winter Equals Big Dollars for Pangnirtung Fishermen." *Nunatsiaq News*, April 24. www.nunatsiaqonline.ca/stories/article/65674cold_winter_equals_big_dollars_for_pangnirtung_fishermen/.

———. 2012b. "New Study Links ADHD in Inuit Kids to Mercury." *Nunatsiaq News*, October 1.

Nunatsiaq News. 2013. "China, Korea, EU Woo Arctic Council at Norway Conference." *Nunatsiaq News Online*, January 22. www.nunatsiaqonline.ca/stories/article/65674china_korea_eu_woo_arctic_council_at_norway_conference/.

PPM Public Policy Management Limited. 2010. *Canada's Arctic Gateway: Discussion Paper*, September. www.uwinnipeg.ca/conferences/arctic-summit/arctic-gateway-discussion-paper.pdf.

Standing Senate Committee on Fisheries and Oceans. 2008. "The Coast Guard in Canada's Arctic: Interim Report." June.

Smith, Laurence C. and Scott R. Stephenson. 2013. "New Trans-Arctic Shipping Routes Navigable by Mid-century." *Proceedings of the National Academy of Sciences of the United States of America* 110 (13): 4871-2. www.pnas.org/content/110/13/E1191/1.

Struzik, Ed. 2007. "The True North Strong and Free But Not Cheap." *Toronto Star*, December 1.

———. 2009. "Canada Urged to Take Lead in Polar Research." *Edmonton Journal*, February 25.

Suthren, Victor. 2006. "Sinking the Navy in Afghanistan." *Ottawa Citizen*, November 2.

The Calgary Herald. 2007. "China's Navy Making Waves." *The Calgary Herald*, October 1.

The Globe and Mail. 2006. "Harper Speaks up for Canada's Arctic." *The Globe and Mail*, January 28.

Tonami, Aki and Stewart Watters. 2012. "Japan's Arctic Policy: The Sum of Many Parts." *Arctic Yearbook 2012*. www.arcticyearbook.com/images/Articles_2012/Tonami_and_Watters.pdf.

Toronto Star. 2010. "Charting New Arctic Waters." *Toronto Star*, August 21. www.thestar.com/opinion/editorials/2010/08/21/charting_new_arctic_ waters.html.

United Nations. 2013. "Submissions, through the Secretary-General of the United Nations, to the Commission on the Limits of the Continental Shelf, Pursuant to Article 76, Paragraph 8, of the United Nations Convention on the Law of the Sea of 10 December 1982." www.un.org/depts/los/clcs_new/commission_ submissions.htm.

Vela, Thandiwe. 2013. "'Exceptional' Winter Ice Fishery." *Northern News Services*, February 18. www.nnsl.com/frames/newspapers/2013-02/feb18_13fis.html.

Voutier, Keltie, Bharat Dixit, Peter Millman, John Reid and Adam Sparkes. 2008. "Sustainable Energy Development in Canada's Mackenzie Delta–Beaufort Sea Coastal Region." *Arctic* 61, Suppl. 1: 103–10. http://pubs.aina.ucalgary.ca/ arctic/Arctic61-S-103.pdf.

Wright, David. 2011a. "The Panda Bear Readies to Meet the Polar Bear: China and Canada's Arctic Sovereignty Challenge." Calgary: Canadian Defence & Foreign Affairs Institute. www.cdfai.org/PDF/The%20Panda%20Bear%20 Readies%20to%20Meet%20the%20Polar%20Bear.pdf.

———. 2011b. "We Must Stand Up to China's Increasing Claim to Arctic." *The Calgary Herald*, March 8.

———. 2011c. "The Dragon Eyes the Top of the World: Arctic Policy Debate and Discussion in China." *China Maritime Study* 8, August. www.usnwc.edu/Research---Gaming/China-Maritime-Studies-Institute/ Publications/documents/China-Maritime-Study-8_The-Dragon-Eyes-the- Top-of-.pdf.

Yang, Huigen. 2012. "Development of China's Polar Linkages." *Canadian Naval Review* 8 (3).

Yundt, Heather. 2012. "Canada's North Becomes a Battlefield in Arctic Video Game." *Nunatsiaq News*, February 9. www.nunatsiaqonline.ca/stories/ article/65674canadas_north_becomes_a_battlefield_in_arctic_video_game/.

Zellen, Barry Scott. 2009. *Arctic Doom, Arctic Boom: The Geopolitics of Climate Change in the Arctic*. Santa Barbara: Praeger.

Zhang, Junsai. 2012. Unpublished speech given at Montreal Council on Foreign Relations Luncheon, February 1. http://ca.china-embassy.org/eng/sgxw/ t901201.htm.

7

The Cooperation of Russia and Northeast Asian Countries in the Arctic: Challenges and Opportunities

Tamara Troyakova

INTRODUCTION

In its twenty-first-century geopolitical vision, Russia is ready to take on a new role as a maritime state that will draw its strength from its Arctic coast and watershed. Much has been said and written about the fact that the Asia-Pacific region will determine the development of the world in the foreseeable future. Moreover, recent research and debates show that soon the Arctic region — with its expanses to the Arctic Ocean and adjacent waters of the Atlantic and Pacific Oceans — could determine the vector of economic and geopolitical development (Laruelle 2013; Hara and Coates 2013; Zagorskiy, Glubokov and Khmelyova 2013).

The image of the Arctic as an icy area extending to the outskirts of Eurasia, North America and the islands of the Arctic Ocean with strategic nuclear missiles flying overhead has gradually begun to change. The threat of nuclear war is lessening, and now the prevailing trend is the development of bilateral and multilateral cooperation in the Arctic. The competition today between Russia and other countries is due to the prospects of rich resource development and the development of transport communications in the Arctic area.

The Arctic transportation arteries — the Northern Sea Route (NSR) off the coast of Russia, and the Northwest Passage (NWP) near Canada — have begun to attract the attention of many countries, since these routes from East Asia to Europe and North America are much shorter than the Suez Canal. Global warming, technological advances in shipbuilding and lack of pirates allow shipping companies to make better use of these routes. Although forecasts for ice melt in the Arctic are contradictory, a number of airlines have already expressed interest in the development of cross-polar flights between North America and Asia.

Russia's geographical location allows it to become an important link in the integration processes that are being developed between the Asia-Pacific countries and Euro-Atlantic space. Russia's economic and demographic indicators are modest compared to those of other leading countries, and these indicators are not predicting a huge economic change in the near future. Nonetheless, Russia has a good chance of becoming one of the leading maritime nations due to its growing role in Arctic international relations. These changes will require Russia to become more closely integrated in global commercial and financial networks, to welcome international business involvement and to participate in international bodies that harmonize international shipping, safety, security and environmental regulations. Against the backdrop of the Arctic transformation into the central part of a new geopolitical space, Russia should establish and put into practice the strategies that could promote cooperation with a wide range of actors.

Russia, Canada and the United States have extensive obligations and historical experience in the Arctic. Through being involved in the integration processes in the Asia Pacific, they become guides for the East Asian countries in the Arctic. Over the past 20 years, China, South Korea and Japan have made efforts to gain access to the Arctic Council — the Arctic countries' "club," where issues of Arctic strategic cooperation are discussed. It is obvious that in the near future, these East Asian countries will demonstrate a willingness to change old notions about the place and role of the Arctic region.

The growing influence of existing Arctic organizations and an arrangement of new institutions widen the circle of actors who are ready to participate in Arctic development. Opportunities for international cooperation and competition in the Arctic come from a variety of internal and external legal, economic, natural and cultural factors. It will undoubtedly take decades to reach this point, but the process of developing new concepts and institutions has already begun.

RUSSIA'S PARTICIPATION IN INTERNATIONAL ACTIVITIES IN THE ARCTIC

Russia joined the Council of the Baltic Sea States and the Northern Forum in 1992, the Barents Euro-Arctic Council in 1993, the Conference of Arctic Parliamentarians in 1994 and the Arctic Council in 1996. Over the years, the Arctic Council gained a reputation as a desired institution to discuss different issues of cooperation in the field of environmental protection, oil and mineral resources extraction, shipping, tourism and fishery, urgent problems of the region and preservation of the unique Arctic environment (Arctic Council 2014). In discussions about strengthening the Arctic Council, extremes should be avoided, including any illusions of self-sufficiency or exclusive responsibility of the forum to govern over all Arctic development issues. The important issue for the future will be not only identifying key areas and ways to strengthen the Arctic Council, but also establishing cooperation through its secretariat with specialized regional and universal organizations.

Russia is interested in expanding the power and authority of the Arctic Council. The United States considers the council a forum for cooperation and momentum toward a responsible approach to the region's issues, but does not advocate the plans for altering it into a full-fledged international organization. The council's status, however, is enhanced by the revitalization of the Arctic countries and "non-Arctic" council membership. Its growing role is evident from the May 2013 decision of the Conference of Foreign Ministers — the permanent members of the Arctic Council — to accept India, Italy, China, South Korea, Singapore and Japan as permanent observers to the Arctic Council (Petterson 2013).

In 1997, Russia ratified the UN Convention on the Law of the Sea (UNCLOS), which fixes its external border by a 12-mile zone and its economic border by a 200-mile zone. After the ratification of the convention, discussion of territorial borders in the Arctic commenced. The Russian Federation Government Edict was issued in March 2000, which regulates the activities of various departments in the process of preparation of an application to the United Nations for the expansion of the outer limits of the continental shelf of Russia in the Arctic region.

Russian politicians believe that Russia has reason to claim the extension of its northern possessions, because the country has the largest gateway to the Arctic and a considerable part of the country is located in the Arctic region. Several Arctic expeditions were conducted to prove Russia's rights to expand the shelf boundaries.

Regular scientific research expeditions in the Arctic are conducted, some of which are of promotional character; such as, planting the Russian flag on the Arctic Ocean seabed near the North Pole. The Russian Federation's foreign policy concept of 2013 declares the intentions to establish, in accordance with international law, "the outer boundaries of the continental shelf, thus expanding opportunities for exploration and development of its mineral resources" (Russian Federation 2013).

The main geopolitical interest in the Arctic should benefit the maritime industry. Russia and Canada are the best starting points to control the Arctic space because they have the most extensive lines of the Arctic coast, operate the NSR and the NWP (respectively), and have the largest fleet of icebreakers and unique practical expertise of the navy in the polar circle.

The first task of the legal confrontation is the Arctic countries' protection of their preferential right to define the rules of the game in the Arctic. The second task is to divide the Arctic Ocean among the Arctic countries. Ambiguity in a clean-cut separation of powers to the Arctic Ocean seabed is directly connected with the inability to develop natural resources and the lack of practical navigation. Non-Arctic countries, defending their potential interests in the Arctic, make an attempt to confine the rights of the Arctic countries by appealing to the international legal concept of the "common heritage of mankind."

China

The 2010 agreement on the division of the oil- and gas-rich border line between Norway and Russia exemplifies an important threshold in defining these countries' borders. Russia and Norway have developed a variety of relationships; for example, their first joint military exercise, Pomor-1994, took place in 1994. The resumption of joint military drills in 2010 and subsequent annual training displays tangible evidence of the improvement of Russian-Norwegian relations after mutual settlement of border issues.

For the past 20 years, various committees have been created, different bills have been discussed and many events have been held to ensure the geopolitical interests of Russia in the Arctic and sustainable development of the Arctic zone in general. In July 1998, the Federal Council put the draft federal law On the Arctic Zone of the Russian Federation into debate. It was considered by the State Duma in October 2000, but it remains in the discussion stage. The adoption of such a law would require substantial public funds for its implementation, but it is limited mostly by declarations. For example, the Russian Federation's national security concept, approved in January 2000, states that "mechanisms to maintain livelihoods and economic development of the critical regions and territories in the Far North should be developed as soon as possible" (Russian Federation 2013, 83). Nevertheless, the economic indicators are still low, and the exodus from the Far North continues.

The Cooperation of Russia and Northeast Asian Countries in the Arctic: Challenges and Opportunities

In 2001, the Russian government approved a draft framework for state policy in the Arctic, which was adopted in 2008 as "Foundations of the Russian Federation State Policy in the Arctic for the Period up to 2020 and Beyond" (Government of Russia 2008). Several priorities were formulated in this document: "the use of Arctic resources for socio-economic development, preservation of the Arctic as a zone of peace, stability and cooperation, conservation of fragile Arctic ecosystems and the protection of the interests of the indigenous peoples of the North, the use of the advantages of the [NSR] — the national transport artery of Russia" (ibid.). Several specific decisions at different levels are required to implement this document. It is noteworthy that both the Russian Federation's Council on Arctic issues, which was founded in 2002, and the Interministerial Commission for the Arctic and Antarctic were eliminated two years later. Thus, the possibility of considering the issues at the level of territorial entities is limited, although participation of subnational actors is welcomed and actively developed at the international level. Even at the federal level, the declaration is not always backed up by concrete actions; for example, in April 2013, the reduction of subsidizing the construction of nine new icebreakers was announced and ROSATOM (the Russian Federation's national nuclear corporation), the agency overseeing the project, was asked to seek additional funds for the implementation of the plans on its own.

In February 2013, the development strategy of the Arctic zone of the Russian Federation was approved by Russian President Vladimir Putin. The Arctic zone of Russia includes Murmansk, Nenets, Yamalo-Nenets, Chukotsky and part of the municipalities of Arkhangelsk, Krasnoyarsky and Sakha.

Among the priorities for development are key activities for international cooperation in the Arctic and military security, and defence and protection of the state border of the Russian Federation in the Arctic (Government of Russia 2008). In addition, the document highlights the development of forthcoming expedition activities in order to accomplish large-scale and complex research projects in the Arctic, including: the framework of international cooperation; taking advantage of international scientific and technological cooperation; and providing the participation of Russian scientific and educational organizations in the global and regional technology and research projects in the Arctic (ibid.). A significant part of the document is devoted to intensive development of international cooperation with neighbouring countries in the Arctic, which is seen as one of the driving forces of the program realization.

Implementation of this strategy is considered on the basis of public-private partnerships at the expense of institutions for development, international financial institutions and foreign investment into the future infrastructure; social, innovative and environmental protection; and other projects. The main provisions in this document relate to the problems in the field of foreign policy, military security, economic growth, development of naval policy and transportation routes. However, it is not quite clear where the Russian government expects to find the money for realization of such an ambitious program. There is no funding for this program in the federal budgets for 2014, 2015 or 2016. The Russian authorities expect that the major part of Arctic investments will be made by the biggest corporations, such as state-owned Gazprom and Rosneft, which have the most extensive plans and ambitions connected to this area. Russia experiences more and more serious challenges connected to the deficit of investment resources and currently the Russian Arctic region can hardly expect promised investments from the strategy of Arctic zone development.

The Russian Federation's 2013 foreign policy concept reflects the wording of the 2008 concept: that "Russia is developing forward practical cooperation with the countries of Northern Europe, including the implementation of multilateral mechanisms of joint co-operation projects in the Barents/Euro-Arctic and Arctic region as a whole" (Russian Federation 2013). A new element of the foreign policy concept is the claim that Russia is open to mutually beneficial cooperation with non-regional players, while respecting their independence, sovereign rights and jurisdiction of the Arctic States in the Arctic (ibid.). While the wording is not specific, it is assumed that Russia plans to cooperate with northeast Asian countries. There is concern about the growing influence of Russia on the part of non-Arctic countries, such as China's moves to strengthen trade relations with Iceland and build their own icebreaking fleet.

Russian cooperation with other states and non-state actors speaks about the probability of cooperative or confrontational scenarios. The first scenario, which is based on cooperation within various organizations such as the Arctic Council, sub-regional forums and bilateral consultations, is in the process of discussions, although the confrontational scenario of international cooperation has grounds for development. Russian experts believe that cooperative rather than confrontational patterns of behaviour from key actors will prevail in the Arctic (Konyshev and Sergunin 2011, 148). Marlene Laruelle (2013, 158) also writes that "cooperation with foreign countries is in Moscow's interest, but the fear of losing sovereignty is often perceived as offsetting any advantages occurred."

THE NSR: OBSTACLES AND POSSIBILITIES

Russia's geographical location allows it to become an important link in the integration processes that are being developed between the Asian-Pacific and Euro-Atlantic spaces. There is discussion of a possible use of Arctic routes connecting the Atlantic and Pacific Oceans for regular international transit. The volume of transit along the NSR has grown considerably in the last few years. The number of ships that transited the NSR grew from four in 2009 to 46 in 2012. The first transit of the newly opened (to foreign flag vessels) NSR was completed in the summer of 2009. The number of commercial transits has increased significantly in each succeeding year, with more than 300 movements in the area scheduled for 2013 (ABS 2014).

In January 2013, the Rules of Navigation in the Area of the NSR were approved by the Russian government, and in March 2013, the Russian Federation established the NSR Administration. These are practical consequences of the amendment of the Russian legislation concerning state regulation of merchant shipping in the area of the NSR. Persisting interest in Arctic shipping is explained by its growth in the last years, expectations of international shipping development along the NSR, and the need to ensure safety of the expanding shipping operations and prevent pollution of marine environment. Global demand for Arctic resources will drive the interest in the use of the NSR for commercial shipping and in the extraction of natural resources: "Increasing sea trade volume from globalization and international specialization reinforces the advantages of the NSR" (Lee 2012, 56).

China, South Korea and Japan will enjoy economic benefits from the NSR if they use it in their commercial trade with Europe. However, there are obstacles and risks for commercial shipping in the NSR, such as the problem of environmental pollution of the NSR. Only reasonable scientific evaluations of the pollution situation will be helpful to make corresponding laws and regulations. The icebreaking fee imposed by Russia is also an essential issue for all participants and has to be negotiated. The outcome of negotiations will determine whether or not the NSR will be a popular shipping route.

The Russian Arctic has no modern transportation infrastructure, such as ports, ship maintenance and service facilities. There is a need for the considerable enhancement of search and rescue, and emergency response capabilities. Much work to create an adequate ice-monitoring system and ship-tracking system must be done. Hydrographic and cartographic work also requires considerable investment. The Arctic coastal countries should be prepared to respond to maritime emergencies.

If an international cooperation framework were set up, a comprehensive database of information on the NSR would be possible and would benefit associate countries.

The next issue is a cargo imbalance between East Asian and European countries. It will be necessary to develop industrial parks and new centres near the NSR and in the Russian far east. To solve the problem of the unbalanced shipping trade, new ports must be constructed on the midpoint so that loading and unloading may occur. Russian far eastern ports have the potential to be excellent relay ports for the route in terms of supporting supplies for vessels and connecting into land logistics. The joint participation in such activities by the northeast countries that would use the NSR is much needed.

China is an ultimate leader in the Arctic affairs participation. According to Vyacheslav Karlusov (2012), China's interests in the Arctic is complex, composed of economic issues, including natural resource and logistics interests; geopolitical and closely related military strategy issues; and ecological, climatic and other research interests (ibid.). For Russia, a partnership could involve a joint development of hydrocarbon fields in the Russian Arctic shelf, the modernization of existing ports and the construction of new international seaports throughout the NSR. A Chinese shipping company is planning to organize regular commercial lines through the NSR, followed by an increase in the volume of outbound cargo. Shipping will be provided by Chinese instead of Russian icebreakers.

In 2010, the Japanese Ministry of Foreign Affairs established a task group on the Arctic, which analyzed and monitored the changes taking place in the region in the economy, security, the environment and international maritime law. Despite the dependency of the Russian economy on energy exports, the country lags behind its main competitors in the technology considered necessary for Arctic operations. Japanese know-how in energy extraction and maritime operations could be a vital aid to Russian firms.

In April 2013, South Korean President Park Geun-hye, met with the ministers responsible for navigation, fisheries and maritime affairs, and expressed the need for shipping companies to actively explore the Arctic sea routes. Government cooperation with the private sector can help ensure Busan and other ports become important staging ports in the region. Busan is not only a gateway for South Korea but also a hub port for many northern Chinese and Japanese ports. The option to develop a hub port in North Korea at Rajin seems impossible because of the country's current political situation.

Russian far east ports are better located than Korean, Japanese and Chinese ports in regard to the NSR, due to the shorter distance to and from the main route. The

Russian ports are also potentially connected to land-based logistics system linking Europe and the Asia-Pacific; yet the Russian far eastern ports still have a low capacity and limited nautical accessibility. They still remain gateway ports serving their nearby areas.

With China, South Korea and Japan obtaining the status of permanent observer with the Arctic Council, there are opportunities for further cooperation with Russia in the Arctic. Dialogue and cooperation should continue between Russia, China, South Korea and Japan on many issues in the Arctic, including environmental problems and natural resource development. For Arctic energy to be a viable option of significance for the North Pacific, a stable framework for shipping and investments in infrastructure as well as ships is required.

The global market connection of Russian Arctic natural resources and larger marine access throughout the Arctic Ocean afforded by regional climate change have provided opportunities to exercise the NSR system as a beginning for the commercialization of the route in the near future.

CONCLUSION

It can be argued that the activity of the Russian policy in the Arctic is gradually increasing, but it is still contradictory. This policy can be viewed as a set of functions of the central government, specialized federal agencies, regional authorities and businesses. This activity is poorly coordinated, chaotic and contradictory, and a wide range of participants cannot articulate a coherent strategy. Thus, Russian Arctic strategy is enduring a phase of transformation and adaptation to new geopolitical conditions. It is necessary to form institutions and mechanisms that are adapted to modern realities for the development of the Russian Arctic, with the participation of neighbouring countries. The transformative changes now taking place in the Arctic are tightening the links between this region and the global system.

WORKS CITED

ABS. 2014. "Navigating the Northern Sea Route Advisory." Houston: ABS.

Arctic Council. 2014. www.arctic-council.org/index.php/en/.

Government of Russia. 2008. "The Foundations of State Policy of the Russian Federation in the Arctic for the Period up to 2020 and Beyond." *Rossiyskaya Gazeta*, September 18.

Hara, Kimie and Ken Coates. 2013. "East Asia-Arctic Relations: Boundary, Security, and International Politics: Part I: Academic Workshop." Workshop report, March 2-3, Yukon College, Whitehorse, Yukon, Canada. www.cigionline.org/sites/default/files/EAArctic%20Workshop%20Report%20Part%20I.pdf.

Karlusov, Vyacheslav. 2012. "Arctic Victor of Chinese Globalization." Russian Council. http://russiancouncil.ru/en/inner/?id_4=268#top.

Konyshev, V. A, and A. A. Sergunin. 2011. *Arctic in International Politics: Cooperation or Competition?* [In Russian.] Moscow: Russian Institute of Strategic Studies.

Laruelle, Marlene. 2013. *Russia's Arctic Strategies and the Future of the Far North.* Armonk: M. E. Sharpe.

Lee, Sung-Woo. 2012. "Potential Arctic Shipping." In *The Arctic in World Affairs: A North Pacific Dialogue on Arctic Marine Issues*, edited by Oran R. Young, Jong Deog Kim and Yoon Hyung Kim, 39–60. Busan: Korea Maritime Institute and the East-West Center.

Petterson, Trude. 2013. "Six New Observers to Arctic Council." *Barents Observer,* May 15. http://barentsobserver.com/en/arctic/2013/05/six-new-observers-arctic-council-15-05.

Russian Federation. 2013. Foreign Policy Concept of the Russian Federation, approved by President Vladimir Putin on February 12, 2013. http://mid.ru/bdomp/ns-osndoc.nsf/e2f289bea62097f9c325787a0034c255/c32577ca0017434944257b160051bf7f!OpenDocument,

Zagorskiy A., A. Glubokov and E. Khmelyova. 2013. *International Cooperation in the Arctic.* Russian International Affairs Council Report.

8

From Cold War Thaws to the Arctic Thaw: The Changing Arctic and Its Security Implications to East Asia

Kimie Hara

INTRODUCTION

Unlike Europe, where the Cold War clearly ended with the collapse of the Yalta System, the structure of the regional Cold War confrontation remains profoundly embedded in East Asia. It has gone through political "thaws" or détentes and other notable transformations over the years; yet the foundation of the "San Francisco System" laid in the early post-World War II years essentially continues in East Asia even to the present day. Meanwhile, environmental thaw in the Arctic has been reshaping the world both physically and in international politics.[1]

This chapter considers the changes that the Arctic thaw will bring to the region, and indeed the world, examining the potential for new opportunities for cooperation

---

1   This study builds, in part, on the author's earlier research and publications on the San Francisco System, and accordingly contains some overlapping content. See Hara (2007; 2012).

as well as conflict, and the implications of the evolving situation of the Arctic to political and security relations in East Asia. Taking the San Francisco System as its conceptual grounding, this chapter traces notable developments of post-World War II regional political and security relations in East Asia, with particular attention to the regional conflicts, including territorial disputes; considers possible impacts of the emerging Arctic thaw to the status quo; and concludes with some recommendations for the concerned states to prepare for possible climate change in the security environment involving the East Asian and neighbouring Arctic states.[2]

THE SAN FRANCISCO SYSTEM IN POST-WORLD WAR II EAST ASIA

The Cold War structure of the post-World War II world was often attributed to the Yalta System. This system originated from agreements over the construction of the postwar international order made at Yalta in February 1945 by the leaders of the Allied powers (the United States, the United Kingdom and the Union of Soviet Socialist Republics [USSR]). However, the San Francisco System — the postwar peace treaty between the Allied powers and Japan, signed in September 1951 in San Francisco, along with its associated security arrangements — largely determined the Asian-Pacific postwar regional order (Hara 2007). The San Francisco System may be compared to the Euro-Atlantic's Yalta System, in terms of the three major features of the Cold War: ideology as the fundamental value of social existence; military confrontation including security alliances; and regional conflicts as the frontier of the Cold War confrontation.

Ideology

Ideologically, in the postwar decolonization movements, Asia was politically divided between "free world" and communist blocs, and economically divided between capitalist and socialist blocs under strong US or Soviet influence. The Cold War in Asia, however, developed somewhat differently than the bipolar Euro-Atlantic system in that the People's Republic of China (PRC) emerged as another pole of the communist sphere.

---

2   This study builds, in part, on the author's earlier research and publications on the San Francisco System, and accordingly contains some overlapping content. See Hara (2007; 2012).

From Cold War Thaws to the Arctic Thaw: The Changing Arctic and Its Security Implications to East Asia

Military and Security Alliances

The post-World War II military structure in the region is called the San Francisco Alliance System. In East Asia and the Pacific, with little success in establishing large anti-communist multilateral security alliances like the North Atlantic Treaty Organization (NATO), the United States formed a hub-and-spokes security system of separate arrangements with its regional allies.

Regional Conflicts

Regional conflicts are more characteristic of Asia than Europe. Whereas Germany was the only divided nation in Europe, competition over spheres of interest created several Cold War frontiers in East Asia. The origin of such regional conflicts is deeply rooted in the postwar territorial dispositions of Japan, particularly the San Francisco Peace Treaty. Vast territories, extending from the Kurile Islands to Antarctica and from Micronesia to the Spratly Islands, were disposed of in the treaty. The treaty, however, specified neither their final devolution (i.e., to which state they belong) nor their precise limits, thereby sowing the seeds of various unresolved problems in the region. The major regional conflicts in this region — including the territorial disputes over the Northern Territories/Southern Kuriles, Dokdo/Takeshima, Senkaku/Diaoyu, Spratly/Nansha and Paracel/Xisha, the Cross-Taiwan Strait issue, the divided Korean Peninsula, and the so-called "Okinawa problem" — all derived from the postwar territorial dispositions of the former Japanese empire.

STRATEGIC AMBIGUITY

Close examination of the Allies' documents, particularly those of the United States (which was primarily responsible for drafting the peace treaty), reveals that some, if not all, of these problems were intentionally created or left unresolved to protect US strategic interests against the backdrop of the intensifying Cold War (Hara 2007). During the postwar period leading up to the San Francisco Peace Conference of 1951, the United States carefully prepared the Allies' peace settlement with Japan. Its early drafts were, as a whole, very rigid and punitive toward Japan, reflecting the Yalta spirit of the Allies' cooperation. Those drafts also provided detailed and clear border demarcations specifically to prevent future territorial conflicts. However, as the Cold War intensified, particularly to the extent that it developed into a "hot" war in Korea, the peace terms changed to reflect new US strategic interests. Specifically, Japan and the Philippines had to be secured for the non-communist West and as pro-US allies in East Asia, whereas the communist states were to be contained.

Accordingly, the peace treaty became "generous" and its wording "simple" — but thereby ambiguous, leaving the potential for conflicts to erupt among East Asian states. The peace treaty was the result of careful deliberations and several revisions; issues were deliberately left unresolved.

These regional conflicts — such as those noted earlier — tend to be treated as separate and unrelated issues, yet they emerged as a result of the Japanese peace treaty, which was prepared when the US leadership seriously feared that both South Korea and Taiwan might be "lost" to, or unified by, their communist counterparts. The unresolved problems, derived from the postwar disposition of Japan, continue to divide countries and people in East Asia to this day. Just as the Northern Territories/ Kuriles Islands issue was left between Japan and the Soviet Union as a by-product of the Cold War, seeds of territorial disputes were left between Japan and its partial and mostly communist neighbours of Korea and China respectively.[3] The San Francisco Peace Treaty also concerned the settlement of other past "history" issues, such as war crimes and reparations. These issues also remained owing to the US policy shift to generous and ambiguous peace with Japan, or what some might call its "strategic ambiguity."

COLD WAR THAWS AND THE TRANSFORMATION OF THE SAN FRANCISCO SYSTEM

During the 60 years since the San Francisco agreement, East Asia has undergone notable transformations. After alternating periods of East-West tension and the relaxation of tensions, such as the Cold War thaws of the 1950s and the 1970s, the Cold War was widely believed to have ended by the early 1990s. These changes also affected relations among neighbouring countries in East Asia, with important consequences, but not solutions, for some lingering regional conflicts.

COLD WAR THAW IN THE 1950S

Movement toward an East Asian thaw began to be observed soon after Stalin's death in 1953, with a ceasefire in the Korean War. Watershed events — such as the Indochina ceasefire agreement and the Geneva Conference in 1954, and the Bandung Conference in 1955 — further strengthened this thawing trend. Against the

---

3   The territorial dispute between Japan and China was originally over Okinawa. Chiang Kai-shek's Republic of China (ROC) was demanding Okinawa's "recovery" to China in the early post-World War II years.

backdrop of warming East-West relations, Japan and the Soviet Union began peace negotiations. In 1956, the two countries restored diplomatic relations and agreed, in a joint declaration, to the transfer of the Shikotan and the Habomai Islands to Japan following the conclusion of a peace treaty between them. However, Japan was encouraged (or pressed) by the United States to demand the return of all four of the island groups in its so-called Northern Territories. Indeed, the United States warned that it would not return Okinawa to Japan if its claims to Kunashiri and Etorofu Islands were abandoned.

US support for the four-island-return formula was made with full knowledge that it would be unacceptable to the Soviet Union, thus preventing Japan from achieving rapprochement with the Soviet and communist blocs. The United States feared the thaw would work to the Soviet Union's strategic advantage, and that a Japan-Soviet peace treaty would lead to the normalization of relations between Japan and communist China. Further, if Japan settled the Northern Territories dispute with the Soviet Union, there would be considerable pressure on the United States to vacate Okinawa, whose importance had significantly increased as a result of the United States' Cold War strategy in Asia — especially during the Korean War.[4]

THE PRC IN THE EAST ASIAN COLD WAR

In East Asia, the Cold War developed differently from the Euro-Atlantic bipolar system; rather, a tripolar system, consisting of the United States, the PRC and the USSR, emerged following the Sino-Soviet split. Communist China had been targeted by the US containment strategy since its intervention in the Korean War. With its nuclear development in 1964, China came to occupy the central position in the Asian Cold War. Thus, in 1965, the United States' two regional allies, Japan and South Korea, opened diplomatic relations, setting aside their territorial and other issues. Considering that the emergence of nuclear weapons fundamentally changed the nature of post-World War II international relations and became the biggest factor for the Cold War, the US-China confrontation became truly a "cold war" in lieu of a direct military clash, with fighting taking place in surrogate wars in their satellite states.

Conversely, Sino-Soviet confrontations were initially confined to oral and written communications, but escalated into military clashes along the border, especially over ownership of Damansky Island on the Ussuri River in 1969. This frontier problem did not derive, and was therefore different, from those conflicts that emerged out

---

4   See Hara (2007), particularly chapters 4 and 7.

of the postwar disposition of Japan. Nevertheless, it came to symbolize the height of Sino-Soviet tension that defined the Cold War in East Asia, setting the stage for the dramatic structural transformation during the 1970s thaw, when Sino-US rapprochement occurred.

Thaw in the 1970s

The warming of East-West relations in the early 1970s was similar to that of the 1950s, in that peace was not necessarily achieved in an ideological sense and the relative influence of the United States was declining. Exploiting the Sino-Soviet difference, the United States took major initiatives to "break the ice" this time; US President Nixon's administration entered office with normalizing relations with communist China as its top diplomatic agenda. During this period of détente, several major US allies, including Japan, opened diplomatic relations with the PRC government, which also replaced the ROC at the United Nations.

In parallel with these moves, the focus of the Sino-Japanese territorial dispute shifted to the Senkaku/Diaoyu Islands, where resource nationalism was accentuated by the new energy potential discovered in their vicinity. The United States returned Okinawa to Japan in 1972, inheriting the previous administration's promise. On the reversion of Okinawa, however, the US government took "no position on sovereignty" over the Senkakus; it merely returned administrative rights to Japan, leaving the dispute to Japan and China (US Congress 1971, 91). The ROC government in Taiwan, moreover, maintained that Okinawa was not Japanese territory and opposed its reversion. Again, the United States adopted a policy of strategic ambiguity on the Senkaku issue, despite the fact that it had administered the islands as part of Okinawa throughout its occupation.

The US rapprochement with the PRC represented its recognition of the political status quo — a shift to an engagement policy rather than an end to the Cold War, eventually opening official diplomatic relations in 1978. Under Nixon's administration, communist China continued to be perceived as a threat to US interests in East Asia, and US bases in Okinawa had to be maintained. Thus, leaving the dispute unsettled — by not taking sides with any disputant, and keeping the wedges between the neighbouring states — met US interests, helping to retain its presence and influence in the region. Just as the wedge of the Northern Territories problem was set in place with the four-island-return claim between Japan and the Soviet Union during the thaw of the 1950s, the Senkaku issue was another wedge left between Japan and China during the 1970s thaw.

Japan and the USSR also moved closer during this period, holding a second summit meeting in Moscow in 1971, 17 years after their first meeting in 1956.

The emerging opportunity of the Siberian resource development was one of the biggest factors behind that move. However, before they reached the resolution of the territorial problem or a peace treaty, their relations began to sour, especially in 1978 with the signing of the Treaty of Peace and Friendship between Japan and the PRC, incorporating an "anti-hegemony" clause directed against the USSR (at China's insistence), and the Soviet invasion of Afghanistan. The USSR began a buildup of forces in the Far East, including the disputed islands, which alarmed and deeply offended Japan. In the meantime, the unresolved problems that shared a common foundation in the San Francisco Peace Treaty continued to fester. In addition to a divided China, the newly independent countries — (South) Vietnam, the Philippines, Malaysia and Brunei — joined the territorial disputes in the South China Sea.

REMAINING REGIONAL COLD WAR STRUCTURE

In the global thaw from the late 1980s to the early 1990s, the Cold War was widely believed to have ended. Both US-Soviet and Sino-Soviet rapprochement were achieved, and a remarkable relaxation of tension occurred in East Asia, where expectations soared for a solution to some of the most intractable frontier problems. The Sino-Soviet/Russian border negotiations, ongoing since the late 1980s, finally ended with mutual concessions in the 2000s. None of the regional conflicts that emerged following the foundation of the San Francisco System, however, reached a fundamental settlement. In fact, compared to the Euro-Atlantic region, where the wall dividing East and West completely collapsed, the changes that took place in East Asia left fundamental divisions intact. With the exception of the demise of the Soviet Union, the region's Cold War structure of confrontation basically continued. Today, more than 20 years later, and 60 years after San Francisco, China and Korea are still divided, with their communist or authoritarian parts still perceived as threats by their neighbours and, accordingly, the US military presence and its associated issues, such as the Okinawa problem, continue. Whereas NATO lost its anti-communist drive when it accepted formerly communist Eastern European countries as members, there are no indications that the remaining San Francisco Alliance will either dissolve or embrace North Korea or the PRC.

In retrospect, the term cold war has been used largely in two ways: first as a circumstance, where confrontations between superpowers or conflicting systems are highly strained, and secondly as the structure of such confrontations. The generally accepted view of the end of the Cold War in East Asia is based on the first perception. The relaxation of tension may be a necessary condition for ending Cold War hostilities, but it is an insufficient condition unless accompanied by the demolition of the fundamental structure. In the sense that the fundamental structure of Cold War confrontation remains, the dramatic relaxation seen in East Asia since the late 1980s is more like the periodic thaws than the end of the Cold War per se. As the 1970s thaw rested, in part, on the perceived achievement of Soviet military parity with the United States, China's recent assertiveness in its aspiration to military strength cannot be ignored. The relaxation of tension seen in the Cold War thaws of the 1950s and the 1970s gave way to the deterioration of East-West relations. Similar phenomena have been observed in East Asia, such as US-China conflicts after the Tiananmen incident of 1989, military tensions in the Korean Peninsula and across the Taiwan Strait, the disruption of negotiations between Japan and North Korea to normalize their diplomatic relations, and political tensions involving Japan, China and their neighbours over territorial disputes.

DEEPENING INTERDEPENDENCE IN ECONOMIC AND OTHER RELATIONS

While countries and peoples in East Asia have been divided by politics, history and unsettled borders, they have nevertheless deepened their interdependence in economic, cultural and other relations. Over over the last 60 years, the economic recovery and transformation of East Asian countries from the ruins of war are, in fact, remarkable. Beginning with Japan in the 1950s, followed by the so-called newly industrializing economies in the 1970s and 1980s, and now with China's rise, East Asia (with the exception of North Korea) has become the most expansive centre in the world economy. Economy is indeed the glue connecting the regional states.

Economic-driven multilateral cooperation and institution building developed notably in East Asia with the creation of multiple institutions, especially in the 1990s and the 2000s. This also paved the way for confidence-building measures (CBMs) among neighbouring states. Since the 1990s, progress in CBMs at both governmental and non-governmental levels constitutes a leap beyond the Cold War era, particularly in non-traditional security areas such as the environment, food, energy, terrorism and natural disasters. Nevertheless, the depth of integration pales compared with those of Europe. While the European Community of the Cold War era has long since evolved into the European Union, even the idea of an "East Asian Community" (not an "East Asian Union") is still a future aspiration. As yet, the East Asian countries do not have relationships of sufficient mutual trust. Their countries and peoples are strongly connected economically, but they remain divided politically, and are still in dispute over unresolved problems, including those over territorial sovereignty and borders (Hara 2012). Thus, even though global waves of post-Cold War transformations in international relations such as globalization and regionalism have reached East Asia, they do not necessarily deny the remaining structure of confrontation founded in San Francisco over 60 years ago.

THE ARCTIC THAW AND POLITICAL AND SECURITY IMPLICATIONS

In the latter half of the twentieth century, the dramatic changes of the global political and security environment, such as the emergence of the Cold War, the Cold War thaws and the end of the Cold War, did not bypass East Asia. Yet, unlike Europe, where the Cold War clearly ended with its structural foundation, the collapse of the Yalta System, the San Francisco System essentially remains in East Asia. In the twenty-first century, the Arctic thaw is now reshaping the world both physically and in international politics. This section considers emerging and possible impacts of this Arctic thaw to the status quo in East Asia.

THE EVOLVING SITUATION IN THE ARCTIC AND EAST ASIA

Global climate change is profoundly reshaping the Arctic region today, generating heated discussions on issues such as new marine transportation routes, resource development, border disputes and the environment. With the emerging new northern sea passages (the Northern Sea Route and the Northwest Passage), the Arctic thaw is opening new opportunities to East Asian states. These northern transportation routes can significantly shorten the shipping distance from the Atlantic to the Pacific, from Europe or the east coast of North America to East Asia, leading to potential reductions in shipping time, fuel costs and CO_2 emissions.

Navigational safety could be yet another advantage. The existing maritime transportation route from Europe and the Middle East through the Suez Canal is not always safe, due to uneasy political conditions in the Middle East and piracy en route, especially near Somalia. The northern routes are, therefore, becoming attractive alternatives to East Asian states. Resource development and shipping from the Arctic region to Asia using the passages are becoming realistic as well. With the advancement of technology, resource development in the extremely cold Arctic environment (which used to be impossible) and transporting resources to Asia and other regions are becoming possibilities. Actual production is already underway in some coastal areas (see Figure 1). Melting ice in the Arctic is also an expanding fishing ground.

Figure 1: Resources in the Arctic

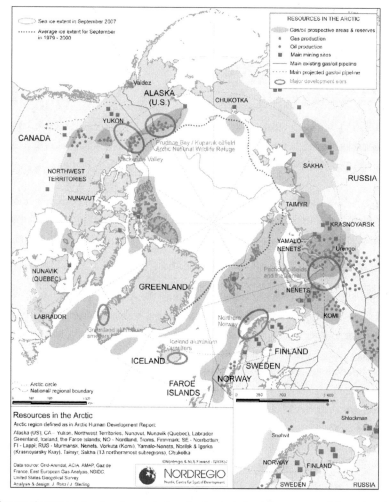

The map shows the main sites of gas and oil production, including infrastructure, mining and sea ice extent in the Arctic.

Source: Nordregio (2013). (Designer/Cartographer: Johanna Roto and José Sterling. www.nordregio.se/Maps--Graphs/05-Environment-and-energy/Resources-in-the-Arctic/)

The East Asian states — particularly the PRC, Japan and South Korea — are becoming increasingly interested in the evolving Arctic region. China is a growing economic giant, now the second-largest economic power, surpassing Japan's GDP in 2011. With the world's biggest population, its energy consumption is also the world's largest, already surpassing the United States. Following the March 2011 Fukushima disaster, Japan is reducing its dependency on nuclear power by looking for alternative energy sources and transportation routes. South Korea, which has a strong shipping industry, is also interested in the evolving Arctic situation. In fact, as non-Arctic states, the PRC, Japan, South Korea, the ROC and even North Korea would all potentially benefit significantly from shorter shipping routes and possible access to alternative energy sources and new fishing ground. They also share environmental and scientific concerns in the Arctic region.

NEW OPPORTUNITIES FOR COOPERATION AND RECONCILIATION

If the Arctic thaw continues, as many scientists and media reports predict, the region's geo-economic and strategic importance to East Asia will further increase and might also provide new opportunities for cooperation, competition and confrontation among East Asian nations. By opening new operative shipping routes across the Arctic, marine traffic and trade volume from Europe and North America to East Asia and further down to Southeast Asia would increase. Associated economic effects, such as invigorating shipbuilding and its related industries, hub ports and coastal cities, could also be expected, thus further energizing the East Asian economy. The East Asian seas could then become vital marine passages, holding the key to all these important developments. While this has a potential to intensify competition and conflict among East Asian states seeking to protect their respective sea lanes, cooperation between and among the neighbours would become more important and necessary to secure the safe passage of their ships cruising and engaging in commercial activities in this region, and establish stability in regional security environment.

The increased Arctic passage marine transportation to Asia would also increase marine traffic near the disputed islands (Northern Territories/Southern Kuriles, and Dokdo/Takeshima, Senkaku/Diaoyu) located in the sea lanes connecting the Pacific Ocean, the Sea of Okhotsk, the Japan Sea/East Sea and the East China Sea. This might motivate the concerned states to effectively manage and even reach some settlement in their territorial and maritime border disputes.

Among the territorial and maritime border problems in East Asia, the evolving situation in the Arctic is likely to bring the largest impact to the Northern Territories/

Figure 2: Sea Lanes Connecting the Arctic and
East Asia, and the Disputed Territories

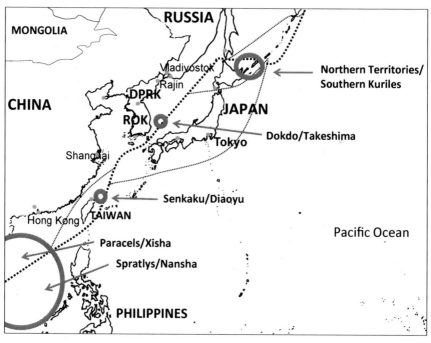

Source: Author.

Southern Kuriles problem between Japan and Russia. In recent years, Russia has successfully negotiated boundary demarcations with many of its neighbours, and Russian President Vladimir Putin has been sending positive signals for resolving the territorial problems with Japan since his first presidency in the 2000s. The evolving situation in the Arctic may provide Japan further incentives to settle this territorial problem.

Japan's negotiating position with Russia over the territorial issue has been reversed over the past two decades. In the early 1990s, with Russia still facing the economic and financial crisis inherited from the collapsed Soviet Union, Japan's attitude, being the then-second-largest economic power, can be described as rather condescending. Japan assumed that Russia was in desperate need of its economic assistance, and thus linked its economic aid to the territorial dispute, which eventually invited criticism even from its Western allies. One major criticism came from former US President Richard Nixon (1993), who condemned Japan for "conditioning aid on Russia's return of four tiny northern islands." Now, however, the inverse is true, as

Russia is a resource-rich capitalist country and the world's foremost oil-production country. It is the biggest Arctic nation, and is active in resource development and production in the Arctic Circle. While Russia has regained its power and influence with the leverage of its rich resources, Japan has been in decline in its negotiating position since the collapse of the "bubble economy," followed by the "lost decade" and the Fukushima disaster.

The opening of the Arctic is already making Russia a very attractive neighbour to Japan. A report produced by Japan's Ocean Policy Research Foundation (OPRF) recognizes the growing importance of developing good neighbourly relations with Russia. It recommends "measures which Japan should take immediately towards sustainable use of the Arctic Ocean," and states that "Russia is the largest coastal country of the Arctic Ocean, and most of the Arctic-related matters in which Japan has interests involve Russia." Further, while the report acknowledges that "there is a difficult problem in the Japan-Russia relationship," it urges the Japanese government to work with Russia to deal with evolving Arctic problems (OPRF 2012). Current Japanese Prime Minister Shinzo Abe's administration appears to be positively exploring points of compromise on the territorial issue with Russia. In April 2013, for example, Abe agreed with Putin to revive the island negotiations by increasing government contact, including reciprocal visits by the leaders and their foreign ministers.[5] However, as past experience has proven, thaws and the potential for resources may not be enough to resolve the nations' territorial disputes.

In 2005, and again in 2012-2013, Japan's relations with South Korea and China deteriorated over the islands disputes, yet these countries have track records of advancing their relations while shelving the territorial disputes. As noted earlier, the economy is the glue connecting regional states. Once policy priority shifts to the economy or other common areas of interest, further cooperation and development may be possible in the areas surrounding the disputed islands. Russia and China have been invigorating their cooperative investment and development in the Rason Special Economic Zone and its Rajin port facing the Sea of Japan (East Sea) in North Korea since 2011, showing a potential to revive the early 1990s regional cooperation involving North Korea (*Sankei News* 2012; *NNN News 24* 2013). This move may further be facilitated by the opening of an operative shipping route in the Arctic. The situation surrounding the nuclear development of North Korea has been one of the most pressing destabilizing factors in the region. Instead of isolating

---

5   For recent developments concerning Japan's relations with Russia, see the Ministry of Foreign Affairs of Japan webpage (2014).

and driving North Korea into a corner where there is no other option but further developing weapons of mass destruction — which would only serve to heighten military tensions — peaceful coexistence or stability of the region may be sought by engaging it and exploring and expanding areas of cooperation.

COOPERATION FRAMEWORK

Finding ways for East Asian neighbours to work together has the potential to create a genuine win-win situation for the states concerned. Some arrangements or governance cooperation may be possible to establish stable regional order in the areas where there are disputed islands and other flashpoints. This could also be connected to development of the 2002 Association of Southeast Asian Nations (ASEAN)-China Declaration on the Conduct of Parties in the South China Sea, where China confronts its neighbours over the Spratlys and Paracel Islands.

Most states have defence programs in order to be prepared for the contingency or development of undesirable security situations. The US military presence is indispensable for its regional allies and also contributes to regional security. This situation seems destined to continue for the foreseeable future. Existing security arrangements that can be applied to the areas covering East Asia and the Arctic include the US hub-and-spoke (i.e., San Francisco) alliance system in the Asia-Pacific and NATO in the Euro-Atlantic. While these systems can be collectively seen as security assurance for allied members, they can also serve as containment networks targeting non-members, specifically Russia, China and North Korea. However, there are other multilateral dialogue frameworks, including some or all of those countries, such as the Six-Party Talks, the ASEAN Regional Forum and the East Asian Summit.

Engagement in Arctic affairs is an emerging common interest among East Asian states and could be a new area of cooperation among them; however, states appear to be in a competing mode, as each country is independently seeking its own way of engaging in Arctic affairs. A unified strategy may become their mutual interest, and it seems worth investigating the possibility of establishing a new cooperative framework, combining the existing China-Japan-South Korea trilateral framework and the neighbouring three Arctic powers of Russia, the United States and Canada, or a similar framework with North Korea (i.e., the existing Six-Party Talks plus Canada). Canada, Russia and the United States have extensive commitments and long histories of engagement in the Arctic. These countries are the major Arctic nations with the gateways to the Pacific, and also have long history of engagement in East Asia. The combination of their northern responsibilities, geography and engagement in East Asia, and East Asia's growing interest in the Arctic, make the nations of both regions key players in determining the future direction of governance and development in the region.

The vulnerable character of maritime security makes it necessary to establish a practice of following and making common rules. That all the concerned states become signatories of the UN Convention on the Law of the Sea (UNCLOS) will be a very important base to solve disputes. In this sense, the participation of the United States, which has not yet ratified UNCLOS, will be an important step.

FROM THAW TO THE NEXT COLD WAR?

Whereas there may be good potential for cooperation among East Asian states in areas such as the development of resources and northern passages, there may also be a danger that tensions among the regional countries may increase, especially in the disputed areas. As seen in the past, similar tensions may rise again from the remaining structure of the Cold War confrontation, where relations among neighbours, including their territorial problems, may be involved in a new power game. The Arctic thaw may become a new factor. As noted earlier, during the warming of East-West relations of the past, the United States did not necessarily facilitate full reconciliation or clear settlement of the territorial problems between Japan and its neighbours. Continued conflicts may still be seen as meeting US interests, as long as they are manageable and do not escalate into a large-scale war. Although an accommodation between Japan and its neighbours is preferable for regional stability, it may not be viewed as beneficial to US interests if it is perceived as likely to reduce or exclude US influence. "Manageable instability" actually helps justify the continued substantial US military presence in the region, not only enabling the United States to maintain its regional influence, but also contributing to operations farther afield, such as in the Middle East and, in the future, possibly the Arctic.

The United States has redirected its strategic focus toward the Asia-Pacific in recent years. It is stepping up its naval presence in the Pacific by shifting a bulk of its naval fleet from the Atlantic as part of the so-called Asia "rebalancing" initiative. On June 2, 2012, US Defense Secretary Leon Panetta announced that "by 2020 the Navy will reposture its forces from today's roughly 50-50 split from the Pacific and Atlantic to a 60-40 split in those oceans" (cited in Neisloss 2012). This includes a troop deployment in Darwin, Australia, and military engagement with the Philippines and other ASEAN countries in the South China Sea. Many have already commented on this shift as counterbalancing China in the Asia-Pacific. However, it may also serve as a possible measure directed to its future defence of the north Pacific and to the Arctic. The premise of the conventional strategy — that the Arctic Ocean is frozen and the cruise of a naval fleet is impossible — now appears to be collapsing. There is a possibility that the Arctic Ocean may serve as a stage of military operation or become an arena of the marine power balance game.

Among circumpolar states, Russia is becoming active in its military activities in the Arctic Ocean, protecting its rights to seabed resources, controlling the Northeast Passage (also called the Northern Sea Route) to prevent foreign intervention, and defending the sea lane to East Asia (OPRF 2012). A statement of principles, approved by then Russian President Dmitry Medvedev in 2008, regards the Arctic as a strategic resource base of primary importance to Russia. Foreseeing the possible rise of tensions developing into military conflict, the document prescribes "building groupings of conventional forces in the Arctic zone capable of providing military security in different military-political conditions" (*Rossiyskaya Gazeta* 2009).

The Northern Territories/Southern Kuriles, located in the northern limit of the ice-free passage and at an important gateway to the Pacific Ocean, were once considered to have vital strategic importance, especially in the late 1970s and 1980s, when the Sea of Okhotsk became a bastion for Soviet missile firing of nuclear-powered submarines.[6] As the southern limit of the ice-free passage moves north due to global warming, these disputed territories might become less important in this sense, but their strategic value might increase in another. Port and military facilities may be strengthened or established to provide a coast guard base to protect sea lanes. Japan is located in such a way that it blocks the access of its neighbouring states to the Pacific Ocean. In 1950, then US Secretary of State Dean Acheson announced the US Cold War defence perimeter to confront communism in the western Pacific, running along the Aleutians to Japan and then to the Philippines. Now China, having successfully demarcated its long northern border with Russia, has shifted the focus of its border defence to its ocean frontiers. It is no coincidence that the "First Island Chain" in the present Chinese defence doctrine overlaps with the Acheson Line.[7]

---

6   For an excellent analysis on Russia's military and the strategic importance of the disputed territories, see Jukes (1993; 2009, 62–82).

7   "The Second Island Chain," running from the Japanese archipelago to the south along the Bonin and Northern Mariana Islands and along the western edge of Micronesia, which used to be called *Nanpo Shoto* and *Nanyo*, respectively, during the period of the Japanese control, overlaps with the US defence line of the early post-World World II (pre-Cold War) years, i.e., when the United States still considered Japan an enemy. For details, see Hara (2007, chapter 4).

According to the OPRF (2012), "If melting ice progresses in the Arctic Ocean and the power game over the naval supremacy of the Arctic Ocean aggravates, along with the US military deployment, operation of the Marine Self Defense Force of Japan would also be affected, e.g. in dealing with the Chinese navy, the Russian Far East fleet near Hokkaido and surrounding ocean area of the Kurile islands." This could mean that the importance of Japan in the US-Asia strategy, and the strategic importance of the Northern Territories and other disputed territories might increase. Thus, there is a possibility that the new security climate change created by the Arctic thaw may re-intensify the remaining structure of the Cold War confrontation. Accordingly, the resolution of territorial problems may become more difficult again.

CONCLUSION AND RECOMMENDATIONS

The Cold War thaws provided opportunities for settling territorial problems and political rapprochement among East Asian neighbours. However, those chances were lost and no definitive settlements have been reached. Divisions in East Asia continue, as does the San Francisco System. Although the system has gone through notable transformations, with the structural foundation for its predominance still in place, the United States continues to hold the most important key to the future direction of the political and security order in the region.

The Arctic thaw is likely to provide new opportunities for regional and intra-regional cooperation, as well as additional sources of conflict. Whereas the Arctic thaw and the opening of the northern sea routes might further stimulate the regional economy — especially in trade and associated industries in East Asia — they would also pose additional challenges in the security environment, especially in the defence of sea lanes from the Arctic to East Asia. Regional and intra-regional security may become a comprehensive concept covering multi-layered areas including traditional, non-traditional, economic and energy security. The East Asian states (especially China, Japan and South Korea), the Pacific-Arctic states (the United States and Canada) and Russia are key players capable of contributing to regional and intra-regional security and stability. Although there are differences among them, these states all share broad areas of interests and cooperation.

Just as the Cold War thaws did not lead to the collapse of the San Francisco System, the Arctic thaw alone may not be enough to bring fundamental change to the continuing structure of confrontation in East Asia. However, the promotion of CBMs in wide-ranging areas can contribute to expanding common areas of interests and cooperation in regional and inter-regional security, as well as preventing misunderstandings and unnecessary confrontations. To prepare for the possible changes that climate change may bring to the Arctic's security environment, there are several measures and adjustments that the concerned states can take:

- The vulnerable character of maritime security makes it necessary to establish a practice of following and making common rules. That all concerned become signatories of the UNCLOS would be a very important base to solve disputes according to rule of law. The United States should ratify the UNCLOS.

- In order to prevent a dangerous situation, such as an accidental military clash and escalation of conflicts thereafter, the concerned governments should build a system of governance cooperation, which would include arrangements of hotlines, regular diplomatic and defence/strategic dialogues, and joint exercises.

- In addition to the existing bilateral and multilateral frameworks, it is worth investigating a new multilateral framework involving coastal states ranging from the Arctic to East Asia, including Canada, the United States, Russia, Japan, China, South Korea and possibly North Korea.

- The academic and intellectual community can play an important and useful role in providing knowledge and ideas to the concerned governments, businesses, non-governmental organizations and other international organizations. From the viewpoint of contributing to the prosperity and stability of the East Asia-Arctic region, further investigation of the topics covered in this project, East Asia-Arctic Relations: Boundary, Security and International Politics, should continue.

WORKS CITED

Hara, Kimie. 2007. *Cold War Frontiers in the Asia-Pacific: Divided Territories in the San Francisco System.* Abingdon: Routledge.

———. 2012. "The San Francisco Peace Treaty and Frontier Problems in the Regional Order in East Asia A Sixty Year Perspective." *The Asia-Pacific Journal* 10 (17).

Jukes, Geoffrey. 1993. "Russia's Military and the Northern Territories Issue." Strategic & Defence Studies Centre Working Paper No. 277.

———. 2009. "Can the Southern Kuriles be Demilitarized?" In *Northern Territories, Asia-Pacific Regional Conflicts and the Aland Experience: Untying the Kurillian Knot*, edited by Kimie Hara and Geoffrey Jukes, 62–82. London: Routledge.

Ministry of Foreign Affairs of Japan. 2014. "Japan-Russia Relations." www.mofa.go.jp/region/europe/russia/.

Neisloss, Liz. 2012. "U.S. Defense Secretary Announces New Strategy with Asia." CNN, June 2. www.cnn.com/2012/06/02/us/panetta-asia/index.html.

Nixon, Richard. 1993. "Clinton's Greatest Challenge." *The New York Times*, March 5. www.nytimes.com/1993/03/05/opinion/clinton-s-greatest-challenge.html?pagewanted=all&src=pm.

NNN News 24. 2013. "Speculation Match of Two Railway Connecting the North Korea and Russia." [In Japanese.]. November 29. www.news24.jp/articles/2013/11/29/10241224.html.

Nordregio. 2013. "Resources in the Arctic." www.nordregio.se/Maps--Graphs/05-Environment-and-energy/Resources-in-the-Arctic/.

OPRF. 2012. "The Measures that Japan Should Take Immediately Towards the Sustainable Use of the Arctic Ocean." [In Japanese.] March. www.sof.or.jp/jp/report/pdf/12_06_02.pdf.

Rossiyskaya Gazeta. 2009. "Principles of State Policy of the Russian Federation in the Arctic up to 2020 and Beyond." [In Russian.] *Rossiyskaya Gazeta*, March 27. www.rg.ru/2009/03/30/arktika-osnovy-dok.html.

Sankei News. 2012. *Hokkyokukai Kiho* ("Seasonal Report of the Arctic Ocean"). [In Japanese.] No. 14, June-August. www.sof.or.jp/jp/monthly/season/pdf/14.pdf.

US Congress. 1971. Senate Committee on Foreign Relations, Okinawa Reversion Treaty: Hearings Before the Committee on Foreign Relations, US Senate, 92nd Congress, 1st Session, on Ex. J.92-1. The Agreement Between the U.S.A. and Japan Concerning the Ryukyn Islands and the Daito Islands.

9

The Business of Arctic Development: East Asian Economic Interests in the Far North

///

Carin Holroyd
••••••••••••••••

INTRODUCTION

Over the past decade, East Asian countries have been showing increased interest in the Arctic. China, Japan and South Korea have all applied for permanent observer status on the Arctic Council. China and South Korea each spend more on polar research than the United States. East Asian countries have begun discussions on joint research, shared visions for the future of the region and potential shipping routes with at least some of the "Arctic Five," as the United States, Russia, Norway, Denmark (via Greenland) and Canada are known. China, in particular, has long-term geopolitical interests in the Arctic and strong feelings that decisions about the region should not be made without its input.

Geopolitics aside, the relatively sudden attention that East Asia has been paying to the Arctic has a strong economic base. East Asian countries, like many others, appreciate the Arctic's potential in terms of resources and the opportunities associated with the opening of navigable waters in the Far North as a result of climate change.

It is scarcely surprising that East Asian nations are keeping an eye on developments and investment opportunities in the Arctic. But the Arctic is only a small part of East Asia's intense global search for long-term supplies of natural resources, including oil, gas and minerals. When East Asian engagement in the Arctic is measured against similar activities in the sub-Arctic, Australia, much of Asia, and Africa, it is clear that the Far North is not central to resource exploration and development strategies.

There are possibilities for East Asia in the Arctic, however, and East Asian states are examining these aggressively. As the Arctic ice melts, the prospects of access to previously inaccessible minerals, oil and gas improve. Estimates are that the region could contain up to 30 percent of the world's undiscovered natural gas and 13 percent of its undiscovered oil (*The Economist* 2012; Chen 2012, 362). The region also contains an abundance of coal, iron, uranium, nickel, copper, tungsten, lead, rare earths, zinc, gold, silver, diamonds and fish (ibid.). Untapped resources of this variety and assumed magnitude cannot be ignored by nations that are dearly lacking in domestic supplies of key energy and minerals.

South Korea and Japan have few energy or mineral resources of their own. Both countries are very dependent on energy from the Middle East and would like to diversify their suppliers. Japan is the world's largest importer of liquefied natural gas (LNG) and third-largest importer of oil; South Korea is the second-largest importer of LNG and the sixth-largest importer of oil (US Energy Information Administration 2013). Until the March 2011 Fukushima nuclear disaster, Japan was planning to increase its nuclear power capabilities significantly and, in combination with renewable energies, was moving away from oil and gas as much as possible. However, as of early 2014, none of Japan's 50 reactors are operating. Newly elected Prime Minister Shinzo Abe has indicated that some will likely be restarted, but public sentiment against nuclear power remains strong. Japan's search for oil and gas is, therefore, intensifying.

China has its own oil but the country's dramatic economic growth has left it desperate for energy. Although it is the world's fourth-largest producer of oil, China is also the second-largest importer. China's domestic oil consumption increased about six percent annually between 2007 and 2011, while its oil production remained stagnant (Salameh 2012). China's energy demands are forecast to continue to grow sharply for the foreseeable future, as a result of increasing urbanization and a rapidly growing middle class. As one example, the number of cars on Chinese roads is projected to jump from 40 million in 2010 to 130 million in 2020 (ibid.).

While energy is of primary importance, access to new sources of minerals is also significant. The potential existence of rare earth minerals, used in the manufacture of many electronic devices, would be vital for Japan, which currently gets it supplies from China. (China currently produces 95 percent of the world's rare earth minerals.) When tensions between the two countries have risen in the past, China has restricted exports of the minerals, leaving Japanese companies in the lurch. Japan and the United States have both filed unfair trade practices complaints with the World Trade Organization about Chinese actions related to rare earth mineral exports.

East Asian countries, like many others, are also carefully considering the impact of the opening of navigable waters in the North caused by warming temperatures. Receding Arctic ice raises the possibility of increased shipping routes through northern waters. The three possible international shipping routes are the Northern Sea Route (NSR) (also called the Northeast Passage) above Russia, the Transpolar Sea Route and the Northwest Passage (NWP), which passes along the northern coast of North America (Hong 2012, 50). It seems likely that both the NSR and NWP could become navigable for a number of months each summer, and some estimate that the Arctic Ocean could be free of ice in the summer season before 2040 (Chen 2012). Both routes substantially reduce the length of the journey between North America, Asia and Europe. According to *The Economist* (2012), the NSR "cuts the voyage from Shanghai to Hamburg by 6,400 km (4,000 miles) compared with the southern journey through the Strait of Malacca and the Suez Canal," while Hong (2012) has written that "sailing through the Northwest Passage, rather than the Panama Canal, can save more than 4,000 nautical miles between German and Japanese ports." As Hong writes:

> Taking into account canal fees, fuel costs, and other variables that determine freight rates, these shortcuts could cut the cost of a single voyage by a large container ship by billions of dollars a year. The savings would be even greater for the megaships that are unable to pass through the Panama and Suez Canals and so currently sail around the Cape of Good Hope and Cape Horn. As well as shorter shipping times, the potential benefits of an ice-free Arctic throughway include the ability to avoid dangerous chokepoints beset by maritime piracy. (2012, 51)

According to interviews conducted with representatives of the users of the main Chinese shipping lines, however, none of these firms see Arctic shipping in their short- or medium-term futures. Despite the potential advantages of the Arctic routes, there are potentially serious concerns including "slower speeds across these routes, higher insurance costs, the high probability of delays, and serious risks of damage to the cargo" (Lasserre 2010).

In 2011, 34 ships used the NSR, up from four the year prior, but this is a very long way from the 18,000 ships that use the Suez Canal (*The Economist* 2012). In August 2012, the first Chinese ship and the world's largest non-nuclear powered icebreaker, the *Xue Long* ("Snow Dragon"), crossed the NSR. While the Chinese government and Chinese shipping companies may not have clear policies for these northern routes, China's concerns about the vulnerability of the Malacca Straits, the narrow stretch of water between Malaysia and Indonesia, through which 80 percent of Chinese oil imports currently pass, ensure that China will be monitoring and paying close attention to their potential evolution (ibid.).

THE LEGACY OF THE INACCESSIBLE ARCTIC

For decades, the Arctic did not attract very much attention from the rest of the world. Little scientific information was available on the region and exploration was limited. Those mining efforts that did occur were expensive, time consuming, difficult and ultimately unsuccessful. Only a small number of projects were completed. The post-World War II era saw improving prospects but limited returns. Russia pushed forward with numerous Arctic resource projects, and several major developments occurred in other parts of the region, but the pace and success of mineral exploitation remained very low. Corporations, national armed forces and academic scientists conducted numerous studies to explore and define the natural environment in the region, but prevailing images of the Far North as a vast, untouched and largely unreachable place predominated. There were reasons for the caution. With a few exceptions, led by the Klondike Gold Rush of 1897–1898, the Far North rarely lived up to its potential. Extreme cold, great distances, the lack of decent infrastructure and the high costs of working in permafrost environments deterred most developers. This was the land largely left to the indigenous inhabitants until the 1960s, in part because the world's resource companies had more accessible fields for resource exploration and development in the temperate zones.

The oil and gas sector led the way in proving that the Far North had great potential. The discovery of developable quantities of oil off Alaska's North Slope in the 1960s changed the general perception of the Arctic, as did the improvement of extraction technologies that made it possible to develop the oil and gas fields off northern Norway. Promising finds of oil and, in particular, natural gas in the Beaufort Sea, raised the prospect of a major pipeline from northern Canada to the country's southern pipeline grid, replicating the Alyeska Pipeline that brought Prudhoe Bay oil from Alaska's Arctic coast to its shipping port, Valdez. The proposed Mackenzie Valley pipeline project foundered on a combination of indigenous politics and economic realities, remaining on the planning table to the present.

Over the past quarter century, a conjunction of factors have challenged the image of the Arctic as inaccessible in terms of resource development. The success of selected oil and gas projects has helped, especially after several attempts in Canada's Arctic islands proved very disappointing. New technologies, particularly those related to the safety and reliability of offshore oil drilling and delivery, improved the prospects for rapid conversion of known oil and gas deposits. The urgent global discussion about peak oil — based on the idea that the world was running out of conventional oil and gas and would be massively short of supplies as early, perhaps, as the mid-twenty-first century — combined with very high energy prices drove resource companies to expand their operations into the now reasonably accessible Arctic regions. A similar combination of increased prices and escalating demand for minerals, driven by a growing population, economic growth in East and Southeast Asia, and globalization more generally, likewise generated the exploration funds and industry interest to expand Arctic exploration and development.

NEW EXPECTATIONS: CLIMATE CHANGE, MARKET DEMANDS AND THE ECONOMICS OF ARCTIC RESOURCES

Climate change, however, was perhaps the most significant single force behind changing attitudes toward the North. Since 1980, the Arctic has been warming twice as quickly as the rest of the planet and the amount of ice in the Arctic Sea has dropped by 12 percent (Chen 2012; Bardsley 2011). As the impact of warming on the Arctic became more evident, many nations began to pay closer attention. The Arctic Five had been discussing border demarcation issues, raising the sensitive issue of national sovereignty, but these talks and negotiations assumed new urgency as the potential of newly available energy and mineral resources became apparent. Suddenly, the boundary work that had been completed under the United Nations Convention on the Law of the Sea (UNCLOS) assumed global importance, with the realization that an unfavourably drawn border could, potentially, leave billions of dollars of accessible resources in the hands of an Arctic neighbour. China, South Korea and Japan, with their substantial energy needs, also began paying close attention to both development prospects and political structures in the region. As Friis Arne Petersen, the Danish ambassador to China stated, "The Arctic has moved up the agenda not only in the Arctic states, but among others who see the opportunities of a more accessible Arctic, including China" (quoted in Bardsley 2011).

EAST ASIAN ARCTIC RESEARCH AND PLANNING

CHINA

Modern industrial countries are increasingly realizing the importance of leading or supplementing their economic development strategies with scientific research. Since the mid-1990s, the Chinese have been taking a definitive interest in Arctic science. The Polar Research Institute of China (PRIC) began Arctic studies in 1999. China acquired the *Xue Long* icebreaker in 1994 and carried out research expeditions in 1999, 2003, 2008, 2010 and 2012 in the Bering and Chukchi Seas (Lasserre 2010, 3). The *Xue Long* has numerous laboratories, and weather observation and navigation equipment on board. China recently commissioned a second icebreaker, to be completed by 2014, that will weigh almost 8,000 tons and will be able to cut through ice close to 5 ft. thick (Myres 2012). The settlement of Ny-Alesund, Svalbard in northern Norway hosts China's permanent Arctic research centre, the Yellow River Station, which opened in 2003. (South Korea and Japan also have scientific bases in Svalbard.) China has been strengthening cooperation with Northern European countries (Iceland, Norway and Sweden) with particular attention to Iceland, whose strategic location as a transshipment port could be a key component of a northern route (Wade 2010).

SOUTH KOREA

South Korea is also becoming actively engaged in Arctic research. In 2004, it launched the Korea Polar Research Institute in Incheon. Recently, the Korean government pledged KRW3.6 trillion (US$3 billion) to offshore and Arctic shipping research, led by the Korea Institute of Ocean Science and Technology. There are also plans to construct an advanced offshore research vessel and to develop a submarine capable of working at a depth of 6,000 m. Since 2010, South Korea has been operating the icebreaker *Araon*, built by Hanjin Heavy Industries. Canada has signed a joint statement with South Korea for access to the *Araon* (Liang 2012).

In August 2012, then South Korean President Lee Myung-bak completed his first Arctic tour and visited Russia, Greenland and Norway. Lee and then Prime Minister of Greenland Kuupik Kleist signed two memorandums of understanding (MOUs) on resource development, geological surveys, and Arctic science and technology, focusing on green growth. Kleist then visited Seoul in December 2012, agreeing to cooperate on the development of new sea routes and sustainable development for Greenland. Greenland is rich in oil, rare earth metals (possessing perhaps the world's largest reserves) and other resources. South Korea has also signed a number of MOUs with Norway. One of the more significant agreements concerns environmentally enhanced shipbuilding. Norway has many large shipping companies, and South Korea many of the largest shipbuilding yards. South Korean-Norwegian discussions also focused on establishing new shipping routes and science and environmental technology cooperation.

JAPAN

The Japanese government founded the National Institute of Polar Research (NIPR) in 1973. The NIPR then established the Arctic Environment Research Centre (AERC) in 1990, with a mandate to build on the country's 30 years of polar research. In 1991, the AERC established an observation centre on Svalbard. Japan has also been active in the field of gas hydrates over fears that melting gas hydrates can hasten climate change. The Japanese have three icebreakers: the *Shirase*, operated by the Japan Maritime Self-Defense Force, and the *Soya* and the *Teshio*, operated by the Japanese Coast Guard as patrol boats in northern Japan (Tonami and Watters 2012, 95). Recently, and building from a major gas hydrates research project in Canada, the Japanese government, the US Energy Department and ConocoPhillips began a joint research project to extract natural gas from methane hydrates beneath Alaska's North Slope. Tests of technology to do so ran from February to April 2012. The US Geological Survey estimates that the amount of methane hydrates in the North Slope could heat more than 100 million homes for 10 years (Belogolova 2012).

While East Asian countries have become very active in Arctic research and diplomacy in the early twenty-first century, actual resource investments have been quite limited. To date, East Asia's economic interest in the Arctic is more speculative and anticipatory than substantial. The region is taking a watching brief on an area that may become economically important and that may possess large and commercializable resource opportunities. The situation is somewhat analogous to Japan's very substantial investment in fusion energy, a highly controversial technology that first showed promise some 20 years ago. The country is now the world's largest supporter of the still unproven nuclear fusion technology, which has attracted increased interest since the 2011 Fukushima nuclear disaster. To date, East Asian Arctic investments fit somewhere in the same category — an uncertain field of considerable potential, requiring a great deal of scientific investigation and national government investment, but with few immediate prospects of commercial return.

EAST ASIA AND ARCTIC TOURISM

East Asian interest in the North and, in particular, the northern lights, has sparked an increase in tourists to Alaska, Yukon, Northwest Territories (NWT) and northern Scandinavia. Although none of the Asian countries are prime sources of northern tourists yet, there is a competition for so-called "Aurora tourists" and their future potential. In 2011, Asian visitors accounted for approximately 12 percent of Alaska's international visitors, excluding Canadians. Of the 154,100 international visitors (from outside North America), 18,000 were from Asia, including 6,000 Japanese and 2,000 Korean visitors (McDowell Group 2012, 1). At US$3,440, the Japanese average per person spending was significantly higher than that of other international visitors (ibid., 6).

Accurate figures for international visitors to Yukon, the NWT and Nunavut are hard to track, as these visitors do not require visas and clear customs in Calgary, Edmonton or Vancouver. Yukon tracks visitor numbers through its visitor information centre in Whitehorse, but this does not necessarily register the total flow of tourists. Based on annual Yukon border crossing statistics, 11,892 visitors came to Yukon from the Asia-Pacific region in 2011; of these, 910 were from China and 929 were from Korea (Yukon Department of Tourism and Culture 2012a). The number of Japanese visitors to Yukon has been declining for a number of years; only 242 Japanese visitors were recorded in 2010, although that number tripled in 2011 (Yukon Department of Tourism and Culture 2012b). Aurora tours in the NWT began in 1989 and grew rapidly until 2000-2001, peaking at over 12,000, but dropped off after the 9/11 attacks (Vela 2012). Now about 6,000 Japanese tourists visit the NWT annually and their numbers appear to be constrained by limited flight availability (ibid.).

Sweden, Norway and Finland all receive thousands of Asian visitors, and despite the difficulty of gauging how many of these tourists venture north, Lapland is a popular destination with Japanese tourists who visit Finland, with the number of overnight stays in the region jumping from around 25,000 in 2010 to over 50,000 in 2012 (Multidimensional Tourism Institute 2014). Chinese tourism in Finland showed a 30 percent increase between 2012 and 2013, with a total of over 117,000 overnights stays in 2013 (YLE News 2014). Winter tourism in Norway is also growing and there has been a recent jump in visitors from South Korea and China

(Ryland 2013). Russia has also become very popular with both Chinese and Korean tourists.

EAST ASIA AND OIL AND GAS

Of all of the resource possibilities in the Arctic, energy has attracted the greatest level of interest. A few examples illustrate the nature and scale of the investment. In December 2010, the Canadian subsidiary of Korea Gas Corporation (KOGAS) bought 20 percent of Canadian energy company MGM Energy Corp.'s 60 percent stake in the Umiak SDL 131 natural gas field in the Mackenzie Valley (MGM Energy Corp. 2010). This US$30 million deal for the 20 percent stake in the gas field, the first ever deal by a South Korean company in the Arctic, stipulates that US$10 million of that is due only if there is a decision to construct the Mackenzie Valley pipeline or another project to commercialize production (ibid.). KOGAS representatives also visited Inuvik in January 2011 to look at the possibility of building a liquefied natural gas (LNG) terminal in Cape Bathurst. The Mackenzie Valley pipeline project is still under consideration (the environmental evaluation has been completed but market conditions have turned against the project) so Koreans are considering converting the gas to LNG[1] and then shipping it to South Korea from an LNG terminal. Building a new terminal would take a few years and shipping logistics would have to be worked out. A new type of icebreaker would be needed, but South Korea's Samsung Heavy Industries has the expertise to construct these vessels. Estimates are that a Polar Class 1 LNG tanker would cost approximately US$700 million (Vanderklippe 2012). They require a 10 cm hull, which is twice as thick as Canada's current ice breakers (ibid.). A Cape Bathurst LNG terminal would discourage construction of a pipeline, but northerners are disappointed that the Mackenzie Valley Pipeline has taken so long — and low oil prices mean that the pipeline is unlikely to be built any time soon.

South Korea also bought into the EnCana shale gas project in northeastern British Columbia (BC) and is now exploring the best means of moving the gas to the Pacific Ocean and then to South Korea. EnCana currently holds a 30 percent share of a proposed LNG terminal in Kitimat; KOGAS agreed to take up to 40 percent of production from the terminal (Kitimat LNG 2009). South Korea's general interest, therefore, remains limited: "Korea merely seeks a stable political and regulatory environment so that it can export resources from the region and build ships for that

---

1   LNG is gas that is cooled to $-162°C$, which reduces its volume, allowing for transport.

very activity.... Korea simply sees the Arctic as a space for scientific research and economic development" (Bennett 2011).

Other East Asian interests have been investing in Canadian oil and gas properties. China National Offshore Oil Corporation, through its local firm Northern Cross (Yukon) Ltd., has been exploring Eagle Plain's natural gas basin in the northern Yukon. The Mitsubishi Corporation of Japan has made a US$450 million investment for a 50 percent share of the Cordova Shale Gas project in northeastern BC, just south of the NWT border. PetroChina Company Limited, KOGAS, the Mitsubishi Corporation and Shell Canada Ltd. are all partners in LNG Canada, a project to develop an LNG export terminal in Kitimat, BC (LNG Canada 2014). The project would include the design and construction of a gas liquefaction plant and the facilities for exporting and storing the LNG (ibid.). The natural gas would come from the northeastern section of BC and the Western Canada Sedimentary Basin, which stretches through Alberta and the NWT and into Manitoba and the northern Yukon (ibid.). These projects are, in the main, sub-Arctic rather than Arctic initiatives. They demonstrate East Asia's strong interest in identifying medium- to long-term energy sources, including across the Canadian North, but in a world that has gone past the peak oil debate, they also suggest that the emphasis has shifted from oil to natural gas and from high Arctic supplies to more accessible sources.

EAST ASIA AND MINERAL PROSPECTS

As part of their global search for mineral supplies, East Asian countries have not ignored the Arctic, although their investments here have been more limited and more cautious than contemporary commentary about rapid Arctic development would have it. An overview of China's recent interest, as the leading East Asian nation in terms of Arctic mineral development, illustrates the nature of the engagement. Chinese companies have begun investigating and investing in mineral exploration and development. However, the Chinese currently only own and operate one northern Canadian mine, the Yukon's Wolverine zinc and silver mine. Chinese exploration and investment, though, is increasing quickly. According to University of Calgary professor Rob Huebert, who follows China's economic and strategic activities in the Arctic, "What we're seeing with the Chinese, in [sic] particularly with their purchases in the North, is that they tend to be long term, they tend to offer a premium....They tend not to buy to own" (quoted in Munson 2012). Yunnan Chihong Zinc and Germanium have signed a US$100 million joint venture with Selwyn Resources to develop a large zinc deposit in the eastern Yukon (ibid.). In northern Ontario, a Baosteel Group subsidiary invested in the Eagle's Nest project, which contains nickel, copper platinum and palladium (ibid.). Jilin Jien Nickel Industry Co. Ltd. purchased two exploration sites in northern Quebec (ibid.).

The most significant potential Chinese northern investment is the Izok Corridor proposal by MMG Ltd., a subsidiary of Chinese state-owned China Minmetals Corp (Weber 2012). The Izok Corridor reaches through large sections of western Nunavut, with the centre located at Izok Lake, about 260 km southeast of Kugluktuk (ibid.). The proposal calls for eight underground and open-pit mines producing lead, zinc and copper, and a processing plant for 6,000 tons of ore a day. The project would have "tank farms for 35 million litres of diesel, two permanent camps totaling 1,000 beds, airstrips and a 350-kilometre all-weather road with 70 bridges that would stretch from Izok Lake to Grays Bay on the central Arctic coast" (ibid.). The company also plans to construct a port that could accommodate ships as large as 50,000 tons that would travel through the NWP (ibid.). Although the mine offers many economic advantages (1,100 jobs during construction and 710 permanent jobs for the 12-year life of the mine), there are significant environmental concerns and the Government of Nunavut is considering ways to maximize the life and economic impact of the resource projects (ibid.). Chinese activity is not restricted to Canada. In Greenland, a British firm funded by Chinese interests is proposing a major €1.7 billion iron ore mine. As has started to happen in Canada, the project is to be staffed largely by Chinese workers — 2,300 in total, a move that would add a full four percent to Greenland's population (Seidler 2013).

EAST ASIA'S GLOBAL RESOURCE SEARCH

East Asia's search for resources in the Arctic is only part of a global search for resources.[2] Over the last two decades, started by Japan; followed by South Korea and accelerated by China's growing interest in and need for natural resources, East Asia has launched a global effort to identify, develop and contract resources for domestic use. Quite often, East Asia's interest in the Arctic is discussed in isolation from this global context. It is the global search for resources that is the crucial driver of regional interest in various remote regions. After all, East Asian nations' interests in Arctic resources are largely defined by the availability of comparable resources from more accessible sources. If access to resources is uncertain or threatened, or if the other supplies begin to dwindle, access to Arctic resources becomes more

---

2   The role of China in the global expansion is described in Moyo (2012).

important. Conversely, if key resources are available reliably, more cheaply and with either ownership by or long-term contracts with East Asian interests — as is the general case at present — regional engagement in the Far North remains speculative and future oriented.

On a global scale, actual East Asian investment in the Arctic is very small compared to its engagement in other economic zones. For example, Chinese and Japanese economic engagement in Zambia alone — a landlocked, comparatively stable African nation — greatly exceeds the current level of their business development efforts in the Arctic. This situation is not likely to change soon. The Arctic political interests of Japan, South Korea and China are forward looking, seeking to ensure that long-term prospects and possibilities are not foreclosed by immediate or short-term political decisions. The Arctic is, in East Asian terms, something of an economic fallback, offering alternate shipping lanes if the existing navigation routes run into greater difficulties and resource possibilities if and when cheaper, more accessible and currently secure supplies run out. The intervening time, for the East Asian governments, is best allocated to research and planning, affording scientists, government and business the opportunity to prepare for the possibility of full-scale resource development in the Arctic.

EAST ASIAN ECONOMIC INTERESTS IN THE ARCTIC

Contemporary East Asian economic engagement in the Arctic is much more prospective than substantial. Countries such as Japan, South Korea and China appear to be committed to laying the groundwork — through research, political involvement and early stage investment — for more substantial long-term participation in regional economic development. In this regard, these nations are not much different than Canada, the United States, Germany, the United Kingdom or many other Western countries. Even with peak energy largely off the table due to the development of shale gas and oil, rapidly growing demand for resources will likely bring Arctic resources into play in a major way. There is, therefore, nothing untoward or even surprising about the current level of East Asian economic interest in the Arctic; rather, it shows the activities of governments known for long-term economic planning and state-owned or state-engaged enterprises with strong track records for securing long-term access to essential resources.

What stands out, of course, is that none of the East Asian countries have Arctic territories of their own, and have only sporadic histories of engagement and interest in the region. If anything, East Asian interests in the Arctic speak volumes to the potential medium-term shortage of natural resources globally. There is a strong need for careful and considered planning for the development of the energy and mineral potential of the last major part of the world to feel the full weight of the developers' hand. Within this global context, each East Asian country has a specific Arctic approach that reflects a combination of its national interests and perceived opportunities in the Far North.

JAPAN'S INTERESTS

Japan has been engaged in polar (Arctic and Antarctic) research for 50 years. While the potential availability of new shipping routes and natural resources in the Arctic are significant to the Japanese, the primary aim of its Arctic work legitimately appears to be the protection and understanding of the Arctic environment. Scientific and environmental interests and a desire to protect the Arctic and ensure it is used peacefully are important to the Japanese. The Japanese government believes it has an important contribution to make, one that is consistent with its strong national preoccupation with global environmental concerns. The Japanese Ministry of Foreign Affairs has created an Arctic Task Force to support Japanese policy development on the area, a sign of continuing interest and commitment (Canadian International Council and Munk-Gordon Arctic Security Program 2011).

Japanese industry is monitoring the amount of ice melting with a view to future resource development. Even here, however, "the Japanese industries that have led the discussion on the extent of the opportunities in the Arctic do not believe, based on current evidence, that there are significant opportunities even if the changes continue to occur. For them, there are too many uncertainties to generate the kind of financial benefits that would encourage them to make the substantial investments required to operate in the Arctic" (Tonami and Watters 2012). The Japanese government has, therefore, not received much pressure from industry to prioritize Arctic issues. In 2012, however, the Japanese Ministry of Land, Infrastructure, Transport and Tourism (which deals with shipping), began investigating the feasibility of a northern sea route, so there is a sense that there may be opportunities. Japan sees itself as being involved with the Arctic over the long term and wants a strong and dependable relationship with all the Arctic states (Ohnishi 2013). As Tonami and Watters (2012) describe it, "one can perhaps view the overarching ambition of Japan's Arctic policy as planting a flag today, to be used tomorrow."

SOUTH KOREA'S INTERESTS

South Korea has also been heavily involved in polar research for decades. Previously, most of its focus was on the Antarctic, but in the last decade it has begun research and conducted expeditions in the Arctic. South Korea's research focuses on climate change and marine species. Economically, the country is interested in potential resource availability, particularly LNG and the ability to ship it to South Korea. An additional unique interest in the Arctic region rests with the shipbuilding industry. South Korean companies, such as Daewoo Shipbuilding and Marine Engineering, and Samsung Heavy Industries, are producers of icebreakers and "pioneers in ice-capable oil and LNG tankers and freighters designs" (Canadian International Council and Munk-Gordon Arctic Security Program 2011). Clearly, South Korea intends to pursue its ongoing commercial interest in Arctic navigation.

CHINA'S INTERESTS

China, while a relative latecomer to the Arctic, has now indicated a strong desire to be included in discussions about the region's future. China does not have an official Arctic strategy, but it has indicated its interest in all the major Arctic areas — from scientific research on climate change and marine species, to the potential availability of natural resources, including energy, and the development of new shipping routes (ibid.). Unlike Japan and South Korea, however, China appears to also be subtly indicating that its position as a global power, with a significant portion of the world's population, mandates that it should be a part of any decisions that might be made about the Arctic's future. China is approaching these discussions with caution and diplomacy, but there appears to be little doubt as to its viewpoint. China is, of course, the East Asian country with the most substantial and fastest-growing global resource interests. In this case, the Arctic is a small part of the country's global resource puzzle, more prospective than immediate, more speculative than dependable.

CONCLUSION

Following the economic rise of Japan after World War II, countries around the globe have been wary of East Asian economic interests and engagement. The current response — one of subtle but significant concern about Chinese, South Korean and Japanese commercial imperatives and strategies — is part of an ongoing international preoccupation with the increasing power of East Asia. Many parts of the world responded similarly to the twentieth-century economic expansion of the United States and, earlier, to the resource-driven European race to colonize the undeveloped parts of the world. The Arctic presents a somewhat different scenario. Although the Arctic states have a firm belief in their territoriality and an agreement to proceed legally and scientifically through UNCLOS to resolve outstanding border issues, other countries view the Arctic (and not just the international sea portions of the Arctic Ocean) as a zone of global economic interest.

The Arctic engagement of China, Japan and South Korea lacks territorial or colonial ambition. East Asian countries clearly want to know that they have reasonable, fair and open access to Arctic resources, which they all see as potentially valuable in the long term. In countries such as Canada (which has a very open approach to foreign investment and the export of resources), there are comparatively few issues beyond a largely unspoken unease about large-scale Asian ownership of natural resources. Greenland, in contrast, has not attracted much resource investment historically, and is eager for foreign interest and has welcomed Chinese commitment to local resource projects. Given the high cost and uncertainty of Arctic resource development — there are as many failed Arctic resource projects as successful ones — global interest and investment are essential if the region's resource potential is going to be tapped in a systematic and appropriate manner.

There is, ultimately, no single East Asian interest or policy approach in the Arctic. China, Japan and South Korea each have different approaches to the region and unique patterns of investment and engagement. On the commercial front, East Asian nations are responding on the basis of the known limitations of the national reserves of natural resources and the absolute requirement that they seek international resource opportunities where and when they can find them. In this case, the Arctic is little different than the vast sub-Arctic resource belt, Africa, Central Asia and the other regions where East Asian companies and nations have sizable investments and deeply entrenched interests.

What is unique about the North is that the area is still comparatively little known, necessitating a great deal of scientific research and commercial exploration to identify and define its resource potential. The shortage of economic infrastructure in the vast region, combined with the high costs and technical challenges of developing resources in the area, requires substantial multinational engagement to be completed successfully.

The economic challenge, for East Asia as for the rest of the world, is to be careful not to overestimate the extent of Arctic resource wealth, nor to underestimate the costs and challenges of bringing the resources to market. East Asia's economic interests in the Arctic appear, appropriately, to be long term and speculative, designed to ensure that China, Japan and South Korea can participate in regional development activity if and when it becomes economically, environmentally and politically viable. When this conjunction occurs, the large-scale investments and the substantial and sustained markets that East Asia can bring to the development agenda will, undoubtedly, be of central importance in the international circumpolar effort to capitalize on the resource wealth in the Arctic.

WORKS CITED

Bardsley, Daniel. "China Hunting for Energy Resources in the Arctic." *The National*, November 9. www.thenational.ae/business/energy/china-hunting-for-energy-resources-in-the-arctic.

Belogolova, Olga. "Arctic Gas Project with Japan Off to Fast Start." *National Journal*, May 2. www.nationaljournal.com/energy-report/arctic-gas-project-with-japan-off-to-fast-start-20120502.

Bennett, Mia. 2011. "South Korea's Growing Role in Arctic Economic Development." Foreign Policy Association blog, April 20. http://foreignpolicyblogs.com/2011/04/20/south-koreas-growing-role-in-arctic-economic-development/.

Canadian International Council and the Munk-Gordon Arctic Security Program. 2011. "Interests and Roles of Non-Arctic States in the Arctic." Seminar, Ottawa, October 5.

Chen, Gang. 2012. "China's Emerging Arctic Strategy." *The Polar Journal* 2 (2). doi:10.1080/2154896X.2012.735039.

Hong, Nong. 2012. "The Melting Arctic and Its impact on China's Maritime Transport." *Research in Transportation Economics* 35.

Kitimat LNG. 2009. "KOGAS Signs MOU with Kitimat LNG." Press release, June 1. www.marketwired.com/press-release/kogas-signs-mou-with-kitimat-lng-997610.htm.

Lasserre, Frédéric. 2010. "China and the Arctic: Threat or Cooperation Potential for Canada?" Canadian International Council China Papers No. 11, June.

Liang, Lee Hong. 2012. "South Korea Pledges $3bn to Offshore and Arctic Shipping Research." *Seatrade Global*, July 20. www.seatrade-global.com/news/asia/south-korea-pledges-$3bn-to-offshore-and-arctic-shipping-research.html.

LNG Canada. 2014. "Our Business." http://lngcanada.ca/our-business/.

McDowell Group, Inc. 2012. *International Visitors to Alaska: Alaska Visitor Statistics Program VI.* Prepared for State of Alaska Department of Commerce, Community and Economic Development.

MGM Energy Corp. 2010. "MGM Energy Corp. Announces Sale of 20% of Umiak SDL 131 for $30 Million to KOGAS Canada Ltd." MGM Energy Corp. press release, December 15. www.mgmenergy.com/upload/news/53/01/press-release-2010-12-15---final.pdf.

Moyo, Dambisa. 2012. *Winner Take All: China's Race for Resources and What It Means for the Rest of the World.* New York: Harper Collins.

Multidimensional Tourism Institute. 2014. Multidimensional Tourism Institute PowerPoint presentation.

Munson, James. 2012. "China North: Canada's Resources and China's Arctic Long Game." iPolitics, December 31. www.ipolitics.ca/2012/12/31/china-north-canadas-resources-and-chinas-arctic-long-game/.

Myres, Connie. "China's Second Polar Expedition Icebreaker to Be Built." Examiner.com, August 2. www.examiner.com/article/china-s-second-polar-expedition-icebreaker-to-be-built.

Ohnishi, Fujio. 2013. "The Emerging Arctic Strategy of Japan: Will the Sun Rise Again in the Arctic?" Presentation given at the Arctic Frontiers 2013 conference, Tromso, January.

Ryland, Julie. 2013. "Airline May Attract More Asian Visitors." *Norway Post*, January 16. www.norwaypost.no/index.php/news/latest-news/27979-airline-may-attract-more-asian-tourists.

Salameh, Mamdouh. 2012. "China Eyes Arctic Access & Resources." USAEE/IAEE Working Paper Series.

Seidler, Christoph. 2013. "The Resource Race: China Dips Toes in Arctic Waters." *Spiegel Online International*, January 25. www.spiegel.de/international/world/growing-chinese-interest-in-the-arctic-worries-international-community-a-879654.html.

The Economist. 2012. "Snow Dragons." *The Economist*, September 1.

Tonami, Aki and Stewart Watters. 2012. "Japan's Arctic Policy: The Sum of Many Parts." *Arctic Yearbook 2012.* www.arcticyearbook.com/images/Articles_2012/Tonami_and_Watters.pdf.

US Energy Information Administration. 2013. "Overview." www.eia.gov/countries/index.cfm?topL=imp.

Vanderklippe, Nathan. 2012. "South Koreans Eye Arctic LNG Shipments." *The Globe and Mail*, August 23.

Vela, Thandiwe. 2012. "Flight Woes Stall Aurora Tourism Growth." *Northern News Services Online*, March 8. www.nnsl.com/frames/newspapers/2012-03/mar9_12fw.html.

Wade, Robert H. 2010. "Iceland Will Play Crucial Role in Arctic Sea Route." *Financial Times*, March 4.

Weber, Bob. 2012. "Harper's Cabinet Mulls Massive Chinese Resource Project in Arctic." *The Globe and Mail,* December 27. www.theglobeandmail.com/report-on-business/industry-news/energy-and-resources/harpers-cabinet-mulls-massive-chinese-resource-project-in-arctic/article6752413/.

YLE News. 2014. "Northern Lights Attract More Hopeful Chinese to Finnish Lapland." YLE News, January 20. http://yle.fi/uutiset/northern_lights_attract_more_hopeful_chinese_to_finnish_lapland/7040261.

Yukon Department of Tourism and Culture. 2012a. *Yukon Visitor Statistics: Year End Report 2011.* www.tc.gov.yk.ca/publications/Year_End_Report_2011.pdf.

———. 2012b. *2011–2012 Tourism Yukon Situation Analysis.* www.tc.gov.yk.ca/publications/Situation_Analysis_2011_2012.pdf.

10

Border Dynamics in Eurasia: Implications for the Arctic Thaw

//

Akihiro Iwashita

INTRODUCTION

Borderland security and stability have gained new momentum on the Eurasian continent with Sino-Russian border cooperation and the establishment of the Shanghai Cooperation Organization (SCO) in 2001 on central Eurasia.[1] In comparison with the previous century, the trends of inland cooperation beyond the former Soviet-China area has moved to other regions, including the Vietnam-China inland border and Tonkin Bay reconciliations. Some border challenges, such as the one between India and China, have yet to be settled, but the relationship is at least stable.

In contrast, border issues arising from sea zones around the Eurasian continent have come into focus, with the conflict zone apparently shifting from the middle tier to the southern tier. Tensions between China and Southeast Asia over the South China Sea are growing. The ongoing hostility, since 2010, between China and Japan in the East China Sea is well known. East Asia has also had to contend with challenges overcoming maritime issues, such as the tense relationships between Japan-South Korea, South Korea-China and Japan-Russia.

---

1   For information about the SCO, please visit www.sectsco.org/EN123/.

As the ice-melting process has accelerated in recent years, the Arctic Sea at the northern tier of Eurasia is also gaining interest as a new available space. The discussion over the Arctic Sea currently focuses on aspects such as military competition, resource hunting and transportation rivalry. There are many actors involved, including the Arctic Five (Norway, Denmark, Russia, the United States and Canada); the Arctic "plus" (Iceland, Sweden and Finland, i.e., Arctic Council members); Arctic stakeholders (the United Kingdom, France, Germany, Poland, Spain and the Netherlands, i.e., Arctic Council observers and permanent participants including indigenous peoples); and, finally, newly active newcomers such as China, South Korea and Japan (i.e., recently admitted observers who have long wanted full observer status in the Arctic Council). The movement from East Asia, in particular, should be paid close attention, as the southern tier rivalry over the maritime area extends to the north. The swing between conflict and cooperation around the Arctic Sea will feature in relations with the southern tier border dynamics, in particular those caused by the developing presence of the East Asian countries.

After reviewing the decade-long trends in continental cooperation over border issues, this chapter explores the possible definition of the seas around the Eurasian continent — including the Arctic Sea, the Bering and Okhotsk Seas, the Sea of Japan, and the East and South China Seas — as a proposed "Sea of Eurasia." Drawing on the proposed characteristics of the Sea of Eurasia and comparing the Arctic with other seas, this chapter focuses on Russia's relations with East Asian countries in the Eurasian maritime context.

BORDER SOLUTION AND STABILITY IN INLAND EURASIA

When there are inland border conflicts in Eurasia, resolution typically involves the SCO. Established in 2001, the SCO, originally consisting of Russia, China, Kazakhstan, Kyrgyzstan, Tajikistan and Uzbekistan, was a promising institution for building Eurasian continental cooperation and, factually, it deserved this reputation. The Shanghai Five was born in the process of confidence building of the former Soviet-Sino borderlands on the basis of the four (Russia, Kazakhstan, Kyrgyzstan and Tajikistan) plus one (China) negotiations. The process produced great results, establishing a "non-militarized zone," implementing a mutual inspection regime on the borderlands and supporting bilateral negotiations over boundary delimitation among the concerned parties (Iwashita 2005).

Figure 1: Ongoing Geopolitical Shift from Inland Border Conflicts to Maritime Conflicts

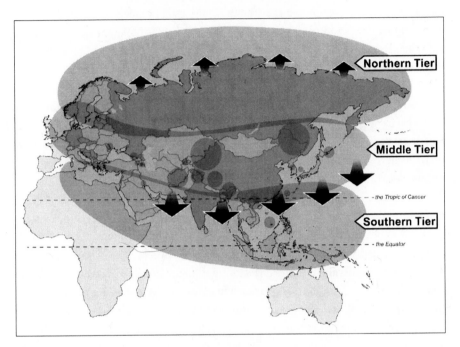

Source: Author.

With the establishment of the SCO, new factors were set in place for border cooperation. For deterring so-called Islamic fundamentalism in Central Asia, the SCO invited Uzbekistan as an additional founding member, a country that shares no borders with China or Russia. The participation of Uzbekistan added a new dimension to the "Shanghai process" that promoted security alignment beyond borders as well as economic and ecological cooperation and other benefits. Uzbekistan, free from the borderland cooperative configuration, brought a kind of balance-of-power approach into the SCO's foreign relations.

From 2004, the SCO's further expansion accelerated the orientation. Inviting India, Pakistan and Iran as observers after Mongolia, the SCO's mission became vague: some casted doubt on the SCO as a co-dominant tool for Russia and China in Central Asia or as a kind of "alliance" against the United States. In 2006-2007, Iranian President Mahmoud Ahmadinejad's grandstanding, in particular, gave the SCO an anti-US and anti-Western orientation (Gill 2001; Menges 2001; Pannier 2007). The SCO has experienced internal challenges, including the fragility of

Pakistan's regime, Mongolia's cool approach, India's lack of strategy toward the organization, as well as Iran's one-sided manner. Additionally, China's plan to let the SCO work as an autonomous economic entity rarely reflects reality, as a variety of individual needs and benefits push members to work for bilateral deals; Russia's ambitions to reshape the SCO in a military context have been rejected by China and other members (Iwashita 2008a).

US foreign policy was defined by long-term indifference and distrust toward the SCO on Eurasia — particularly from 2005, with the SCO's fifth summit in Astana, Kazakhstan, which resolved to terminate the presence of US bases in Central Asia. However, thanks to the SCO's success of keeping "transparency and openness" at its Bishkek Summit in 2007 (Feigenbaum 2007; Katz 2007), US-SCO relations did not worsen, offering hope that the United States would take greater interest in the SCO for peace in Afghanistan under US President Barack Obama's "reset" policy toward Russia.

The SCO provides a good example for reviewing the current ambivalence between competition and cooperation in Eurasian maritime affairs with US involvement. The phenomena are also true for the maritime politics around Eurasia (i.e., in the southern Eurasia seas). The SCO has swung between "openness" to outsiders, with full cooperation of the participants on border issues, and "exclusiveness" toward outsiders, with competition among big players such as Russia, China and Uzbekistan. The SCO faces many challenges in inland Eurasia. Axes on central Eurasia consist of US access from the south (engaging India) as China-Russia deny access toward would-be US involvement. The 2005 Astana SCO declaration, which would have included a plan to block US military access to Central Asia, the 2006 Iranian anti-US provocation fanned by President Ahmadinejad and US counter-reactions were typical phenomena on these axes. Since the end of 2007, there has been an interim peaceful coexistence between the United States and the SCO, but an effective format for cooperation has yet to be identified. Rather, following the calming of conflicts, US indifference toward the SCO is again apparent, as is the lack of new dynamism within the SCO itself, as no new full members have been invited.

EAST ASIA AND THE EURASIAN SEAS: REALITIES OF THE SOUTHERN TIER RIVALRIES

Axes for competition or cooperation are also being formed in the sea areas around the Eurasian continent. One example of this is US access with Japan toward Eurasia activated from the southern seas (even now the US State Department is not as enthusiastic about the "South Asia-Central Asia corridor" as it once was under the Bush administration). The quadrangle collaboration between the United States, Japan, Australia and India has recently been officially announced, and the supposed target is China. The conceptual gap between the United States and China, namely "freedom of navigation" and "access denial" over the East Asian Sea and Pacific Ocean, is mainly featured in this context (Bush 2010). In a broader sense, the axis seems similar to the inland conflictual scheme.

It is interesting to see how Russia will behave in the matter. In a Eurasian sense, Russia prefers enclosure and access denial, but Russia is a partly developed sea power succeeding the Soviet Union's Cold War superpower capabilities. As long as the United States recognizes Russia's influential zone over the maritime area, Russia might share its sea interests with the United States. One important reason for this is that Russia is a US neighbour, sharing the Bering Strait and the Arctic. However, it seems doubtful that the United States would be prepared to respect Russia's exclusive management of their seas anytime soon. It was unwilling to do so in the Cold War period, and the accord was just a product of the Cold War compromise and realist thinking of the interim balance of powers.

Russia's relations with China are more complex. On one hand, inland relations between Russia and China are stable and cooperative. In terms of borderland collaboration, for example, the Bolshoy Ussuriysky Island/Heixiazi Island dispute was settled in 2004, with Russia transferring some control of the island to China; spatial cooperation is not developing rapidly, but progress is steady (Iwashita 2008b). On the other hand, Russia has concerns about the future advancement of China's influence in the Eurasian seas, and Chinese activities in the South and East China Seas and the Pacific Ocean are being cautiously surveyed. Russia would not welcome China's march toward the Sea of Japan and the Okhotsk up to the Arctic, as Russia wants to monopolize this area with Norway, Canada, Denmark and the United States. Russia would face a dilemma between island cooperation and maritime competition (Dodds 2014).

India also faces a challenge. Conventional wisdom suggests that the rivalry between India and China over the development of power naturally suggests a conflictual relationship, which would make US-Indian-Japanese cooperation natural, however, the matter is not necessarily set in stone. Sino-India border disputes were calmed recently, though both countries still engage in frequent verbal exchanges. Some Indians harshly criticize China, while others assert that China is not a threat. The latter camp emphatically differentiate India from Japan's current "Sinophobia" (Khan 2011; Panda 2011).

The maritime discourse also shows there are some similarities between India and China, echoes of which are found in India's claims on the sea order during the 1970 and 1980s. India kept the exclusive economic zone (EEZ) out of other powers' military performances as the United States demanded. India did not allow foreign powers to do scientific surveys within its EEZ and pushed for non-military use on the continental shelf. In short, India followed the principle of the Eurasian concepts of enclosure and exclusiveness in maritime activities. If China and India were to agree to divide the sphere of influence on the seas as well as inland, there would be a collaboration of access denial. It is naive for politicians to emphasize a natural partnership in Indian-Japanese or Indian-US relations simply because they share a common value such as "democracy" (Baru 2012). Sino-India relations could just as easily share the common interest of access denial against an outsider. Who knows which is more relevant or likely to unite countries, "values" or "interests"?

Finally, China's possible metamorphosis should not be ignored. The stereotype of rivalry between maritime and inland powers must not be depended upon. Russia, India and China were traditionally continental forces, but with maritime zones to be exploited, particularly after the United Nations Convention on the Law of the Sea order, there is no telling what axes may be formed in the future. In this sense, the problem should be clarified as conflicts between *developing* maritime powers and *developed* maritime powers. Developing powers feel that the sea is largely controlled by developed powers, and they want to reshape the sea order to be more advantageous for them.

A transformation of China's attitude may be possible. First, from the lesson of the Soviet shift of preference toward a wider available maritime space during the 1970s, a developing sea power could change its stance as it strengthens its power projection in sea areas. This suggests that China could "share" its sea interests with the United States after building up enough power to manage the western Pacific Ocean and the northern part of the "Eurasia Sea." Even if China does not leave the Eurasian nature of "enclosure" on spaces, the maritime order would be reshaped dramatically. If a "Group of Two" (G2) scenario between the United States and China developed into a collaborative relationship, the fact that the maritime order would be dominated by the G2 could not be excluded. How would Russia, India and Japan react in such a scenario?

Japan is surrounded by seas: the Sea of Okhotsk to the north, the Sea of Japan to the west, the East China Sea to the south and the Pacific Ocean to the east. This gives the country an apparent geopolitical role as a maritime power in greater Eurasia.

Currently, Japan plays a proactive role in the management of sea security policy and shares maritime borders with Russia, South Korea and China.

Conventional wisdom dictates that Japan and the United States should be allies as developed sea powers — a fact that holds true for the management of the Pacific Ocean. However, Japan's interests on the maritime order do not align with US interests, particularly regarding the Eurasian seas. The primary reason for this misalignment is that Japan has challenging boundary disputes with its neighbours, including territorial issues such as the Northern Territories and Takeshima, and EEZ issues, including energy resource exploitation in the East China Sea (Furukawa 2011). This means that Japan must soon delimit maritime borders with Russia, China and South Korea to keep the space under its exclusive control, while it continues to share its interests of "freedom of navigation" in the Pacific and Indian Oceans. In addition, the United States is indifferent to the border issues between Japan and its neighbours and just wants the concerned parties to keep the space stable and available to outside powers. The United States' recent "cool" discourse over the Senkaku boat incident in 2010 could conflict with Japan's interests. In this sense, Japan should be defined as a developed, but specifically a Eurasian, sea power. Japan could help by playing an intermediary role between the United States and China and other Eurasian powers.

The US and Sino-Russian contradictions are often seen in various international issues. As far as any mutual distrust among the United States, Russia and China is concerned, India could also play the role of intermediary in Eurasia. This represents a real chance for India to cooperate with Japan, as India has considerable experience with inland cooperation and is increasing its presence in the Eurasian seas. India's role in Eurasia must be defined in the reordering of the Eurasian seas, as well as the continental spaces. A new multi-vectored interaction involving India, the United States, Japan, China and Russia should be pursued for stability and prosperity in a maritime commons beyond the divided areas.

LESSONS FROM CENTRAL/INLAND EURASIA TOWARD THE SEAS

The time has come to create a new type of maritime cooperation in the Eurasian seas. This section returns to the issue of SCO ambivalence and examines how it could be overcome. When US-SCO relations hit bottom in 2006 and 2007, I issued a proposal called "Eurasian Interaction Initiative" for the SCO (Iwashita 2007). The main points of the proposal are as follows:

- Using SCO Charter article 14, the SCO should activate a "dialogue partner" status to involve a new concerned country. This would make the SCO more transparent, and help the organization to acquire more prestige.

- Start an ad hoc status at the summit: "guest" (e.g., Afghanistan). This move would help to prevent potential conflicts with the West.

- Pre-summit interactions would help the SCO to gain a future perspective — a key component that could become a future all-around Eurasian forum.

- Establishing a "SCO plus alpha" format: from a "guest" toward a "partner." Such a move would calm unnecessary noise for "balancing" around the SCO through a build-up of mutual confidence mechanisms with non-member states and groups.

- Linking the SCO and other regional organizations such as the South Asian Association for Regional Cooperation, the Association of Southeast Asian Nations and the Six-party Talks. This would help to strengthen the positive aspects of constructive regional cooperation under global support.

The proposal relied on the experiences of a "contact group" and "guest" with/on Afghanistan and encouraged outside powers to involve the activities of Eurasian inland cooperation in a constructive way. Another key aspect concerned the formation of the "dialogue partner" category. Then, the SCO categories of dialogue partner, "observer" and "full-fledged" member were not adequately explained in the terms. Therefore, my proposal was to develop the "partner" or "guest" status to engage any countries that have interests in collaborating with Central Asia and its neighbours in SCO activities.

The proposal was partly realized. In 2008, the dialogue partner category was established, but only Belarus and Sri Lanka joined. The guest category worked, but only Turkmenistan and a few international organizations were invited. It is difficult to determine the success of the functions. The Obama administration discussed the possibilities of a US commitment to the SCO, but there is probably little chance of this being realized, as a dialogue partner must respect the SCO Charter clause that lists "terrorism, extremism and separatism" as the "three evils." The United States views this clause as a message against US foreign activities in Central Asia.

The only available option would be to use guest status for the previous intensive interactions between SCO members and outside powers. An "SCO plus alpha" format has yet to be established. The SCO plus alpha format with the guest status suggested might include the "SCO plus Japan," the "SCO plus European Union" and the "SCO plus United States." It should be combined like the "SCO plus three." Institutionalization of SCO cooperation with outside powers is a must and even some Chinese researchers support the idea. The time has come for central Eurasia to develop a security commons for all members of the international community. At the very least, we must begin to develop true interaction to halt any unnecessary play-up of "misperceptions" that provoke conflict between the Eurasian inland powers and those outside.

How might the SCO experience be applied to the Eurasian seas, in particular to the southern tier? At the "Energy, Transportation and Economic Links in Eurasia: Emerging Partnerships" conference held at the Institute for Defense Studies and Analyses in New Delhi on January 16-17, 2012, I suggested a new proposal on maritime cooperation, which would see Mumbai serving as a centre for the new organization. Mumbai can cover the Persian Gulf and the Middle Eastern parts of the Eurasian seas, as well as the Southeast and East Asian Seas in collaboration with Kolkata. India is geographically positioned at the centre of the proposed Sea of Eurasia. The concept of a "greater Eurasia," encompassing both continental and maritime spaces, would produce various forms of new expertise on the Eurasian continent and the seas surrounding it, and would help overcome the geopolitical power contradiction on the continental and maritime axes and the stereotype of the US-Eurasian conflict between enclosure and freedom.

India is not only at the proposed centre of the Eurasian seas, but also at a knotted place between central Eurasia toward the seas. This means that a proposed Mumbai Cooperation Organization (MCO), which would include the United States and Japan as full-fledged members, as well as China and Russia, would need to cooperate with the SCO. New Delhi could play a key role in marrying both inland and maritime functions neatly, and the joint program could lead the SCO to a new horizon of Eurasian continental collaboration involving the outside great powers and, in turn, the results could add a thoughtful dimension to the concrete plans of the newly born MCO on the basis of the inland coordinated experiences. With collaboration between the two institutions, a transportation corridor between the hearts of the continent and the wider ocean would have the potential to develop.

THE ARCTIC AS A "EURASIAN SEA": ENGAGING RUSSIA WITH EAST ASIA

How, then, should Arctic rivalry and cooperation be viewed? As the introduction illustrated, Arctic rivalry and cooperation is multifold. Interestingly, Canada's position in the Arctic seems extreme; its assertiveness sounds more "Eurasian" than other Eurasian (or European) concerned parties. Canada exclusively monopolizes the Northwest Passage by claiming the sea lanes belong to its "internal waters," it shares exclusively only with concerned parties (e.g., the Arctic Five) and, finally, it persistently excludes East Asian countries from the current Arctic stakeholders.

The United States seems to hold the key to unlocking the Canadian monopolization of the Arctic. Until now, the United States has been inactive in the Arctic competition and factually recognizes the status quo of the Canadian monopoly. This situation might be changed if the United States offers more openness and availability of the Arctic, as it did in the Eurasian continent and seas. The United States could press Canada to open the transportation route, but it is unlikely to do so, unless such a move appeals specifically to US interests. The challenge is that the United States has a slightly different perception of the North American continent, as the historic Monroe Doctrine demonstrates. The United States does not want other powers to be involved in North American governance, regardless of its commitments (or non-commitments) to other continents. If the United States would back the logic of the Arctic as "a space open to all," Eurasia (Europe) would move closer toward Arctic collaboration. In short, a tilt on the competition and cooperation among the Arctic Five is decisive for the future.

A key for overcoming the Eurasian-North American rivalry remains not only with the United States but also with Russia. Russia holds an exclusive idea on its own Arctic use on the basis of the notorious "sector zone" to the pole, but its "win-win (fifty-fifty)" deal on the Arctic EEZ with Norway and cooperative plans on the Northern Sea Route (also called the Northeast Passage) for transportation with East Asian countries are more open and transparent when compared to Canadian exclusivity (Adomanis 2012). As far as the exit from the Russian Arctic Sea to the Pacific is concerned, Russia-US cooperation over the 82 km Bering Strait is critical for the future availability of the Arctic route to the south.

The featured zone should be the Bering down south to the Okhotsk Sea, the Sea of Japan and the western Pacific. As explained in the previous sections, Japan's Eurasia maritime seas have been kept as available space in this context and, in particular,

Japan-Russia relations must make progress on a southern-to-northern maritime zone (figure 2).

The seas around the Japan-Russia islets are the most important route for the north-south corridor of the Sea of Eurasia. Japan has struggled with making sea boundaries and management with South Korea, China and Russia. A calming of the disputed zones with these nations is crucial to future maritime cooperation, including in the Arctic. Japan-Russia relations are especially pivotal because the area covers the Okhotsk Sea, the Sea of Japan and the Pacific Ocean, covering adjunct spaces from the Bering to the southern tier on the existence of the so-called Northern Territories/South Kurile border challenges. The management of the border issues around Japan, although the territorial claim is bilateral per se, goes beyond bilateral interests, and stability and control should be managed by all of the concerned parties to avoid potential military conflicts and incidents.

Figure 2: Maritime EEZs Claimed by Russia, China, India and Japan

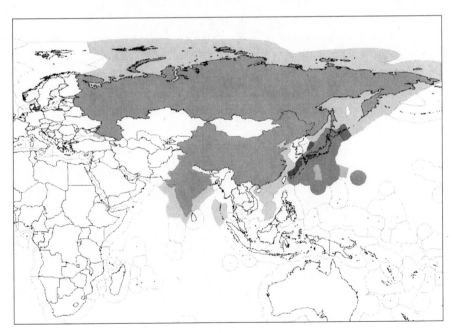

Source: Author.

CONCLUSION: COOPERATION TOWARD A "GREATER ARCTIC"

The lessons drawn from the inland and southern tier cooperation in Eurasia must be applied to the region to foster collaboration between the southern and northern tiers of Eurasia, including the Arctic. The project can be sold as a kind of "Greater Arctic" cooperation. The region consists of East Asian countries that hope to engage themselves in further Arctic-related activities. According to the lessons from the Eurasian inland and southern tiers, the formula of the "Arctic Council plus East Asia" would make sense for a future agenda. A country like Canada, which has been reluctant to accept more observers from outside the region to the Arctic Council, might agree to the agenda if clear borders between the inside and outside were drawn in the formula.

In this case, the city of Vladivostok, Russia's window to East Asia and host of the 2012 Asia-Pacific Economic Cooperation summit, would have one of the best geopolitical positions. The city has good relations with Japan, the United States (West Coast and Alaska), China, South Korea and other Asian countries. The city seems an ideal place to establish an institution, such as a "Vladivostok Cooperation Organization," building a community and managing the East Asian parts of the seas in liaison with Arctic collaboration. This initiative on East Asia and the Arctic, as well as the proposed Mumbai cooperation on the East and South China Seas and the Indian Ocean on the southern tier, would definitely reshape the new world order in and beyond Eurasia.

The last question that arises is this: could the developing trend of inland stability on the continent really be followed by a corresponding growth in maritime stability to the north? New Eurasian initiatives including the Arctic could provide a wonderful way forward, and should be pursued soon.

WORKS CITED

Adomanis, Mark. 2012. "Russia and Norway's Increasing Cooperation in the Arctic." *Forbes*, May 5. www.forbes.com/sites/markadomanis/2012/05/05/russia-and-norways-increasing-cooperation-in-the-arctic.

Baru, Sanjaya. 2012. "The importance of Shinzo Abe." *The Hindu*, December 19. www.thehindu.com/opinion/op-ed/the-importance-of-shinzo-abe/article4214264.ece.

Bush, Richard. 2010. *The Perils of Proximity: China-Japan Security Relations*. Washington, DC: Brookings Institution Press.

Dodds, Klaus. 2014. "Squaring the Circle: The Arctic States, 'Law of the Sea,' and the Arctic Ocean." *Eurasia Border Review* 5 (1).

Feigenbaum, Evan. 2007. "The Shanghai Cooperation Organization and Future of Central Asia." Speech given at The Nixon Center, Washington, DC, September 6. http://2001-2009.state.gov/p/sca/rls/rm/2007/91858.htm.

Furukawa, Koji. 2011. "Bordering Japan: Toward a Comprehensive Perspective." *Journal of Borderlands Studies* 26 (3).

Gill, Bates. 2001. "Shanghai Five: An Attempt to Counter U.S. Influence in Asia?", *Newsweek Korea*, May 4.

Iwashita, Akihiro. 2005. "The Shanghai Cooperation Organization and an Emerging Security System in Eurasia." In *Regional Integration in the East and West: Challenges and Responses*, edited by A. Duleba and T. Hayashi. Bratislava: Research Center of the Slovak Foreign Policy Association.

———. 2007. "The Shanghai Cooperation Organization and Japan: Moving Together to Reshape the Eurasian Community." In *Toward a New Dialogue on Eurasia: The Shanghai Cooperation Organization and Its Partners*, edited by Akihiro Iwashita. Sapporo: Slavic Research Center.

———. 2008a. "Border Dynamics in Eurasia: Sino-Soviet Border Disputes and the Aftermath." *Journal of Borderlands Studies* 23 (3): 69–81.

———. 2008b. "The Shanghai Cooperation Organization: Beyond a Miscalculation on Power Games." In *Japan's Silk Road Diplomacy: Paving the Road Ahead*, edited by Christopher Len, Uyama Tomohiko and Hirose Tetsuya. Washington, DC: Central Asia-Caucasus Institute and Silk Road Program.

Katz, Mark. 2007. "The Shanghai Cooperation Organization: A View from the US." In *Toward a New Dialogue on Eurasia: The Shanghai Cooperation Organization and Its Partners*, edited by Akihiro Iwashita. Sapporo: Slavic Research Center.

Khan, Shamshad Ahamad. 2011. "Indo-Japan Strategic Cooperation: Issues, Expectations and Challenges." In *India-Japan Dialogue: Challenges and Potential*, edited by Akihiro Iwashita. Sapporo: Slavic Research Center.

Menges, Constantine. 2001. "Russia, China and What's Really on the Table." *The Washington Post*, June 29.

Panda, Rajaram. 2011. "Changing Dynamics of India-Japan Relations: Future Trends." In *India-Japan Dialogue: Challenges and Potential*, edited by Akihiro Iwashita. Sapporo: Slavic Research Center.

Pannier, Bruce. 2007. "Eurasia: U.S. Security Expert Talks about SCO Exercises, Summit." Radio Free Europe/Radio Liberty, August 20.

11

The Arctic and Geopolitics

///

David A. Welch
....

PRELUDE: WHAT IS THE ARCTIC, AND WHAT IS "GEOPOLITICS"?

The words "Arctic" and "geopolitics" are fixtures of the English language, although the former undoubtedly enjoys wider usage; "geopolitics" is a term that one is most likely to encounter either in academic social science or in media commentary on global affairs. Yet neither is particularly well defined. This is no coincidence. If you look up "Arctic" on Wikipedia, you will see that it has both natural science definitions and social/political definitions. Everyone agrees that the waters of the Arctic Ocean count, but the application of the label to southward land masses and peripheral minor seas and bays is inconsistent and occasionally contested. The contestation is often political — which is where geopolitics comes in.

The word "geopolitics" was originally coined in 1899 by a Swedish political scientist and rapidly developed into a subfield of its own (Dodds 2007). To some extent, it was a case of putting old wine in new bottles: statesmen, military thinkers, scholars and commentators had long been aware of the importance of geography in world politics. What many regard as the seminal work of geopolitics — Alfred Thayer Mahan's *The Influence of Sea Power Upon History* — had, in fact, been published almost a decade earlier (Mahan 1890). Nevertheless, the word gave the subject a quasi-scientific cachet that helped to establish "claims to intellectual legitimacy and policy relevance" (Dodds 2007, 26). The term was taken up with particular gusto

◇◇◇◇◇◇◇◇◇◇◇◇

by those whom we would identify today as "realists," preoccupied with the art and science of promoting national interest defined in terms of power by manoeuvring for territorial advantage. Primarily politically conservative, early geopolitical thinkers offered justifications for hard-nosed power politics, formal and informal empire, and the high levels of armament required to pursue them.[1] In recent years, however, the term has been embraced by scholars in a wide variety of disciplines, including those who work in a critical or postmodern vein, and whose politics are as likely to be post-colonial as early geopolitical thinkers' were pro-colonial (Dalby and Ó Tuathail 1998; Kelly 2006; Ciută and Klinke 2010; Ó Tuathail, Dalby and Routledge 2006).

Whatever the politics of geopolitics may be, practitioners all share a concern with relating space to politics. Politics is (or should be) about protecting things worth protecting, providing public goods and doing today what needs to be done to enable our children to have a better tomorrow. Not surprisingly, in the field of political science, geopolitics falls squarely in the subfield of international security studies. Differences between old-style and new-style geopolitics can be understood, to some extent, as differences between traditional and non-traditional understandings of security. And so a good place to begin a discussion of the Arctic and geopolitics is to identify what is at stake in the region, looking through both traditional and non-traditional security lenses.

Defining "the region," however — as I indicated at the outset — requires disambiguation. It will suffice for my purposes here simply to define the Arctic as that part of the Earth above the Arctic Circle — i.e., north of 66°33'44". This has the advantage of including territory from all eight member states of the Arctic Council. This arbitrary delineation does not mean, of course, that the issues I discuss here are not of concern to other countries or to the people or territories of the Arctic Council members (that vast majority of both in every case)[2] that lie outside the region.

What *are* my purposes here? Quite simply, to show that, from a traditional security perspective, the Arctic is completely uninteresting geopolitically, and while it is interesting from a non-traditional security perspective, it is truly important only in the one respect that happens to attract the least attention and action from policy makers. Moreover, it is the one respect that forces us to look in the other direction.

---

1 In addition to Mahan, a particularly influential figure was Halford Mackinder (1904); see also Dodds and Sidaway (2004).

2 The one partial exception is Denmark, whose territory, if one includes Greenland, is predominantly above the Arctic Circle, but whose population is almost entirely below it.

Security is not at stake in any meaningful sense *in* the Arctic, but is very much at stake *because* of it.

TRADITIONAL SECURITY

Early geopolitical thinkers were concerned almost entirely with the security of the state against military attack from another state. This understanding of security dominated the field of international relations right up until the end of the Cold War. During the Cold War, the Arctic had geopolitical value in this traditional sense as a result of the premium the superpowers placed on the early warning of transpolar strategic bomber or ballistic missile attack, which required building, manning, supplying and maintaining radar sites in harsh, remote northerly locations. Now that the Cold War is over, however — and in view of technological advances that have shifted the monitoring burden to space-based and unmanned sensors — the region has lost this particular "hard" security value. Arguably, even during the Cold War, the Arctic had relatively little real hard security value, owing to the fact that neither superpower harboured intentions of nuclear attack. The dangers of nuclear war were almost entirely a function of accident, inadvertence, misperception and unintended escalation — any of which would have resulted in massive casualties south of (not north of) the Arctic Circle, regardless of early warning capabilities.

The Arctic never was — and, for the foreseeable future never plausibly will be — a significant theatre of non-nuclear war. No matter which school of military thought one belongs to, it is impossible to imagine that significant military operations in the Arctic will ever be feasible or desirable. Climate, terrain, sea ice, remoteness from economic and population centres and lack of forward base infrastructure all make the Arctic inhospitable for military operations no matter whether one favours decisive engagement (as did Sun Tzu and Jomini), destruction of the enemy's "centre of gravity" (as did Clausewitz) or an "indirect approach" to war through flanking and manoeuvre (à la Liddell Hart) (Clausewitz 1989; Handel 1992; Holmes 2007; Liddell Hart 1929; Sun Tzu 2009; Swain 1990; Wood 2008). The most that can be said for the Arctic's traditional military value is that once in human history — during World War II — Arctic waters served an important logistical function. By means of convoys from Atlantic ports to Arkhangelsk and Murmansk, the Allies helped to keep the Soviet Union supplied in its fight against Hitler (Schofield 1977). It is difficult to imagine the conflict that would require Arctic transit routes in the twenty-first century; Europe and North America are members of a security community, and while the Northern Sea Route (NSR) might be useful for shipping supplies to combatants in East or Southeast Asia, it is implausible to imagine that it would play more than a marginal role given trans-Pacific alternatives.

The Arctic is an inhospitable military environment for exactly the same reasons that it is inhospitable for large-scale human habitation. The 10 largest cities in the Arctic have a combined population of fewer than 900,000 — roughly the same as that of Canada's capital city, Ottawa — and one-third of the population lives in Murmansk, which enjoys the odd status of being ice-free year round, thanks to the Gulf Stream (The World Geography 2011). In any case, there is little in the Arctic to fight over. There is but one territorial dispute (between Canada and Denmark over Hans Island, a 1.3 km² barren rock notable primarily as a source of binational mirth), and while there are a few maritime jurisdiction disputes, there is no indication that any of them is more than a low-grade management issue.[3]

Despite all this, one occasionally encounters alarmist accounts of traditional security threats in the Arctic. These have an air of implausibility across the board, and often trade on mixing up very distinct concepts such as sovereignty and security.[4] They can be useful in bureaucratic political games, however; the Canadian Navy, for example, used the putative US and Russian submarine threats to Canada's Arctic sovereignty to help justify the purchase of four used Upholder class submarines from Britain in 1998, never explaining to the Canadian government, Parliament or people what exactly they intended to do with them if they encountered unwelcome foreign submarines in waters that Canada liked to think of as its own, nor explaining why they were buying diesel-electric submarines that were almost entirely unsuited to Arctic operations. The purchase has proven to be a complete debacle, and yet the "submarine threat" canard refuses to die (Huebert 2012; *The Economist* 2012).

NON-TRADITIONAL SECURITY

While traditional understandings of security privileged the protection of the state as the "referent object" against the threat of military attack, the field of security studies has recently embraced a variety of non-traditional conceptions with a much wider variety of threat/object pairs. We owe the useful distinction between

---

3   Notably, all of the countries involved in actual or potential maritime jurisdiction disputes in the Arctic are either signatories to the UN Convention on the Law of the Sea or are tacitly observing its provisions, which include various requirements for the peaceful settlement of disputes. See Permanent Court of Arbitration (2009).

4   See, for example, Huebert (2009) and CBC News (2009).

"threat" and "referent object" to the Copenhagen School of International Relations, which also brought us the concept of "securitization" — i.e., the process by which problems become elevated from run-of-the-mill political problems to "security" problems warranting extraordinary effort and resources, often justifying the suspension of normal rules (Buzan, Wæver and de Wilde 1997). Five of the more commonly discussed non-traditional security issues of potential relevance to the Arctic are human security, cultural security, energy security, economic security and environmental security.

The concept of human security was first articulated in the United Nations Development Programme's (UNDP's) 1994 *Human Development Report*, which argued that individual human beings were the primary referent objects and that threats to their security were context-specific (1995). Critics were quick to notice flaws in this early conceptualization, not least of which was that it was radically subjective, provided indeterminate guidance for policy, and was difficult to distinguish from both "human rights" and "development" (Daudelin and Hampson 1999; Howard-Hassman 2012; Paris 2004). But it did have the effect of sensitizing both policy makers and publics to a range of issues that caused high levels of death, misery and morbidity, but that had not attracted sustained attention and resources during the Cold War owing to the preoccupation with avoiding World War III. These issues included (*inter alia*) substate conflict, landmines, small arms and light weapons, human trafficking, food insecurity, disease and violence against women.[5]

In recent years, there has been a minor surge of interest in the human security of Arctic peoples (Daveluy, Lévesque and Ferguson 2011; Heininen and Nicol 2007; Hynek and Bosold 2010; Lukovich and McBean 2009). The issues, of course, are not exactly the same as they are, say, in Sub-Saharan Africa or Afghanistan, but they are real. They primarily concern the relative material quality-of-life disadvantages Arctic indigenous peoples experience vis-à-vis the non-indigenous populations of Arctic countries. Life expectancy is shorter and rates of infant mortality, suicide, substance abuse, spousal abuse and sexual abuse are all typically significantly higher. To some extent, these issues are a function of cultural dislocation — the loss of indigenous languages, the erosion of traditional cultural practices and so forth — but

---

5   The three countries that took up human security most energetically in their foreign policy platforms were Canada, Japan and Norway. For a representative Canadian operationalization, see Department of Foreign Affairs and International Trade Canada (DFAIT 2002). The Harper government has distanced itself from human security because it is so closely identified with the previous Liberal government and, in particular, with former Liberal Foreign Affairs Minister Lloyd Axworthy (Davis 2009).

by any measure, the most important factor has been the effective colonization of the Arctic by non-Arctic peoples and the sense of disempowerment and humiliation that this brings. The experience and the pathology may not be unique to Arctic peoples — it is a sad fact that indigenous peoples everywhere suffer similar disadvantages, deprivations and depredations — but the effects are especially noticeable in the Arctic precisely because of the delicacy of the relationship between the land and the people and the combination of small numbers and high dispersion. There are relatively few buffers to cultural conquest in the Far North.

Climate change is, by all indications, an accelerant for human and cultural security challenges. With the warming of the Arctic and the retreat of the ice, traditional ways of life become harder to maintain even where there is the will to do so. One of the great unknowns is food security. The same may be said of food supplies everywhere — climate change models are notoriously sensitive to assumptions, specifications and inputs — but in the Arctic, there is relatively little room for error. It is a particularly delicately balanced ecological zone (Duhaime 2002; Duhaime and Bernard 2008; Wesche and Chan 2010).

Energy security is a rather different kind of problem for the Arctic than it is for the rest of the world. The Arctic's energy needs are modest in absolute terms, and climate change is unlikely to have a dramatic effect on them, either in terms of supply or demand. But climate change may well make the Arctic more important for the rest of the world's energy security and economic security. It may do so in two primary ways: first, by increasing the commercial viability of exploiting Arctic oil and natural gas deposits, fishing grounds and ore deposits; and second, by opening up new transportation corridors. For Arctic peoples, this represents something of a mixed blessing. On the one hand, investment in resource extraction and transportation brings the promise of jobs and improvements to infrastructure and overall wealth; on the other hand, it threatens to accelerate the erosion of traditional cultures and increase the danger of environmental catastrophe.

How likely are these to happen? With respect to resource extraction, it is worth bearing in mind that the Arctic has always been the big payoff lurking just around the corner. Nowhere and never has it lived up to its resource extraction hype. The reasons for this are complex, but harshness, remoteness and lack of infrastructure have always been factors. Tellingly, a fairly recent major study of the future of natural gas refers only five times to the Arctic, once in neutral terms and four times to warn of the difficulties of Arctic gas exploitation (Victor, Jaffe and Hayes 2006, 128-9,

142n, 144, 394).[6] A warmer Arctic may well increase the commercial viability of Arctic fisheries, but there are many uncertainties both about sustainability and the degree to which local populations would benefit vis-à-vis foreign multinationals higher up the value-added chain. Climate change will certainly increase the number of days during which Arctic shipping routes are open each year, but neither the Northwest Passage (NWP) nor the NSR across the top of Russia is likely to become a major shipping artery anytime soon (Lasserre 2011). The prospects for the latter are certainly much better than for the former, for a variety of reasons: it is ice-free a larger proportion of the year; it offers more of a distance savings for a dramatically higher volume of shipping; and it boasts a much more highly developed shipping infrastructure in terms of available ports, icebreaker services, and so forth (Pettersen 2013; Headland 2010). And yet even the NSR's prospects seem modest at best. The unpredictability of sailing conditions represents a deterrent to container shipping, which is highly just-in-time oriented; introduces speed uncertainties, which has a strong effect on scheduling and fuel efficiency; increases insurance costs; and requires shippers to take on expensive Russian pilots (Ho 2011; Khon et al. 2010; Liu and Kronbak 2010; Schøyen and Bråthen 2011; Verny and Grigentin 2009).[7] In addition to being geographically less attractive, the NWP is far less hospitable than the NSR; climate models suggest that it is likely to be ice-free far less often and vulnerable to persistent icing at crucial choke points (Howell et al. 2008). If shipping through either route increases dramatically, it will probably take the form of bulk rather than container shipping — which poses especially acute environmental dangers in case of accident (Lasserre 2011, 806-7).

This last point raises the important issue of environmental security. Commentators univocally note the particular sensitivity and fragility of Arctic ecosystems both to pollution and to disruption. The Arctic and the Antarctic are the two regions of the Earth that have the lowest net energy input, owing to low solar forcing and limited inter-zonal energy transport mechanisms.[8] This significantly extends the time required for biotic adjustment. Put another way: the Arctic would take many times

---

6   See also Moe (2012).

7   Even relatively optimistic assessments of the commercial viability of the NSR flag serious obstacles such as these; see, for example, Xu et al. (2011), but cf. Lee (2012).

8   The major exception to this is the Atlantic Conveyor, which transfers heat from the Gulf of Mexico to Northern Europe via the Gulf Stream — the mechanism that keeps Murmansk ice-free year round at the moment. This "heat pump" is vulnerable to fresh water hosing caused by glacial melting, particularly in Greenland. See, for example, Kageyama et al. (2010).

longer than a tropical or semi-tropical zone to recover from an oil spill or similar disaster. This unusual vulnerability points toward the importance of ensuring that development of the Arctic takes place within the context of strict environmental regulations and robust regional environmental governance.

WHAT'S MISSING FROM THE ARCTIC GEOPOLITICS DISCOURSE?

The discussion to this point would suggest that the Arctic is a region with great potential, but fraught with danger. This is true enough, but the point might be misconstrued. One might be tempted to say that the takeaway is simply to ensure that the development of the Arctic takes place in a cooperative, coordinated, appropriately governed fashion. Traditional geopolitics may not be at stake in the Arctic, but non-traditional geopolitics most certainly is, and it is tempting to draw the lesson that we must move forward gingerly to maximize the benefits and minimize the costs.

This is not the lesson.

It is true that human, cultural, energy, economic and environmental security are all at stake in the Arctic, and that we must take care to avoid harm where possible. But in the grand scheme of things, these are all relatively minor problems:

- Owing simply to the relatively small numbers of people concerned, Arctic *human security issues* pale in comparison to human security challenges elsewhere. In view of the horrific levels of organized violence and exploitation that millions of people experience on a daily basis in failed states around the world, the challenges that Arctic populations face seem more like policy failures than acute security problems.

- *Cultural security* is, in any case, a questionable concept, as culture is inherently dynamic; it cannot be protected from change, and it is difficult to imagine the normative argument that it *ought* to be protected from change. At most, one can argue that it ought to be protected from artificially rapid change, which is demonstrably psychologically disruptive.

- *Energy security* is a challenge around the world, but no more so in the Arctic, and there is little reason to think, despite the perennial hoopla, that the Arctic will be the cure for energy security challenges elsewhere.

- Likewise with respect to *economic security*: the Arctic is more likely to depend upon the national policies of Arctic countries than on grandiose development initiatives originating elsewhere. As for the economic security of the rest of the world, the marginal contribution of Arctic resources in a warming world is not likely to have a material impact, particularly in view of the enormous increase in demand for resources that we will likely see from populous, rapidly developing countries such as India.

- As far as *environmental security* is concerned, the Arctic is certainly a uniquely vulnerable region; but given the likelihood that it will never live up to its resource development and transportation hype, and in view of the fact that environmental disasters such as blowouts, oil spills, tailing pond leakages and other extractive industry accidents will only have local (if unusually persistent) effects, it is hard to make the case that the Arctic will be the site of the most egregious environmental disasters in the years to come.

What really makes the Arctic important from a geopolitical perspective is the threat it poses to *ecospheric security*. This is a conception of security that has yet to make its way into the mainstream of even non-traditional security discourse.[9] The ecosphere is that part of the Earth that does (or could) support life, and its health depends crucially on atmospheric homeostasis and adequate biodiversity — the latter of which, according to prominent climate scientists, may be a precondition for the former.[10] At no time in known history has the planet experienced a more rapid rise in greenhouse gases or a faster increase in mean surface temperature. True, it has been hotter at times, and the atmosphere has borne more carbon; but the crucial consideration is the rate of change. An elastic band will stretch much farther without breaking if pulled slowly, but we are stretching atmospheric chemistry at an unprecedented rate as a result of fossil fuel emissions. The Arctic is relevant here because vast quantities of powerful greenhouse gases — carbon dioxide and methane, in particular — are locked up in permafrost. A rapidly warming Arctic has the potential to shift from a net carbon sink to a net carbon source (Schaefer et al. 2011), accelerate warming worldwide, increase the frequency and severity of wildfires (which, in turn, are powerful causes of warming) (Mooney 2013), increase the frequency and severity of extreme weather events in other climate zones (Greene and Monger 2012), and both alter and amplify global climate feedbacks (Sommerkorn and Hassol 2009).

---

9   The term "environmental security" results in more than 700,000 hits on Google; the term "ecospheric security" results in eight, three of which are from my University of Waterloo course on security ontology.

10   The seminal article is Lovelock and Margulis (1974).

Less ominous than ecospheric catastrophe, but still of concern on a scale that dwarfs any of the local security challenges facing the Arctic, is sea-level rise caused by polar warming (Hansen and Sato 2012; Kinnard et al. 2011; Levermann et al. 2013; Livina and Lenton 2013; Rignot et al. 2011). Arctic sea ice is not a major issue here, except as regards thermal expansion and the effect of salinity dilution on heat transport mechanisms. But the Greenland and Antarctic ice caps are a major issue, as both currently sit on land and are not at the moment displacing their own volume in water. Estimates of the mean global sea-level rise we could expect as a result of polar ice cap melting are, of course, uncertain, but even a relatively modest rise will swamp island states such as Vanuatu and the Maldives wholesale, and will disproportionately affect Asia, the most populous continent and increasingly the engine of the global economy (see Figure 1).

The Arctic is not itself a site of interesting geopolitical value; but it has enormous, generally unappreciated geopolitical value to non-Arctic regions both as a proverbial canary in a coal mine and as a potential climate change time bomb in its own right. Ironically, if we do not find a way to wean ourselves off carbon, the Arctic may itself actually become one of the few remaining places on the planet capable of sustaining human habitation (Hansen et al. 2013; Lovelock 2006a, 2006b; Morgan 2009). Needless to say, there is no Arctic-governance fix to this. It is a global problem requiring an urgent, concerted global solution. This is a problem for which traditional geopolitical lenses and traditional geopolitical rivalries are pointless distractions — and, for this very reason, are serious security threats in and of themselves.

Figure 1: Population, Area and Economy Affected by a 1m Sea-Level Rise

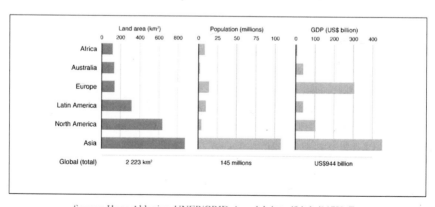

Source: Hugo Ahlenius, UNEP/GRID-Arendal, http://bit.ly/117XpTz.

WORKS CITED

Buzan, Barry, Ole Wæver and Jaap de Wilde. 1997. *Security: A New Framework for Analysis*. Boulder, CO: Lynne Rienner.

CBC News. 2009. "Battle for the Arctic Heats Up." CBC News, February 27. www.cbc.ca/news/canada/battle-for-the-arctic-heats-up-1.796010.

Ciută, Felix and Ian Klinke. 2010. "Lost in Conceptualization: Reading the 'New Cold War' with Critical Geopolitics." *Political Geography* 29 (6): 323–32.

Clausewitz, Carl von. 1989. *On War*, translated by Michael Howard and Peter Paret. Princeton: Princeton University Press.

Dalby, Simon and Gearóid Ó Tuathail, eds. 1998. *Rethinking Geopolitics*. New York: Routledge.

Daudelin, John and Fen Osler Hampson. 1999. *Human Security and Development Policy*. Ottawa: CIDA Policy Branch Strategic Planning Division.

Daveluy, Michelle, Francis Lévesque and Jenanne Ferguson, eds. 2011. *Humanizing Security in the Arctic*. Edmonton: CCI Press.

Davis, Jess. 2009. "Liberal-Era Diplomatic Language Killed Off." *Embassy*, July 1.

DFAIT. 2002. "Freedom from Fear: Canada's Foreign Policy for Human Security." http://bit.ly/1lUuWv1.

Dodds, Klaus. 2007. *Geopolitics: A Very Short Introduction*. New York: Oxford University Press.

Dodds, Klaus and James D. Sidaway. 2004. "Halford Mackinder and the 'Geographical Pivot of History': A Centennial Retrospective." *The Geographical Journal* 170 (4): 292–7.

Duhaime, Gérard ed. 2002. *Sustainable Food Security in the Arctic: State of Knowledge*. Edmonton: CCI Press.

Duhaime, Gérard and Nick Bernard, eds. 2008. *Arctic Food Security*. Edmonton: CCI Press.

Greene, Charles H. and Bruce C. Monger. 2012. "An Arctic Wild Card in the Weather." *Oceanography* 25 (2): 7–9.

Handel, Michael I. 1992. *Masters of War: Sun Tzu, Clausewitz, and Jomini*. London: Frank Cass.

Hansen, James and Makiko Sato. 2012. "Update of Greenland Ice Sheet Mass Loss: Exponential?" www.columbia.edu/~jeh1/mailings/2012/20121226_GreenlandIceSheetUpdate.pdf.

Hansen, James, Makiko Sato, Gary Russell and Pushker Kharecha. 2013. "Climate Sensitivity, Sea Level, and Atmospheric CO_2." http://arxiv.org/pdf/1211.4846v2.

Headland, R. K. 2010. "Ten Decades of Transits of the Northwest Passage." *Polar Geography* 33 (1–2): 1–13.

Heininen, Lassi and Heather N. Nicol. 2007. "The Importance of Northern Dimension Foreign Policies in the Geopolitics of the Circumpolar North." *Geopolitics* 12 (1): 133–65.

Ho, Joshua. 2011. "The Opening of the Northern Sea Route." *Maritime Affairs: Journal of the National Maritime Foundation of India* 7 (1): 106–20.

Holmes, Terence M. 2007. "Planning Versus Chaos in Clausewitz's on War." *Journal of Strategic Studies* 30 (1): 129–51.

Howard-Hassmann, Rhoda E. 2012. "Human Security: Undermining Human Rights?" *Human Rights Quarterly* 34 (1): 88–112.

Howell, Stephen E. L, Adrienne Tivy, John J. Yackel and Steve McCourt. 2008. "Multi-Year Sea-Ice Conditions in the Western Canadian Arctic Archipelago Region of the Northwest Passage: 1968–2006." *Atmosphere-Ocean* 46 (2): 229–42.

Huebert, Rob. 2009. "Canadian Arctic Sovereignty and Security in a Transforming Circumpolar World." Canadian International Council Foreign Policy for Canada's Tomorrow No. 4. http://celarc.ca/cppc/224/224620.pdf.

———. 2012. "Submarines, Oil Tankers, and Icebreakers: Trying to Understand Canadian Arctic Sovereignty and Security." *International Journal* 66 (4): 809–24.

Hynek, Nicola and David Bosold, eds. 2010. *Canada's Foreign & Security Policy: Soft and Hard Strategies of a Middle Power.* Don Mills, ON: Oxford University Press.

Kageyama, Masa, André Paul, Didier M. Roche and Cédric J. Van Meerbeeck. 2010. "Modelling Glacial Climatic Millennial-Scale Variability Related to Changes in the Atlantic Meridional Overturning Circulation: A Review." *Quaternary Science Reviews* 29 (21-22): 2931–56.

Kelly, Phil. 2006. "A Critique of Critical Geopolitics." *Geopolitics* 11 (1): 24–53.

Khon, V, I. Mokhov, M. Latif, V. Semenov and W. Park. 2010. "Perspectives of Northern Sea Route and Northwest Passage in the Twenty-First Century." *Climatic Change* 100 (3-4): 757–68.

Kinnard, Christophe, Christian M. Zdanowicz, David A. Fisher, Elisabeth Isaksson, Anne de Vernal and Lonnie G. Thompson. 2011. "Reconstructed Changes in Arctic Sea Ice over the Past 1,450 Years." *Nature* 479 (7374): 509–U231.

Lasserre, Frédéric. 2011. "Arctic Shipping Routes: From the Panama Myth to Reality." *International Journal* 66 (4): 793–808.

Lee, Sung-Woo. 2012. "Potential Arctic Shipping: Change, Benefit, Risk and Cooperation." In *The Arctic in World Affairs: A North Pacific Dialogue on Arctic Marine Issues*, edited by Oran R. Young, Jong Deog Kim and Yoon Hyung Kim, 39–67. Seoul and Honolulu: Korea Maritime Institute and East-West Center.

Levermann, Anders, Peter U. Clark, Ben Marzeion, Glenn A. Milne, David Pollard, Valentina Radic and Alexander Robinson. 2013. "The Multimillennial Sea-Level Commitment of Global Warming." *Proceedings of the National Academy of Sciences of the United States of America* 110 (34): 13745–50.

Liddell Hart, B. H. 1929. *The Decisive Wars of History: A Study in Strategy*. London: G. Bell.

Liu, Miaojia and Jacob Kronbak. 2010. "The Potential Economic Viability of Using the Northern Sea Route (NSR) as an Alternative Route between Asia and Europe." *Journal of Transport Geography* 18 (3): 434–44.

Livina, V. N. and T. M. Lenton. 2007. "A Recent Tipping Point in the Arctic Sea-Ice Cover: Abrupt and Persistent Increase in the Seasonal Cycle since 2007." *Cryosphere* 7 (1): 275–86.

Lovelock, James. 2006a. "The Earth Is About to Catch a Morbid Fever That May Last as Long as 100,000 Years." *The Independent*. http://ind.pn/12yGf1l.

———. 2006b. *The Revenge of Gaia: Earth's Climate in Crisis and the Fate of Humanity*. New York: Basic Books.

Lovelock, James E. and Lynn Margulis. 1974. "Atmospheric Homeostasis by and for the Biosphere: The Gaia Hypothesis." *Tellus* 26 (2): 1–9.

Lukovich, Jennifer aand Gordon McBean. 2009. "Addressing Human Security in the Arctic in the Context of Climate Change through Science and Technology." *Mitigation and Adaptation Strategies for Global Change* 14 (8): 697–710.

Mackinder, Halford J. 1904. "The Geographical Pivot of History." *The Geographical Journal* 23 (4): 421–37.

Mahan, Arthur Thayer. 1890. *The Influence of Sea Power Upon History, 1660-1783*. London: S. Low, Marston, Searle & Rivington.

Moe, Arild. 2012. "Potential Arctic Oil and Gas Development: What Are Realistic Expectations?" In *The Arctic in World Affairs: A North Pacific Dialogue on Arctic Marine Issues*, edited by Oran R. Young, Jong Deog Kim and Yoon Hyung Kim, 227–51. Seoul and Honolulu: Korea Maritime Institute and East-West Center.

Mooney, Chris. 2013. "More Wildfires = More Warming = More Wildfires." *Mother Jones*, July. www.motherjones.com/environment/2013/07/global-warming-wildfire-permafrost-feedback.

Morgan, Dennis Ray. 2009. "World on Fire: Two Scenarios of the Destruction of Human Civilization and Possible Extinction of the Human Race." *Futures* 41 (10): 683–93.

Ó Tuathail, Gearóid, Simon Dalby and Paul Routledge, eds. 2006. *The Geopolitics Reader*, 2nd ed. London: Routledge.

Paris, Roland. 2004. "Human Security: Paradigm Shift or Hot Air?" In *New Global Dangers: Changing Dimensions of International Security*, edited by Michael Brown, Owen R. Coté, Jr., Sean M. Lynne-Jones and Steven E. Miller. 249–64. Cambridge, MA: MIT Press.

Permanent Court of Arbitration. 2009. "Ad Hoc Arbitration Under Annex VII of the United Nations Convention on the Law of the Sea." Permanent Court of Arbitration. www.pca-cpa.org/showpage.asp?pag_id=1288.

Pettersen, Trude. 2013. "Preparing for Record Season on the Northern Sea Route." *Barents Observer*. http://barentsobserver.com/en/business/2013/06/preparing-record-season-northern-sea-route-06-06.

Rignot, E, I. Velicogna, M. R. van den Broeke, A. Monaghan and J. Lenaerts. 2011. "Acceleration of the Contribution of the Greenland and Antarctic Ice Sheets to Sea Level Rise." *Geophysical Research Letters* 38.

Schaefer, Kevin, Tingjun Zhang, Lori Bruhwiler and Andrew P. Barrett. 2011. "Amount and Timing of Permafrost Carbon Release in Response to Climate Warming." *Tellus Series B-Chemical and Physical Meteorology* 63 (2): 165–80.

Schofield, B. B. 1977. *The Arctic Convoys*. London: Macdonald and Jane's.

Schøyen, Halvor and Svein Bråthen. 2011. "The Northern Sea Route Versus the Suez Canal: Cases from Bulk Shipping." *Journal of Transport Geography* 19 (4): 977–83.

Sommerkorn, Martin and Susan Joy Hassol, eds. 2009. *Arctic Climate Feedbacks: Global Implications*. Oslo: World Wildlife Fund International Arctic Programme.

Sun Tzu. 2009. *The Art of War*, translated by John Minford. New York: Penguin Books.

Swain, Richard. 1990. "B. H. Liddell Hart and the Creation of a Theory of War, 1919–1933." *Armed Forces & Society* 17 (1): 35–51.

The Economist. 2012. "Rock Bottom." *The Economist* Americas View blog, March 7. www.economist.com/blogs/americasview/2012/03/canadian-submarines.

The World Geography. 2011. "10 Largest Cities Within the Arctic Circle." The World Geography, December 10. www.theworldgeography.com/2011/12/10-largest-cities-within-arctic-circle.html.

UNDP. 1995. *Human Development Report 1994*. New York: Oxford University Press for the UNDP.

Verny, Jerome and Christophe Grigentin. 2009. "Container Shipping on the Northern Sea Route." *International Journal of Production Economics* 122 (1): 107–17.

Victor, David G, Amy Jaffe and Mark H. Hayes, eds. 2006. *Natural Gas and Geopolitics: From 1970 to 2040*. Cambridge: Cambridge University Press.

Wesche, Sonia and Hing Chan. 2010. "Adapting to the Impacts of Climate Change on Food Security among Inuit in the Western Canadian Arctic." *EcoHealth* 7 (3): 361–73.

Wood, Jason D. 2008. "Clausewitz in the Caliphate: Center of Gravity in the Post–9/11 Security Environment." *Comparative Strategy* 27 (1): 44–56.

Xu, Hua, Zhifang Yin, Dashan Jia, Fengjun Jin and Hua Ouyang. 2011. "The Potential Seasonal Alternative of Asia–Europe Container Service Via Northern Sea Route under the Arctic Sea Ice Retreat." *Maritime Policy & Management* 38 (5): 541–60.

12

East Asian States and the Pursuit of Arctic Council Observer Status

//

James Manicom and P. Whitney Lackenbauer
••

INTRODUCTION

The tremendous changes taking place in the Arctic have attracted worldwide attention, often to the discomfort of Arctic states and peoples.[1] The growing interest of East Asian states in regional issues is clear evidence of this trend. All three major East Asian states — China, Japan and South Korea — have active polar research programs and applied for permanent observer status at the Arctic Council in 2009. Their interest has met with concern in several quarters, not least because of China's perceived belligerence in its own claimed maritime areas and because of the misperception that it claims some portion of the Arctic Ocean (Chang 2010).[2] Combined with wrinkles over the European Union's bid for Arctic Council observer status and the growing global attentiveness to Arctic issues by countries as diverse as Italy, India and Singapore, recent scholarship has focused on the potential hidden

---

1   This paper is an extension of ideas presented in Manicom and Lackenbauer (2013).

2   Vice-Admiral Yin Zhou was actually speaking in the context of China's broader maritime strategy and referring to the area in the central Arctic Ocean that is beyond national jurisdiction. See Luo (2010).

agendas of non-Arctic states (particularly China) vis-à-vis the region's resource potential (Lasserre 2010; Jakobson 2010; Wright 2011a). Although other applicants (such as Japan) argue that the Arctic Council should welcome their ongoing participation, particularly given their strong track record in polar scientific research, these participants' perspectives on navigation and shipping in Arctic waters may conflict with some Arctic coastal state positions (Byers 2012; Wright 2011b). This chapter begins to explore the attitude of East Asian states toward Arctic governance by focusing on their bids for observer status in the Arctic Council — a status extended to China, South Korea, Japan, India, Singapore and Italy at the Arctic Council meeting in Kiruna, Sweden on May 15, 2013 (Arctic Council Secretariat 2013, 6).

The Arctic Council is a unique regional governance forum that is wrestling with growing international exposure. It consists of eight Arctic member states with voting rights and six non-voting permanent participants (PPs) representing indigenous peoples of the region who shape the agenda and bring expertise to the council's work. They are joined by observer states and non-governmental organizations (NGOs) that attend ministerial, senior arctic official, and working group meetings. They also contribute to the council's activities, which, to date, have focused mainly on sharing scientific data and mitigating environmental problems.

Although widely considered the primary multilateral forum for addressing regional governance questions confronted by Arctic states and inhabitants, commentators continue to debate the Arctic Council's mandate and membership. In light of the much-publicized impacts of global warming on the Arctic environment, as well as rising interest in emerging maritime transit routes and access to natural resources, China, Japan, India, Singapore, Italy and the European Union expressed interest in joining the council as observers.[3] Problematically, no clear mechanism to incorporate new observers existed until 2011, leading some commentators to question the underpinnings of the Arctic Council itself, given that it was never intended to be a formal, legally binding institution (Koivurova 2009; Koivurova and VanderZwaag 2007). After a period of considerable reticence, Nordic countries issued statements of unanimous support for granting observer status to these non-Arctic applicants in early 2013. Even Norway, which China sanctioned following the Nobel Peace Prize awarded to Chinese dissident Liu Xiaobo, expressed its support for China's bid at the January 2013 Arctic Council meeting in Tromso, Norway.

---

3   Several of these countries had previously secured ad hoc observer status on a biannual basis.

Despite the favourable consensus reached at the Kiruna meeting in May 2013, council members remain cautious about the practical role that observers should play in the institution's activities. The five Arctic coastal states (Canada, Denmark, Norway, Russia and the United States) are wary of any attempt to bring non-coastal state interests to bear on maritime delimitation in the Arctic Ocean, not least because boundary delimitation processes can be lengthy and politically charged (Manicom 2011). The European Union and various scholars have recommended an Antarctic Treaty model to manage regional issues, but the Arctic Council member states have soundly rejected this proposal in favour of the existing United Nations Convention on the Law of the Sea (UNCLOS)-based regime that acknowledges coastal state sovereignty and sovereign rights in the Arctic Ocean (Airoldi 2008; Koivurova, Molenaar and VanderZwaag 2010).

The PPs, meanwhile, express concern when states (or international organizations) do not appear sensitive to the interests of Arctic indigenous peoples. For example, Terry Audla, president of Inuit Tapiriit Kanatami (ITK), suggested in February 2013 that the applications from China and the European Union needed to be looked at "more closely" to ensure that the countries would respect Aboriginal rights (quoted in Gregoire 2013). Most notably, indigenous representatives have vigorously protested EU restrictions on trade in marine mammal products — which helps to explain their opposition to extending observer status to the European Union (Arctic Athabaskan Council 2008). Former ITK leader Mary Simon (2011) asserted that "Inuit will welcome the presence of the EU in the Arctic Council when and if the EU strikes down its legislation aimed at destroying an important and traditional element of our economy." The council shelved the European Union's application at the Kiruna meeting pending the outcome of this dispute (Arctic Council Secretariat 2013, 6).

This chapter examines East Asian nations' pursuit of observer status at the Arctic Council. It begins with a general reflection on their interests in the Arctic, followed by a brief background on council observers (including the criteria for this status laid out in the 2011 Nuuk Declaration) and the formal applications by China, Japan and South Korea. Despite concerns that Asian state involvement in the Arctic Council may dilute the power of member and permanent states, denying Asian states observer status — and thus forcing them to pursue Arctic discussions in other fora — would undermine the council's place as the premier regional forum for high-level discussion. The real challenge will lie in accommodating non-Arctic states' rising ambitions and perceived stake in regional issues in a manner that reconciles global interests with those of Arctic states and peoples.

EAST ASIAN INTERESTS IN THE ARCTIC

By virtue of their geographic location and export-oriented economies, China, Japan and South Korea perceive Arctic issues in similar ways. All three states justify their circumpolar interests in global terms: the changing climate in the Arctic affects weather patterns in all states; year-round shipping through the Northern Sea Route (NSR) could bring global shifts, which would affect local waters and regional logistics patterns; and finally, all three countries perceive access to energy resources through a security lens and have proven that they are prepared to pay a premium for secure supplies (Vivoda and Manicom 2011; Herberg 2004). Although an effort to locate these countries' Arctic interests in their wider foreign policy interests is beyond the scope of this chapter, it is worth considering that the Arctic does not factor very highly on these agendas relative to other national and regional priorities, including bilateral relations with some Arctic states.

CHINA

China's interests in the Arctic relate to scientific research, particularly climate change, shipping and resource exploitation. The Arctic states view China's Arctic ambitions with more apprehension than any other state, primarily because of the misinterpretations of its views on sovereignty and sovereign rights in the Arctic.

Viewed through the lens of China's official statements, its two primary Arctic concerns relate to climate change and associated scientific research efforts. Speaking to Norway's High North Study Tour in 2010, Assistant Foreign Minister Liu (2010) argued that China is exposed to Arctic weather patterns by virtue of geography. The Arctic region is an ideal place to conduct scientific research on the global climate. To this end, China established a research station at Svalbard in 2004 and has been conducting polar research trips using its icebreaker (the *Xue Long*) with greater tempo for over a decade.

Liu (2010) classified economic interests, such as shipping and energy issues, as another Chinese priority. Roughly 46 percent of the country's GDP comes from international trade, making the NSR's shorter distance to Europe — offering approximately 3,455 nautical miles in savings compared to the Suez Canal and Malacca Strait routes — particularly appealing. Furthermore, 80 percent of China's imported oil travels through the Malacca Strait, making the prospect of blockade a legitimate source of anxiety for Chinese leaders (Lanteigne 2008). The opening of the NSR could allow China to diversify the direction of its resource imports and secure access to new import sources in the Arctic. Furthermore, although Arctic shipping may not be amenable to the just-in-time delivery of manufactured products, the NSR's shorter distance is appealing as Chinese manufacturers seek to open new markets in the European Union (Weber 2010).

Yang Jian, vice president of the Shanghai Institute for International Studies, suggests that China views Arctic affairs in two broad categories: regional issues that are appropriately managed by the Arctic states, given China's respect for the sovereignty and sovereign rights of the Arctic countries; and those with global implications. In the latter case, he argues that:

> China maintains that global Arctic affairs need to be handled through global governance and multi-party participation, because such trans-continental issues as climate change, ice melting, environmental pollution and ecological crisis all pose serious challenges to humankind as a whole and cannot be solved by any single country or region. Instead, solving them requires that all nations work together to provide the necessary public goods that Arctic governance entails. Certainly, countries of the region bear more responsibilities in Arctic affairs, yet non-Arctic countries also have their interests and responsibilities to assume. As an important international body leading the governance of Arctic issues, the Arctic Council should provide *an inclusive and open platform* that can bring in all the positive forces to facilitate good governance for the Arctic and for the planet. Such is the rationale behind China's bid for permanent observer status in the Arctic Council. (Yang 2012; emphasis added)

As a function of these interests, there is little doubt that China perceives itself as an Arctic stakeholder capable of contributing to Arctic governance.

JAPAN

Japan's interests in the Arctic also relate to scientific research, shipping and resource exploitation. Japan has had an active polar research program for over 50 years and set up a research station at Svalbard in 1991. In terms of shipping, Japan boasts the world's third-largest economy and relies heavily on trade to transport goods as part of a regional and increasingly global supply chain. Similarly, Japan relies heavily on imported oil and liquefied natural gas (LNG) to meet its energy needs, a condition that has been exacerbated since the country shut down its nuclear reactors after the "Triple Disaster" in March 2011. Japanese scholars note the 40 percent reduction in distance that the NSR offers over current routes, and also point out that the NSR avoids the threat of piracy in Southeast Asia and the Gulf of Aden (Ishihara 2012). This is enticing to a country that perceives energy supplies as a security issue (Energy Security Study Group 2006). Japan is also interested in resource exploitation in the Arctic, and the state-backed Japan Oil, Gas and Metals National Corporation is close to financing stakes in waters off northeast Greenland and in Siberia (Ocean Policy Research Foundation [OPRF] 2012a, 8).

Although Japan has not yet produced an Arctic policy document, its official statements have a common point of departure: it is interested in the Arctic because of the changing climate, which creates, according to Hidehisa Horinouchi (2010), Japan's Director-General of International Legal Affairs Bureau, "new potential for international cooperation in the Arctic" in the areas of newly open passages and the development of natural resources. Japan's stated Arctic interests include the environment, navigation, natural resources and the international legal framework. The OPRF, a Japanese think tank, adds national security and contributions to international order to this list (OPRF 2012a, 13-14).

Japanese sources also indicate that emerging legal norms in the Arctic affect Japan, which, along with Arctic coastal states, is actively engaged in the process of making claims to an extended continental shelf and joined Canada, Denmark and the United States in protesting Russia's first submission to the UN Commission on the Limits of the Continental Shelf (UNCLCS) in 2001, albeit on different grounds. Although Arctic states affirmed their adherence to UNCLOS principles in 2008, Japan has interests in navigation as a self-identified "maritime state" that run counter to the views of some Arctic states. In addition to its long-standing contributions to the Arctic Council, Japan vigorously pursues Arctic-related issues in the International Maritime Organization. Japanese think tanks, such as the OPRF, have been active in the mapping and surveying of the NSR since the late 1990s (Ship & Ocean Foundation 2001).

SOUTH KOREA

South Korea is the world's largest shipbuilder, the second-largest importer of LNG and the world's fifteenth-largest economy. Its interests are similar to China and Japan, as they relate to shipping and resource exploitation. No other non-Arctic country stands to benefit as much from the surge in Arctic shipping as South Korea, whose shipping industry is already leading the way in the construction of LNG and bulk carriers with ice-breaking capabilities (Korea Offshore & Shipbuilding Association 2011, 10). Secure Arctic shipping supports South Korea's trade relations with the

European Union and facilitates LNG imports from Russia and Norway. South Korea signed a memorandum of understanding with Norway on Arctic shipping in September 2012 and has already taken delivery of gas condensate from Russia and kerosene from Finland (Bennett 2012). Like Japan and China, South Korea also perceives energy supply as a security issue and is investing in frontier energy projects worldwide, including in the Arctic (see Shin 2012). Executives from Korea Gas Corporation, the state-owned gas company, visited Inuvik in 2011 to explore the feasibility of building an LNG terminal at Cape Bathurst, Northwest Territories, in case their preferred option (the Mackenzie Valley pipeline) fails (Vanderklippe 2011; Bennett 2011).

South Korea's polar research program is more modest than that of Japan or China, but it is expected to grow dramatically over the next decade. South Korea opened the King Sejong station in Antarctica in 1989 and the Dasan research station at Svalbard in 2002. It launched its first icebreaker, the *Araon*, in 2010. It will complete a new Antarctic station in 2014 and is a world leader in the study of meteorites, 70 percent of which strike near the South Pole.

Clearly, East Asian states see themselves as having considerable Arctic interests. Furthermore, two of these states are democratic countries that are members of the Group of 20 and the Organisation for Economic Co-operation and Development. Nevertheless, in advance of the May 2013 Arctic Council ministerial meeting held in Kiruna, Sweden, citizens of the Arctic countries indicated lingering mistrust of Asian intentions for the circumpolar north — much of which is directed toward China. According to recent survey data, citizens of Arctic states ranked China as their least-preferred partner in Arctic affairs (save Russia, which ranks the United States as its least-preferred partner) (Ekos Research Associates 2011, 57). Because this survey did not include other non-Arctic states, it is unclear whether this mistrust is unique to China or extends to other non-Arctic states. In a separate poll of "Asia practitioners" conducted by the Asia-Pacific Foundation of Canada (2013, 10), a greater Chinese role in Arctic governance was favoured over a greater role by India, Singapore and South Korea. This may reflect a wariness of "latecomers" arriving on the Arctic scene, with their motivations still unclear and their record unproven.

THE ARCTIC COUNCIL AND THE OBSERVER STATUS QUESTION

Observer status is open to non-Arctic states, governmental organizations (e.g., parliamentary) and NGOs. When the Arctic states created the Arctic Council in

1996, the "permanent" observers included France, Germany, the Netherlands, Poland, Spain, the United Kingdom, the UN Development Programme and the International Arctic Sciences Committee. According to council rules, observers participate in meetings at the discretion of the member states and the permanent participants, do not enjoy any decision-making power and sit adjacent to (but not at) the main table. They can, however, propose ideas with permission from a member state and can contribute to the work of the council's six working groups. If observers engage in activity that is at odds with the Arctic Council Declaration, they can be suspended. Other states that do not have official observer status but want to attend Arctic Council meetings need to apply annually and can be accepted on an ad hoc basis.

Recently, actors that perceive themselves as having lasting interests in Arctic issues, such as the European Union, have pushed for a mechanism to allow them to become "permanent" observers. This desire partly reflects the burdensome application process for ad hoc observer status that begins 180 days before the biannual meeting. Aspiring observers must catalogue their ability to contribute to the council's work — an exercise that some perceive as insulting, particularly if they have been active in the working groups. In 2009, China, the European Union and South Korea all applied for observer status, indicating that they sought it on a permanent basis.[4] The council rejected their applications because it did not have a mechanism to add new observers to the group. Accordingly, the council set to work developing criteria that would guide its consideration of future applications (along with the existing criteria that observers contribute to the work of the council).

The Nuuk Declaration, reached at the Seventh Ministerial Meeting of the Arctic Council on May 12, 2011, set out criteria stipulating that observers must:

- accept and support the objectives of the Arctic Council defined in the Ottawa declaration;

- recognize Arctic states' sovereignty, sovereign rights and jurisdiction in the Arctic;

- recognize that an extensive legal framework applies to the Arctic Ocean, including the Law of the Sea, and that this framework provides a solid foundation for responsible management of this ocean;

---

4   In addition to the three East Asian states examined in this chapter, Italy, Singapore, India and the European Union have also applied for observer status, along with five intergovernmental organizations and NGOs, including Greenpeace and the Association of Oil and Gas Producers.

- respect the values, interests, culture and traditions of Arctic indigenous peoples and other Arctic inhabitants;

- have demonstrated a political willingness, as well as financial ability, to contribute to the work of the PPs and other Arctic indigenous peoples;

- have demonstrated their Arctic interests and expertise relevant to the work of the Arctic Council; and

- have demonstrated a concrete interest and ability to support the work of the Arctic Council, including through partnerships with member states and PPs bringing Arctic concerns to global decision-making bodies.

In addition, the Nuuk Declaration placed constraints on observers' participation in the council. The statement reaffirmed that observers are there to observe and may not make statements. They are expected to contribute to the working groups and may, at the discretion of the chair, make statements and submit documents. At ministerial meetings, observers could submit written statements but could only propose projects through an Arctic state or PP. Furthermore, the level of financial contribution provided by the observer to a working group or project may not exceed that provided by the Arctic states, unless permitted by the Senior Arctic Officials. Furthermore, observer status is subject to review every four years, at which time observer states are expected to reiterate their interest in retaining this status and to share information about their activities in and contributions to the Arctic Council.

APPLICATIONS BY EAST ASIAN STATES FOR OBSERVER STATUS

China has participated as an ad hoc observer to the Arctic Council since 2007. In late 2011, it submitted a formal application to become an observer in accordance with the prevailing criteria and procedures. Although these applications are not public documents, official Chinese statements provide insight into the country's rationale for and interest in seeking this status. On November 6, 2012, Lan Lijun, China's ambassador to Sweden, argued that the participation of more non-Arctic states as observers would have a "positive significance to the work of the council" (Lan 2012). He recognized that much of the region fell under national jurisdiction of Arctic states, which had specific interest in issues such as environmental protection, resource exploration, indigenous affairs and socio-economic development. His message was reassuring: "The participation of observers does not prejudice the dominant role of Arctic states in the council....The participation of observers in the work of the council is based on the recognition of Arctic states' sovereignty, sovereign rights and jurisdiction in the Arctic as well as their decision-making power in the council" (ibid.).

Issues like climate change and international shipping, however, transcend the region. Arctic and non-Arctic states have common interests in addressing these global issues, Lan suggested, and could do so through improved communication and cooperation. "By accepting observers and therefore enhancing its openness and inclusiveness, the Council will help the international community to better appreciate its work, thus expanding its international influence," he argued. "Its exchanges and cooperation with the observers will help it review trans-regional issues from a broader perspective, which will facilitate effective settlement of relevant issues through international cooperation. This model of cooperation has been effective in addressing issues such as climate change and international shipping, and deserves further promotion. The council should well respond to the desire expressed by relevant parties to participate in the work of the council as observers" (ibid.).

Casting China as a "near Arctic state," Ambassador Lan also emphasized the significant impact that climate change and resource development in the Arctic had "on China's climate, ecological environment, agricultural production as well as social and economic development" (ibid.). Accordingly, China continues to invest in scientific research in the region — something best accomplished through cooperation with other states. The ambassador's message sought to reassure the member states that China's participation would not destabilize the council or the region. In reaffirming the importance of "communication and dialogue with Arctic states on Arctic issues to enhance mutual understanding and trust," as well as China's willingness and ability "to contribute to the work of the council and to strengthen cooperation with states in the Council for the peace, stability and sustainable development in the Arctic region," the ambassador's remarks corroborate recent findings that China fears being excluded from Arctic institutions (ibid.; Jakobson and Peng 2012).

The Japanese delegation issued a statement to the 2011 Arctic Council ministerial meeting, arguing unequivocally that it was doing its best to meet the criteria set out by the council. Japan is particularly proud of its polar research credentials and uses these to link its work on the environment and sustainable development with the Arctic Council mandate. The delegation's official statement argued that "with the knowledge and experience acquired through the aforementioned research activities, Japan believes that it can contribute to the work of the Arctic Council in a constructive way" (Delegation of Japan 2011). In 2012, Japan raised the profile of its participation by sending Senior Vice Minister of Foreign Affairs Shuji Kira to attend a meeting in Stockholm with the Swedish chair and the observers. Speaking to the Nuuk criteria, Kira stressed Japan's participation at the working group level, particularly in the Arctic Monitoring and Assessment Program (AMAP), and then reiterated Japan's polar research credentials (Kira 2012). Kira also mentioned Japan's own indigenous people, the Ainu, as evidence that Japan respects the values of the Arctic indigenous people and clearly stated Japan's recognition of the sovereignty of Arctic countries. Kira further noted that Japan had been present as an observer at the first Arctic Environmental Protection Strategy meeting in 1996.[5] While intended to indicate the long-standing nature of Japan's interest in the council's work, this may speak to a deeper Japanese resentment of the need to go through the process of requesting observer status at all. One Japanese diplomat pointed out that Japan has been active in the region for longer than many Arctic countries and thus does not see itself as a newcomer to Arctic politics, particularly since Japan was present at the council's creation.[6]

South Korea has been an ad hoc observer to the Arctic Council since 2008. Like the other East Asian states, Korean officials place tremendous weight in their scientific research credentials, in particular membership to international bodies like the Inter-Agency Standing Committee, the International Arctic Social Science Association (both Arctic Council observers) and the Association of Polar Early Career Scientists. In particular, Korean scientific capacity and credentials are perceived to intersect with the work of the Arctic Contaminants Action Plan, AMAP, the Conservation of Arctic Flora and Fauna, and the Protection of the Arctic Marine Environment working groups. Discussions with officials at the Korean Polar Research Institute (KOPRI) reveal excitement at the prospect of engaging the council more fully, although Arctic policy coordination is centred in the Korean Ministry of Foreign Affairs. South Korea appears willing to cooperate with any working group partner to boost its profile in the council. Indeed, one Korean official revealed tremendous pride in South Korea being the only ad hoc observer present at a council meeting on ecosystem management in October 2012.[7]

---

5   By this, the ambassador likely means the first meeting of the Arctic Council, which absorbed the Arctic Environmental Protection Strategy in 1996.

6   Pers. comm., official in International Legal Affairs Bureau, MoFA, July 27, 2011, Tokyo.

7   Pers. comm., KOPRI official, December 4, 2012, Seoul.

CHALLENGES FOR THE ARCTIC COUNCIL

The question of whether to include non-Arctic states presented a considerable challenge to the Arctic Council. All East Asian states see themselves as maritime states, and as such, are aware that the council is not the only, or even the most important, pillar of Arctic governance. Other global and regional organizations — including the International Maritime Organization, the International Arctic Science Committee, the International Association of Classification Societies, the Conference of Arctic Parliamentarians, the Barents Euro-Arctic Council and the United Nations — have competencies that overlap, or are not even covered by the Arctic Council's mandate (Takei 2011, 62–8). According to some Chinese scholars, this diversity of institutions suggests that "a political valid and legally binding Arctic governance system has yet to be established" (Cheng 2011). In the earliest official Chinese statement on the Arctic, Assistant Minister of Foreign Affairs Hu Zhenyue insisted that "Arctic countries should protect the balance between the interests of states with shorelines in the Arctic Ocean and the shared interests of the international community" (cited in Campbell 2012, 3). Indeed, the OPRF advocates that Japan contribute to international governance in the Arctic through the entirety of relevant international bodies, because "the importance of the appropriate management of the Arctic Ocean is not only the concern of coastal states, but that of the whole world" (OPRF 2012b, 8). The OPRF (2012a, 15) thus favours leveraging the entirety of relevant international institutions to foster a coherent governance arrangement in the Arctic.

A second and related challenge relates to East Asian state perceptions that Arctic states seek to exclude them from Arctic governance. Some Chinese scholars criticized the Nuuk criteria as raising the political threshold for non-Arctic states to join the council, at a time when "it is unimaginable that non-Arctic states will remain users of Arctic shipping routes and consumers of Arctic energy without playing a role in the decision-making process" (Cheng 2011). Some Koreans also harbour inherent suspicions of council efforts to establish a regime for Arctic shipping that does not include user states. In this view, "countries whose interest would be affected by this development have a good reason to be vigilant and try to have their views reflected in the new regime" (Lee 2011). Japanese scholars have expressed concerns that coastal states are exploiting international maritime law (specifically Article 234 of UNCLOS, which allows coastal states wider environmental jurisdiction over ice-covered waters) to raise rent from shipping in Arctic waters (OPRF 2012a, 14-15). On this basis, if the council had rejected East Asian bids for observer status, it would have perpetuated the perception that Arctic governance is biased against them. East Asian states will lobby hard to represent user state interests on issues such as environmental regulations, shipping protocols and flag state responsibilities, whether inside the Arctic Council or not. Some Asian commentators even argue that observer status in the Arctic Council increases one's obligations without a comparable increase in rights (Guo 2013).

Although the decision at the Kiruna meeting mitigates these concerns, two other challenges remain. First, Arctic states and PPs remain wary that East Asian countries could operate as a bloc to increase their influence in the council. There is already considerable collaboration occurring elsewhere. The OPRF views Arctic cooperation with Russia as a possible way for Japan to improve relations with its sometimes truculent neighbour, despite identifying Russia as the only state that is overtly militarizing the circumpolar region (OPRF 2012b, 9). Similarly, some scholars argue that Russia is the primary target of Chinese cooperative efforts as the former seeks to diversify its energy partners and the latter tries to amass as many resources as possible (Alexeeva and Lasserre 2012, 66–68). South Korea and China are already engaging in collaborative research activities in the north (Yonhap News Agency 2009). Furthermore, South Korea and Japan collaborated on ecosystem surveys in the Bering and Chukchi Seas in 2007, and all three states collaborate extensively with Russia on research in the North Pacific Ocean. Given the cost of Arctic resource exploitation, it is reasonable to conclude that natural economic complementarities exist between Arctic and East Asian states (Hong 2011). Scientific cooperation, however, as an inherently apolitical activity, may not be an accurate indicator of such behaviour. Indeed, several Japanese scholars view the greater maritime activity associated with the opening of the NSR as a threat, given their past experiences with Russian and Chinese naval activity (Ishihara 2012, 3; Akita 2011). Significant mistrust persists between the three East Asian states, stemming in large part from their own maritime disputes and tumultuous political relations. Therefore, concerns by Arctic states and PPs that these states might be capable of acting as an "East Asian bloc" remain speculative at best. Although these three states have similar interests in the Arctic, this does not suggest that they are capable of polar policy coordination — at least not in the near future.

CONCLUSION

This overview of East Asian interests in Arctic governance yields several general conclusions. First, scholars need to discern East Asian states' official Arctic interests because these states have not articulated Arctic strategy documents. Given the hyperbole surrounding "the rise of Asia" and its Arctic implications, it is unlikely that the Arctic states would find any official articulation of East Asian state strategy reassuring. In the case of China, its Arctic policy is tied up with broader maritime policy, which — if released soon, as analysts expect — may shed some light on the issues (Chen 2012). Accordingly, East Asian states should not be expected to articulate Arctic strategies any more than Arctic states should be expected to articulate strategies specifically for East Asia in dedicated policy documents.

Second, East Asian states do not perceive Arctic issues through an Arctic lens. Arctic issues are best situated as "maritime or "polar" issues. In principle, these "user states" favour open access and limited coastal state jurisdiction over adjacent waters. As a function of their own jurisdictional claims in their own region, however, these states understand and are sympathetic to coastal state interests. All three have lodged claims to extended continental shelves with the UNCLCS, and are unlikely — upon sober reflection — to oppose them in the Arctic as long as coastal states meet the established technical criteria.

Third, all three states understand the importance and the influence of Arctic indigenous peoples but are unsure how to engage them. The PPs, either individually or collectively, may consider developing their own strategy for engaging new observers to ensure their interests are protected and pursued with maximum effect.

On balance, the extent to which Arctic and East Asian states' interests conflict on circumpolar issues may be overblown. Nevertheless, Arctic states will need to be cognizant of areas where long-time behavioural benchmarks by East Asian states conflict with their circumpolar priorities. All three East Asian states have dubious records as responsible managers of global fish stocks, yet the size and scope of their industries make them key variables in any regional management organization. Furthermore, China in particular has demonstrated that its national economic goals come ahead of its environmental commitments — domestically and around the world (Brady 2012, 15). Finally, all East Asian states will remain ardent supporters of free access to Arctic waters for international shipping. These policies reflect their global outlook and are unlikely to be sacrificed as the cost of inclusion in the Arctic Council, given that Asian states can pursue their Arctic interests elsewhere if need be.

The Arctic Council's decision to admit new observers is just the tip of the proverbial iceberg. The real challenge will come in maintaining the current structure of the council as new actors clamour for a say in scientific research, resource development, transportation and regional governance more generally. Some Asian commentators have indicated that they consider observer status as a foot in the door to leverage greater influence over time. The challenge for Arctic states lies not in excluding Asian states from regional conversations, but in striving to educate non-Arctic states about why the existing system of governance is appropriate and relevant. Alienating Asian states will feed perceptions that the Arctic countries view the region as a private backyard, dismissing international interests and simply dividing the spoils amongst themselves. Instead, the Arctic community should strive to inculcate an Arctic consciousnes among East Asian nations that is sensitive to the region's unique attributes. During its tenure as chair of the Arctic Council from 2013 to 2015, Canada must look at the region through global, regional and national lenses to ensure that its interests, those of the council and those of a growing array of interested stakeholders are balanced and maintained.

WORKS CITED

Airoldi, Adele. 2008. *The European Union and the Arctic: Policies and Actions*. Copenhagen: Nordic Council of Ministers.

Akita, Hiroyuki. 2011. "Japan in Middle as Russia, China Set to Spar over Arctic." *Nihon Keizai Shimbun*, October 31.

Alexeeva, Olga V. and Frédéric Lasserre. 2012. "The Snow Dragon: China's Strategies in the Arctic." *China Perspectives* 3.

Arctic Athabaskan Council. 2008. "Europe and the Arctic: A View from the Arctic Athabaskan Council." Presentation to Nordic Council of Ministers, Arctic Conference: Common Concern for the Arctic, Ilulissat, Greenland, September 9–11.

Arctic Council Secretariat. 2013. *Kiruna Declaration*. Kiruna, Sweden, May 15.

Asia Pacific Foundation of Canada. 2013. "Charting Canada's Relations with Asia in the Arctic." *Points of View Asia Pacific Opinion Panel*.

Bennett, Mia. 2011. "South Korea's Growing Role in Arctic Economic Development." *Foreign Policy* Blogs, April 20. http://foreignpolicyblogs.com/2011/04/20/south-koreas-growing-role-in-arctic-economic-development/.

———. 2012. "South Korea and Norway Sign Memoranda of Understanding on Arctic Shipping and Shipbuilding." *Foreign Policy* Blogs, September 18. http://foreignpolicyblogs.com/2012/09/18/south-korea-and-norway-sign-memoranda-of-understanding-on-arctic-shipping-and-shipbuilding/.

Brady, Anne-Marie. 2012. "Polar Stakes: China's Polar Activities as a Benchmark for Intentions." *China Brief* 12 (14).

Byers, Michael. 2012. "Asian Juggernaut Eyes our 'Golden' Waterways." *The Globe and Mail*, August 29.

Campbell, Caitlin. 2012. "China and the Arctic: Objectives and Obstacles." US-China Economic and Security Review Commission Staff Research Report. April.

Chang, Gordon. 2010. "China's Arctic Play." *Foreign Policy*, March 9.

Chen, Gang. 2012. "China's Emerging Arctic Strategy." *The Polar Journal* 2 (2): 258–371.

Cheng, Baozhi. 2011. "Arctic Aspirations." *The Beijing Review* 4 (August).

Delegation of Japan. 2011. Statement at the Seventh Ministerial Meeting of the Arctic Council. May 12.

Ekos Research Associates. 2011. *Rethinking the Top of the World: Arctic Security Public Opinion Survey*. Toronto: The Walter and Duncan Gordon Foundation and the Munk School of Global Affairs.

Energy Security Study Group. 2006. "Interim Report." Agency for Natural Resources and Energy press release, July 13. www.enecho.meti.go.jp/english/archives_2006.htm.

Gregoire, Lisa. 2013. "Arctic Council Should be Cautious about New Observer Hopefuls: Inuit Org President." *Nunatsiaq Online*, February 1. www.nunatsiaqonline.ca/stories/article/65674arctic_council_should_be_cautious_about_new_observer_hopefuls_inuit_or/.

Guo, Peiqing. 2013. "An Analysis of New Criteria for Permanent Observer Status on the Arctic Council and the Road of Non-Arctic States to Arctic." *International Journal of Maritime Affairs and Fisheries* 4 (2): 2–38.

Herberg, Mikkal. 2004. "Asia's Energy Insecurity: Cooperation or Conflict?" In *Strategic Asia 2004-05: Confronting Terrorism in the Pursuit of Power*, edited by Ashley J. Tellis and Michael Wills, 339–377. Seattle: The National Bureau of Asian Research.

Hong, Nong. 2011. "Arctic Energy: Pathway to Conflict or Cooperation in the High North?" *Journal of Energy Security*, May. www.ensec.org/.

———. 2012. "The Melting Arctic and its Impact on China's Maritime Transport." *Research in Transportation Economics*, 35 (1): 50–7.

Horinouchi, Hidehisa. 2010. "Japan and the Arctic." Statement at the Japan-Norway Polar Seminar, April 26.

Ishihara, Takahiro. 2012. "Japan Should Play a Constructive Role in the Arctic." Association of Japanese Institutes of Strategic Studies-Commentary No. 151, June.

Jakobson, Linda. 2010. "China Prepares for an Ice-Free Arctic." SIPRI Insights on Peace and Security No. 2010/2.

Jakobson, Linda and Jingchao Peng. 2012. "China's Arctic Aspirations." *SIPRI Policy Paper* 34 (November).

Kira, Shuji. 2012. Statement by Parliamentary Senior Vice-Minister of Foreign Affairs at the Meeting between the Swedish Chairmanship of the Arctic Council and Observers. November 6.

Koivurova, Timo. 2009. "Limits and Possibilities of the Arctic Council in a Rapidly Changing Scene of Arctic Governance." *Polar Record* 46: 146–56.

Koivurova, Timo and David VanderZwaag. 2007. "The Arctic Council at 10 Years: Retrospect and Prospects." *UBC Law Review* 40 (1): 121–94.

Koivurova, Timo, E. J. Molenaar and David VanderZwaag. 2010. "Canada, the EU and the Arctic Ocean Governance: A Tangled and Shifting Seascape and Future Directions." *Journal of Transnational Law and Policy* 18 (2): 247–88.

Korea Offshore & Shipbuilding Association. 2011. *Shipbuilding Korea 2011.*

Lasserre, Frédéric. 2010. "China and the Arctic: Threat or Cooperation Potential for Canada?" Canadian International Council China Papers No. 11, June.

Lanteigne, Marc. 2008. "China's Maritime Security and the Malacca Dilemma." *Asian Security* 4 (2): 143–61.

Lan, Lijun. 2012. Statement by H.E. Ambassador Lan Lijun at the Meeting between the Swedish Chairmanship of the Arctic Council and Observers, November 6.

Lee, Jae-min. 2011. "Arctic Ocean in the Heat." *The Korea Herald*, August 9.

Liu, Zhenmin. 2010. "China's View on Arctic Cooperation." Ministry of Foreign Affairs of the People's Republic of China, July 30. www.fmprc.gov.cn/eng/wjb/zzjg/tyfls/tfsxw/t812046.htm

Luo, Jianwen. 2010. "Navy Major General: China Cannot Afford to Lose Out on Developing the Arctic Ocean." [In Chinese.] *Zhongguo Xinwen She*, August 28.

Manicom, James. 2011. "Maritime Boundary Disputes in East Asia: Lessons for the Arctic." *International Studies Perspectives* 12 (3): 327–340.

Manicom, James and P. Whitney Lackenbauer. 2013. "East Asian States, the Arctic Council and International Relations in the Arctic." CIGI Policy Brief No. 26, April.

OPRF. 2012a. *The Arctic Conference Japan Report.*

———. 2012b. *Actions and Measures Japan is to Take with a View to Ensuring Sustainable Use of the Arctic Ocean.*

Shin, Hyon-Lee. 2012. "S. Korea Seeks Bigger Role in Arctic." *The Korea Herald*, May 16.

Simon, Mary. 2011. "Canada's North and Beyond – the EU and the Arctic Council." Mary Simon's Blog, October 18.

Ship & Ocean Foundation. 2001. *The Northern Sea Route: The Shortest Sea Route Linking East Asia and Europe.* Tokyo: Yoshio Kon.

Takei, Yoshinobu. 2011. "Who Governs the Arctic Ocean? A Reply from an International Law Perspective." *Ocean Policy Studies* 9 (July).

Vanderklippe, Nathan. 2011. "South Koreans Eye Arctic LNG Shipments." *Globe and Mail*, April 19.

Vivoda, Vlado and James Manicom. 2011. "Oil Import Diversification in Northeast Asia: A Comparison between China and Japan." *Journal of East Asian Studies*, 11 (2): 223–254.

Weber, Bob. 2010. "Little Interest in Arctic Shipping." *The Canadian Press*, June 30.

Wright, David. 2011a. "The Dragon Eyes the Top of the World: Arctic Policy Debate and Discussion in China." *China Maritime Study* 8, August. www.usnwc.edu/Research---Gaming/China-Maritime-Studies-Institute/Publications/documents/China-Maritime-Study-8_The-Dragon-Eyes-the-Top-of-.pdf.

———. 2011b. "We Must Stand Up to China's Increasing Claim to Arctic." *Calgary Herald*, March 8.

Yang, Jian. 2012. "China and Arctic Affairs." 2012 Arctic Yearbook commentary. http://arcticyearbook.com/index.php/commentaries#commentary2.

Yonhap News Agency. 2009. "South Korea, China Agree on Joint Research in Arctic Ocean." November 18.

Contributors

Ken Coates is Canada Research Chair in Regional Innovation at the Johnson-Shoyama Graduate School of Public Policy. Raised in the Yukon, with a B.A. (history) from the University of British Columbia (UBC), M.A. (history) from Manitoba and Ph.D. (history) from UBC, Ken has worked at universities across Canada and in New Zealand. He was the Founding Vice-President (Academic) of the University of Northern British Columbia and held administrative posts at the University of Waikato (New Zealand), the University of New Brunswick at Saint John, the University of Saskatchewan and the University of Waterloo. His co-authored work, *Arctic Front: Defending Canada in the Far North*, won the Donner Prize in 2009. He was recognized by the Canadian Society for Civil Engineering for his work on the history of the Alaska Highway and has received awards from the Manitoba Historical Society, the BC Historical Society and the Yukon Historical and Museums Association. Ken is the president of the Japan Studies Association of Canada. His research focuses on Aboriginal rights, science and technology policy, and northern development.

Kimie Hara is professor and the Renison Research Professor at the University of Waterloo, where she is also director of East Asian Studies at Renison University College. She specializes in contemporary international relations of the Asia-Pacific region, border studies, Cold War history, and Japanese politics and diplomacy. Her books include *Cold War Frontiers in the Asia-Pacific: Divided Territories in the San Francisco System* (Routledge, 2007, 2012), *Japanese-Soviet/Russian Relations since 1945: A Difficult Peace* (Routledge, 1998, 2012), *Japanese Diplomacy through the Eyes of Japanese Scholars Overseas* (Fujiwara-shoten, 2009, in Japanese), and *Northern Territories, Asia-Pacific Regional Conflicts and the Åland Experience: Untying the Kurillian Knot* (Routledge, 2009, 2013, edited with Geoffrey Jukes). She has held visiting fellowships/professorships at Kyoto University, the University of Tokyo, the International Institute for Asian Studies/University of Amsterdam, the East-West Center, Stockholm University and the Institute of Oriental Studies of the Russian Academy of Science.

Carin Holroyd is associate professor, Department of Political Studies, University of Saskatchewan. After completing a degree in Asian studies at the University of British Columbia, she studied at Chaminade University of Honolulu/ Sophia University of Japan and then received her Ph.D. in political science from the University of Waikato in New Zealand. She has worked for the Asia Pacific Foundation, Kansai Gaidai University, CIGI, the University of Waterloo and the University of Saskatchewan. She has published widely on political economy in Asia, including *Government, International Trade and Laissez Faire Capitalism* (a study of trade with Japan) and the co-authored books *Japan and the Internet Revolution, Innovation Nation: Science and Technology in 21st Century Japan, Digital Media in East Asia: National Innovation and the Creation of a Region* and the forthcoming book *Digital Planet: Government Policy and Digital Media*. Carin was involved with the establishment of the University of Northern British Columbia, where she negotiated agreements with several Arctic partners, and has travelled extensively in the Canadian and circumpolar North.

Akihiro Iwashita, professor at Hokkaido University and chief editor of *Eurasia Border Review*, is a leading researcher on border studies. His studies on the Sino-Russian borderland and on the Japan-Russian "Northern Territories" issue are renowned by both foreign and local experts. In 2006, he was awarded the prestigious Osaragi Jiro Prize for Commentary for his timely book *Hoppo ryodo: 4 demo 0 demo 2 demo naku* ("Japanese Northern Territorial Issues: Neither Four nor Zero, nor Two," Tokyo: Chuokoron-shinsha, 2005). His book was highly acclaimed by the selection committee for its probing analysis of one of the most difficult and sensitive issues in Japan's diplomacy, and has sold over 20,000 copies. His research on the Sino-Russian border solution was also deeply praised and was awarded the 2007 Japan Society for the Promotion of Science award. The book has been published in English and Russian, and excerpts have also been published in Chinese. He now belongs to leading academic organizations on border studies such as the Association for Borderlands Studies, where he is vice president; Border Regions in Transition, where he was the twelfth conference organizer; and vice president of the Japan International Border Studies Network.

P. Whitney Lackenbauer is associate professor and chair of the Department of History at St. Jerome's University (University of Waterloo). He is also a fellow with the Canadian Defence & Foreign Affairs Institute, the Arctic Institute of North America, and the Laurier Centre for Military and Strategic Disarmament Studies. His recent books include *The Canadian Rangers: A Living History, 1942–2012* (2013), *Canada and the Changing Arctic: Sovereignty, Security and Stewardship* (co-authored 2011), *Canada and Arctic Sovereignty and Security: Historical Perspectives* (edited 2011), *A Commemorative History of Aboriginal People in the Canadian Military* (co-authored 2010), *The Canadian Forces and Arctic Sovereignty: Debating Roles, Interests, and Requirements, 1968–1974* (co-edited 2010), and *Arctic Front: Defending Canada in the Far North* (co-authored 2008, winner of the 2009 Donner Prize for the best book on Canadian public policy). He was a Fulbright Fellow at Johns Hopkins University in 2010 and a Canadian International Council Research Fellow at CIGI in 2008-2009, when he completed a major report entitled *From Polar Race to Polar Saga: An Integrated Strategy for Canada and the Circumpolar World.*

James Manicom joined CIGI as a research fellow in August 2012. He is an expert in East Asia, the Arctic and global security, with a specialty in maritime issues. James holds a B.A. in international relations from Mount Allison University and an M.A. and Ph.D. in international relations from Flinders University in Australia. Prior to joining CIGI, James studied in Tokyo at the Ocean Policy Research Foundation through a Japan Foundation fellowship. He also taught international relations at the Canadian Forces College, where he still teaches occasionally, and Flinders University. He held a Social Sciences and Humanities Research Council of Canada post-doctoral fellowship at the Balsillie School of International Affairs and remains affiliated with the Asian Institute in the Munk School of Global Affairs at the University of Toronto. James' current research focuses on ocean governance and China; it explores the country's changing interaction with the rules and institutions that govern international behaviour at sea. At CIGI, James is contributing to the development of the Global Security & Politics Program and working on research projects that explore Arctic governance and East Asian security.

Gerald (Jerry) McBeath trained at the University of Chicago (A.B., 1963, A.M., 1964) and at the University of California, Berkeley (Ph.D., 1970). At Berkeley, he became a Sinologist, attending the Inter-university Consortium of Chinese Language Studies (Stanford Center) in 1967-1968, and used both Mandarin and the Amoy dialect to conduct dissertation research on the Philippine Chinese. He is fluent in Chinese (speaking, reading and writing [haltingly]), and speaks some Japanese and Filipino. Since 1976, Jerry has worked at the University of Alaska Fairbanks, where he is professor of political science and department chair. His research interests comprehend studies of Alaska and US government/politics, federalism, circumpolar northern studies, domestic and foreign policies of China and Taiwan and environmental politics (domestic, comparative and international).

Fujio Ohnishi is an assistant professor, College of International Relations, Nihon University, Japan. He was a research fellow for Policy Research Department, Ocean Policy Research Foundation, where he worked for several Arctic research projects. He was also a visiting researcher both at the Barents Institute in Norway from 2008 to 2009 and the Åland Peace Institute in Finland from 2004 to 2005. His current research interest ranges from regional cooperation in the Nordic contexts to international politics in the Arctic. His recent publications include: "Arctic Environmental Protection Strategy (AEPS) and the Diplomacy of Finland," *Studies in International Relations* 34-1 (2013), 49–58 [In Japanese]; "Climate Change and the Present Arctic Issues: Broadened Economic Possibilities and Challenges for Japanese Diplomacy," *Intelligence Report* 59 (2013), 34–49 [In Japanese]; "The Politics of the Barents Euro-Arctic Council (BEAC) and its Prospects: From Sub-Regional Cooperation to Frontier Cooperation?" *Russian Eurasian Economy and Society* 972 (2013), 24–38 [In Japanese]; "Military Trends in the Arctic," *Arctic Ocean Quarterly* 16 (2013), 61–67 [In Japanese]; "Regional Cooperation in the Arctic," *Arctic Ocean Quarterly* 16 (2013), 45–53 [In Japanese]; "Struggle for the Framework of Arctic Governance: The Issue of Observer Status in the Arctic Council," *Arctic Ocean Quarterly* 15 (2012) 39–51 [In Japanese]; "Comments on Chapter 6: Japanese Perspective," in *The Arctic in World Affairs*, edited by Oran. R. Young et al. (KMI Press, 2012).

Young Kil Park has been a director of International Marine Affairs and Territory Research Center of Korea Maritime Institute (KMI) since March 2013. He earned his Ph.D. (Seoul National University, 2009), the title of which was "Universal Jurisdiction in International Law: A Reconsideration of the Concept and its Practical Implications." He was a visiting researcher at the School of Politics, International Relations, Philosophy and the Environment at Keele University in 2003 and attended the Rhodes Academy in 2011. His academic interests include various fields of international law, such as the law of the sea, modes of territorial acquisition, human rights law, international criminal law and Arctic governance. His current work focuses on the law of the sea issues in East Asia such as maritime delimitation, territorial disputes and development of the continental shelf. His recent publications in English include: "Different Voices on Military Activities in the EEZ," *KMI International Journal of Maritime Affairs and Fisheries* 3 (2011); "Republic of Korea v. Araye," *American Journal of International Law* 106 (3) (co-author, 2012); and "The Legal Assessment of the Illegal Fishing Activities of Chinese Fishing Vessels: A Focus on Detention of Foreign Vessels," *Korean Journal of International and Comparative Law* 1 (1) (co-author, 2013).

Contributors

Kai Sun is associate professor at the School of Law and Politics, and research fellow at the Institute of Polar Law and Politics, Institute of Marine Development, Ocean University of China. His current research explores the transformation of and China's participation in Arctic governance.

Tamara Troyakova is associate professor and head of the International Studies Department at Far Eastern Federal University, where she is teaching courses on Russian foreign policy. Her research interest is primarily Russian cooperation with East Asian countries. Recent publications in English include *The Russian Far East and the Asia-Pacific: State-Managed Integration* and "From APEC 2011 to APEC 2012: American and Russian Perspectives on Asia-Pacific Security and Cooperation" (with Artyom Lukin), and in Russian, "Russia and Northeast Asian Countries Cooperation in Arctic: Current Situation and Future Development."

David A. Welch is a CIGI senior fellow, chair of global security at the Balsillie School of International Affairs and professor of political science at the University of Waterloo. He is also founder of the Japan Futures Initiative. David's 2005 book, *Painful Choices: A Theory of Foreign Policy Change*, was the inaugural winner of the International Studies Association ISSS Book Award for the best book published in 2005 or 2006, and his 1993 book, *Justice and the Genesis of War*, won the 1994 Edgar S. Furniss Award for an outstanding contribution to national security studies. He is the author of *Decisions, Decisions: The Art of Effective Decision-Making* and co-author of *Vietnam If Kennedy Had Lived*; *The Cuban Missile Crisis: A Concise History*; *On the Brink: Americans and Soviets Reexamine the Cuban Missile Crisis*; and *Cuba on the Brink: Castro, the Missile Crisis, and the Soviet Collapse*. David is co-editor of *Intelligence and the Cuban Missile Crisis*, and his articles have appeared in numerous journals, including *Asian Perspective*, *Ethics and International Affairs*, *Foreign Affairs*, *The Georgetown Journal of International Affairs*, *Intelligence and National Security*, *International Security*, *International Journal*, *International Studies Quarterly*, *The Journal of Conflict Resolution*, *The Mershon International Studies Review*, *The Review of International Studies*, and *Security Studies*. He received his Ph.D. from Harvard University in 1990.